BY KENT POLITSCH

LEGENDS AND LEGACY

75th ANNIVERSARY

Yellow: Legends and Legacy
Commemorating 75 years of service

www.yellowcorp.com

Produced and printed in the United States of America.
First Edition 1999

Dedicated to the employees of Yellow, past and present, and to their families.

ISBN 0-9676585-0-0

Jacket and book design by Muller+Co., Kansas City, Missouri.

Acknowledgements

James F. Filgas and L.L. Waters gathered many facts about Yellow's early growth during their research, interviews and continuous updating of the company's history. They co-authored and published Yellow in Motion as recently as 1987, their latest edition. Drs. Filgas and Waters, retired professors at the University of Michigan and Indiana University respectively, have preserved important details that enable us to understand how Yellow changed over the past 75 years.

Before their effort began, though, a dedicated employee uncovered and recorded many stories that helped all of us. Now deceased, William Glenn, who worked with many employees still active in the company, interviewed A.J. Harrell, the founder, and Evans Nash, president between 1944-1950. He wrote a 33-page unpublished document about those conversations in 1958, which I used reverently. It is a valuable resource for the company.

My mission from the outset was to tell Yellow's story, which I found in dozens of documents, but enjoyed most the legends shared by people. I am grateful to the following contributors who gave me their time.

Ralph Amoss, Reid Armstrong, Frank Averella, Jim Bair, Ray Beagle, Larry Berkowitz, Ralph Bollinger, John Braklow, Jere Brandt, Lloyd Brandt, Bill Brooks, George Brooks, Mike Brown, Bob Burdick, Forrest Burm, John Burton, Jim Carlin, Rex Clarkson, Dick Clepper, Howard Dean, Steve Defenbaugh, John Dehan, John Deichert, Frank DiPaula, Rosemary Donley, Al Evans, Jim Felkner, Ritchie Gallimore, Ron Gilleran, Jim Glenn, Harry Gorden, John Henry, Newton Graves, John Grimes, Kevin Grimsley, Charlie Harrel, David Hughes, Sam Kimmey, Carol Kirchhoff, Dave Knisley, John Koehler, Mike Ladd, Dave Letke, Harold Marshall, TJ Mehaffey, Bill Martin, John McKelvey, Don McMorris, Karen McQuitty, Steve Murphy, Maury Myers, Harold Nichols, Bruce Payne, Roger Payne, Carleta Pool, Jim Porto, George Powell, Jr., George Powell III, Steve Richards, Dan Robeson, Mark Robeson, Steve Rogers, Kermit Scarborough, Carl Sheets, OJ Simpson, Wally Smith, Curvin Snellbecker, Jerry Stouse, Bill Wisniewski, Dick Wright, Denny Yuede and Bill Zollars.

I received help in gathering information from industry organizations including Motor Freight Carriers Association, American Trucking Associations and Oklahoma Trucking Association. At MFCA, I would like to recognize Elisabeth Barna, Linda Barber, Art Bunte and Tim Lynch for their contributions. Likewise, I used recollections offered by retired ATA officials Neil Darmstadler, Dick Few and Bob Halladay, which were critically important and appreciated.

I also received help from Sharon Burns of The Daily Oklahoman and from the Oklahoma Historical Society. Ms. Burns' newspaper article about my search for people who knew Yellow's Oklahoma City beginnings, and then photos I found in the historical society's files, led me to Jan Cooke and Pauline Severs, descendants of Yellow's founders. From them I learned important facts about the Harrell brothers that made the story richer in detail.

Most significant to this work was the constant support and editing by Roger Dick, Manager of Corporate Communications for Yellow Corporation, and further review by G. Fred Wickman, Editor of YFS Week.

Finally, I would like to express my appreciation to Yellow Corporation Chairman, President and CEO Maury Myers. His trust and support in this effort allowed me to accomplish a lifetime ambition, to sit down and write a book about something important, which I believe Yellow's story is.

Foreward

Bill Graves
Governor
State of Kansas

Trucks brought Midwestern states like Kansas into the mainstream of America's economy within the past 75 years. Before that, we were isolated prairies, wonderful places for homesteaders, farmers and hardy individuals searching for opportunity in oil fields and mineral mines. Riches were here, but conveniences were not, until trucks began to shrink the size of our vastness.

Railroads had come much earlier and even made legend of our cities Atchison and Topeka and cow towns like Dodge City. They tempted civilization to test our spaces. But not until the truck brought everyday supplies to our small towns as well as our cities did our state begin to participate in the nation's mainstream of trade.

I am proud to say that my family had an instrumental part in making Kansas a more livable place because of a single truck that became a few and then by the 1970s a very prosperous fleet of many. Graves Truck Line employed hundreds of people and moved millions of dollars of commerce from Nebraska, across Kansas to Oklahoma, Colorado and into Texas.

In my youth I learned what it meant to load a trailer high and tight for efficiency and to protect a customer's wares. I learned that drivers and dock laborers faced many physical and safety challenges in the act of doing their jobs. And I learned that businesses in cities like Wichita, Topeka, Salina, Overland Park and Kansas City depend heavily on truck lines to move products to market on schedule and intact, otherwise those businesses fail to please their customers.

The role of transportation is vital to each state and province in North America. Manufacturers and retailers survive in crowded cities or remote towns equally because there are reliable truck lines to move their goods to markets worldwide. The speed and dependability with which commerce moves today is miraculous compared to what it was like at the beginning of this century. Trucks are a major part of this amazing transformation.

Yellow Freight System officially became a headquarters resident of Kansas in 1973. However, Yellow's familiar and oddly "orange" trucks have traversed our state's highways and roads since the early 1930s.

Kansas was the second state served by Yellow Transit Company Freight Lines as it expanded from Oklahoma. In addition to serving our communities with reliable freight transportation for all those years, the Yellow name became well known because of its philanthropic and civic leadership. It is a valued asset in Kansas that we proudly share with the rest of the continent.

For the state and all citizens it serves, I extend my congratulations to Yellow, its employees and shareholders for completing 75 years of dedicated service. I encourage the company to face the challenges of the future with the same wisdom and skill its employees and management have demonstrated in the past. We, the people of Kansas and all citizens of a global marketplace, are depending on Yellow to serve us well.

It is a new era in transportation, one that depends as much on information technology as it does on tractors and trailers. It offers us all new opportunities to enrich our lives through progress built on imagination. The future can be as potent as the past when we have forward-looking people running companies like Yellow.

I am honored to contribute these few words and invite every reader to examine one of America's true success stories. I know firsthand the trials and tribulations experienced by people like the Harrell brothers, three generations of Powells, whom I have known well and long, and now Chairman Maury Myers and Yellow Freight System President Bill Zollars, two energetic and inspiring leaders.

Each generation of leaders has elevated this transportation company to new levels of success by overcoming great odds. It is a wonderful story told honestly. I hope you enjoy it.

Bill Graves
Governor
State of Kansas

Introduction

One reason why North America's economy grew to dominance in the 20th century is because of truck transportation and a superior highway system. Efficient, dependable transportation of goods to market created a prosperous culture. (photo by Steve Uzzell)

Trucks, especially 18-wheelers, are majestic vehicles. They cause children to gawk and motorists to curse. They are loved, hated, valued and criticized. But the most important thing to remember as you read this book is that according to the Eno Transportation Foundation, 79 percent of all revenue generated by freight transportation is produced by trucks. The remaining 21 percent is split among the railroads (7.0%), boats, barges and ships (5.0%), air carriers (4.5%), through pipelines (1.7%) and other various means (2.1%). That is how important the truck and the highway system is to this nation.

Trucks have been around for one century. By today's standards, the original vehicles were primitive. They were faster than horse-drawn wagons, but not much.

As the truck evolved and improved, it became more important. It was more versatile compared to other cargo transporters. By mid century it surpassed the train to become the dominant freight carrier.

Changes are important in telling the story of Yellow Freight System. The truck enabled convenient distribution to every community in America. Industrial leaders observed that better roads meant larger trucks could move more products faster and more efficiently, so highway development became an economic priority. With better highways, cities expanded. Suburbs blossomed. Commerce decentralized. Extraordinary dynamics shaped the marketplace, which in turn constantly reshaped the transportation industry.

Today, Yellow Freight System is one of more than 50,000 companies paid to move products to market via a truck. Rugged individuals who drive the trucks and handle the freight create the company's public image. Likewise, shippers' opinions are based on how easy it is to get help from customer service representatives, cargo claims adjusters, inside sales agents, account managers, sales assistants, terminal managers and others. Images and opinions are drawn from the company's cultural. The culture has a direct link to the past.

How did the company develop? Who were the important decision-makers that shaped the company? What motivated them? And how did they address the common challenges facing every organization that has been around for 75 years; things such as the stock market crash of 1929, supply shortages caused by World War II, labor strikes and industry deregulation?

For Yellow, the answers unravel with the understanding that like other older truck lines, the company started as a basic trade. The Harrell brothers of Oklahoma City bought two trucks and hired drivers because the community needed freight transportation to other cities in the state. The Harrells asserted that fact as a result of frequent requests to carry express items in their buses that ran from Oklahoma City to Tulsa.

The Harrell family portrait when they lived in Olney, Ill. Jacob Harrell had traded his farm for a livery stable, which he operated a few years before his family started heading west. (from left to right: A.J., Clema, Marvin, Jacob, Cleve, and Sarah Harrell)

A.J. Harrell, the man given the most credit for Yellow's early success as a truck line, had a fourth-grade education but street learning that made him very wise. After a visit to the 1904 St. Louis Worlds Fair, the 22-year-old set his sights on the West, but got no farther than Oklahoma City. The city, still wild and unruly when he arrived, attracted his entrepreneurial spirit. He stayed to make his mark.

He was crafty and conservative with his money. If there were anyone who held onto the first dollar he made, it would have been A.J. Harrell. He was proud of his money-making abilities regardless of the trade he engaged in – horse trading, hauling oil rig parts in mule-drawn wagons, taxicabs, bus lines, filling stations, cattle ranching, real estate, oil drilling, or running a truck line. He did everything intensely, sternly and successfully. His story is fascinating, but probably quite similar to hundreds of others of his day. It was an era in which the truck became an icon of American hustle.

They were all tradesmen, though, not true businessmen in the modern sense. They had in their minds to move freight, watch operating costs and charge a competitive rate to attract the right amount and right kind of cargo going to the right destinations.

Today, that simple tradesman approach is not enough. To keep alive what A.J. Harrell started, new leaders at Yellow have had to master many skills in a dynamic process. Marketing professionals, researchers, economists, telemarketers, industrial engineers, accountants, investment relations experts, human resource specialists, authorized hazardous materials handlers, intermodal analysts, international freight forwarders, computer programmers and analysts and Internet web masters are some of the trained and professional people who help run a transportation company.

There also were historic events so big that they did more than influence the company's development; they

This page — *Sleeper tractors have been a part of trucking for more than 30 years. Yellow returned to using the sleeper in the 1990s to improve speed efficiency on certain routes.*

Page 1 — *Long before the sun has had time to burn off the morning haze, Yellow's trucks are moving North America's commerce. (photo by Steve Uzzell)*

shaped it. Some will be obvious, like government deregulation and union organization of employees. Less obvious but just as profoundly influential was the development of the Interstate Highway System.

Transitioning from one moment to the next was never easy. Certainly, there were those in the organization that resisted change vehemently and in so doing, became intolerant, disillusioned and unproductive. Presumably, they sought personal happiness elsewhere.

For the most part, people at Yellow have embraced the direction chosen by owners, presidents, chairmen and other key leaders. They supported decisions with hard work and dedication to the company's success. It was a simple formula.

Hidden in facts about an individual company is a much bigger story about how we act as human beings. Rightfully, we view things first from a "me" perspective. Does this job, this company, this industry provide what I need for my family, my ego and my personal aspirations? But, in a broader, more charitable view, does what I do make a difference in the world? The answer to the first question is individualistic, but the answer to the second is universal. And it's yes, what people do at Yellow does make a difference.

This book is not a heavy-handed way to boast about the contribution because that is a vain, and therefore dull story to tell. This is just the legend and legacy of the founding and 75 year history, which have many nuances that make it unique.

Yellow Freight System has been a leading provider of freight transportation for many of its 75 years. Its service to commerce has made an important contribution to the quality of life we enjoy all across North America. It is no coincidence that as Yellow and other freight transportation firms grew and improved service quality, the North American economy grew and prospered.

Look around. Every manufactured item within your sight got there by way of a truck. The industry and its individual companies – Yellow being one of the best – moves products cheaper and better today than ever before. That is an important reason why we in America live so well.

HARVEY ST.

Oklahoma Roots

Aspirations

The year is 1916. Taxicabs are lined up at the rail station along Santa Fe Avenue in Oklahoma City. Nearby are horse- and mule-drawn wagons. A train's iron wheels lock and bring the machinery to a stop. Drivers jockey coyly to greet the boomtown's new arrivals as passengers step down from the railcars into the hissing engine's trail of steam. Competition is fierce to see who can assist travelers with baggage and transportation to their final destination.

Cleve Harrell is in the middle of the driver pack. He holds his hand up hoping to attract a customer. His older brother, A.J., is a few feet away, but oblivious to Cleve's attempts to solicit a fare. A.J. is too busy trying to close a sale. He is in an animated negotiation with three men studying one of the hack teams, trying to get A.J. to lower his price.

If you could freeze time, and place A.J. and Cleve together, you could easily tell they were brothers. Both are broad-shouldered and stand about the same height. Their hair is dark and thick. Their faces are chiseled and ruddy from long days in the sun when they were farm boys in Illinois.

A.J. – Arthur Jacob – looks the sterner of the two. His dark, penetrating eyes verify his serious nature. Born in 1882, A.J. is already a seasoned businessman.

G.C. "Cleve" Harrell is two years younger. He is more passive. Perhaps shy. His confidence is weakened by a hint of frailty due to a youthful bout with polio.

Observing A.J. and Cleve in their separate endeavors is another brother, Marvin Harrell. He waves to them as he walks to his job with Missouri, Kansas and Texas Railroad. He is a yard clerk. Marvin is a decade younger than A.J., but already his hair is thinning. He doesn't appear as rugged as the other two. Instead, he looks more studious and urbane.

Although together in Oklahoma, the Harrells did not come as a family. A.J. was the first to make the newly chartered territory his home in 1904. Cleve followed in 1906, a year ahead of Oklahoma statehood. Then came Marvin and the rest of the Harrell family in 1909, including their father, Jacob, and their sister, Clema, and her husband, Bliss Waggoner. Within a decade, the entire clan would be working for a company started by the two oldest brothers. It will be called Yellow Cab Transit Company, known today as Yellow Freight System.

Page 2 — *Boomtown Oklahoma City attracted the Harrell brothers. By 1910, A.J. (left) and Cleve (right) made part of their living driving hack teams. They would reunite in 10 years to start a transportation company that eventually became Yellow Freight System. Marvin (center) would then join them after gaining experience as a railroad clerk. (photo courtesy of Jan Cooke)*

1924

- Calvin Coolidge is elected President.
- Consumer products introduced include Kleenex, and Wheaties, the Breakfast of Champions.
- The Eveready Hour is the first sponsored network radio program. All live.
- Little Orphan Annie first appears as a newspaper comic strip on a campaign against communism.
- Rhapsody in Blue is first performed by George Gershwin at New York's Aeolian Hall.

After starting, succeeding and selling a city bus company, Yellow Cab Transit Company began intrastate bus service between Oklahoma City and Tulsa in the mid-to-late 1920s. The bus carried express cargo shipments as well as passengers.

Coming Up "Yellow"

A.J. Harrell was a hardy entrepreneur who did business with cash in hand. He was crafty and shrewd, but some who remember him say he had a warm and humorous side as well.

By 1920, A.J. was in partnership selling horses and mules. Oklahoma badly needed the animals. People were feverishly drilling for oil. Those not active in pursuit of oil built prosperous new businesses to cater to those who were. Suppliers and merchants filled the city quickly. Everyone relied on horses and mules to haul goods over raw open land being carved by unpaved roads and streets.

When not selling the animals or the wagons they pulled, A.J. Harrell was among the freight haulers, transporting heavy equipment to the oil rigs. He was also a part-time bookkeeper.

Cleve Harrell had no doubt that he would make his fortune in transportation. It just wouldn't happen quickly. He arrived in Oklahoma with very little money so he could not afford a motor vehicle. He worked as a school janitor and occasionally hauled freight in horse-drawn wagons, like his brother. Occasionally, he also transported passengers with his hack team. After 10 years he had saved more than $1,000 and was able to buy an open-bodied Model-T Ford. He was closing in on his dream.

Cleve began driving his four-cylinder car as a taxicab in early 1916. The next year the United States entered World War I and Oklahoma became training ground for soldiers. Cleve committed his Model-T to hauling army personnel from train station to base and back. When the war ended, he returned to his regular taxi fares, only this time he decided to differentiate himself from all the other drab black cars.

Cleve Harrell hand-painted his Model-T yellow and called his one-man business Yellow Cab, a name he reportedly registered with the state of Oklahoma. The legendary claim is that Cleve was the originator of the Yellow Cab concept that was copied successfully in metropolitan America.

Yellow Cab of Oklahoma City had a good reputation known broadly across America, especially within the taxicab industry. That reputation was based on the quality of service, not just the name. Harrell prided himself on courteous, uniformed drivers and spotless, fumigated vehicles.

On the streets of Oklahoma City, though, Cleve and his first yellow cab were taunted and ridiculed by the other drivers. They called the man and his car

1925

- The world powers sign an agreement to bar the use of poison gas in war.
- 3M creates Scotch Tape.
- The first "motel" opens in San Luis Obispo, Calif.
- Synthetic rubber is first made by a chemist at Notre Dame University.
- The worst tornado in U.S. history hits Missouri, Illinois and Indiana, killing 689 people.

"Banana," but his ploy worked. Regular customers sought his yellow Model-T in spite of its airy discomforts on rainy and cold days, because Cleve offered the kind of personal service customers wanted.

Cleve added two more yellow taxicabs to his business by 1921 and gave the company the official name of Yellow Cab & Baggage Company. His marketing slogan was "prompt and efficient night and day taxi and baggage service." When he wanted to expand further, he asked A.J. to finance his growth and join him in the business. A.J. obliged. They formed a partnership, keeping the Yellow Cab & Baggage Company name.

By then, the Harrell brothers were 39 and 37 years old, respectively. Each had been modestly successful following separate paths. And now they had a chance to do better as a team.

With Cleve focused on the taxicabs, A.J. began to look at other transportation opportunities in Oklahoma City. Bus service was an obvious consideration. Demand for public transportation between downtown and the state capitol, 20 blocks to the north, grew steadily. According to the Harrells, prior bus service had been erratic.

Once permission was granted by the city council, Yellow Cab expanded. The addition of city bus service prompted the brothers to incorporate on December 31, 1924. A.J. and Cleve Harrell registered the name Yellow Cab Transit Company, naming Cleve as president and A.J. as secretary. Incorporated under a new name, they still continued to promote the taxi service as Yellow Cab & Baggage Company. The buses carried the corporate name.[1]

The Harrell brothers operated the city bus line for about 15 months before selling it. Its success gave rise to a new idea – bus service between cities.

The company bought several separate state permits until A.J. and Cleve had woven together authority to transport passengers between Oklahoma City and Tulsa, the state's largest and fastest growing communities. The intercity bus service, like their city bus line, was immediately successful, and led to another profitable sale in 1929.[2]

Pioneering Spirit

As the company grew, the Harrells set up their operations at the intersection of Santa Fe and California, near the train station. Their business address was 113 S. Santa Fe. The building they used for offices, garage and warehouse has since

A.J. Harrell was proud of his Yellow Transit equipment. He expected his drivers and mechanics to keep it looking well scrubbed and running in top condition.

1926

Ford Motors introduces an 8-hour work day and 5-day work week.

E.I. duPont introduces improved waterproof cellophane that will revolutionize packaging.

Charles Lindbergh, 24, flies the first air mail route between St. Louis and Chicago.

Greyhound is incorporated to compete with intercity passenger rail service.

Cushioned cork-centered baseballs are introduced to the sport.

YELLOW TRANSIT CO. FREIGHT LINES
CHICAGO
ST. LOUIS
KANS. CITY
TULSA
OKLA. CITY
DALLAS
FT. WORTH
HOUSTON
WEE ROOMS 50¢-75¢
SIMPSON SELLS Fords
YELLOW TRANSIT CO. FREIGHT LINES
CHICAGO ST. LOUIS
TULSA OKLAHOMA CITY
FT. WORTH HOUSTON
YELLOW TRANSIT CO. FREIGHT LINES
YELLOW TRANSIT CO. FREIGHT LINES
YELLOW TRANSIT CO. FREIGHT LINES
YELLOW TRANSIT CO. FREIGHT LINES
LOW TRANSIT CO.
FREIGHT LINES

been razed. The vacant property awaits new life at the edge of an attractive downtown redevelopment. The railroad tracks bisecting downtown Oklahoma City are a continuing link to the past.

While in its prime, the original site of Yellow Cab Transit Company took on many functions. It was an active transportation center. Around it sprung many small businesses, including a small restaurant that took the Yellow Cab name – Yellow Cab Café.

The company building was spacious. A.J. turned it into a warehouse for consolidating freight from numerous area truck lines. He established a new enterprise he called Union Truck Depot. Through it, he observed how truckers operated, which spawned yet another business venture.

Yellow Cab Transit Company bought two White straight trucks in 1926, primarily to do local deliveries for Union Truck Depot. Using his relationship with Oklahoma regulating authorities, A.J. was able to secure rights between Oklahoma City and Tulsa, a route with which he was familiar because of the company's intercity bus line.

Even before the trucks were purchased, the Harrells' buses had been carrying express shipments for the oil fields. Their express rates were posted in the Union Truck Depot rate pamphlet. It cost a shipper $1.25 to send a 75-pound express item via Yellow Cab Transit Company between the two cities. Seventy-five pounds was the maximum weight allowed by the Oklahoma Corporation Commission. Oklahoma City & Eastern, the only other transportation firm with Oklahoma City-Tulsa authority, would carry items at first class rates for $1.02 per hundred weight. Fourth class was the minimum charge allowed at $.56 per hundred weight.

Yellow Cab Transit began hauling intercity freight on a regular basis with the addition of the two White trucks. Many of the items were already familiar to the Harrells – parts for oil rigs. The freight business struggled originally, partly because it received less attention than the taxi enterprise and other ventures, and partly because the national economy was slumping.[3]

Mounting concern about the economy did not stop the Harrells. They began to look for ways to control their expenses. Their frugality led them to another opportunity. The solution they settled on for controlling costs was to gain access to wholesale oil and gasoline supplies. They spun their search into their next venture. They began to buy and construct gasoline filling stations.

Page 6, top — *The first Yellow Transit Company terminal was located near the intersection of S. Santa Fe and California in downtown Oklahoma City. (photo courtesy Oklahoma Historical Society)*

Page 6, bottom — *These two White trucks were the first Yellow Cab Transit Company vehicles to carry freight exclusively. They remained part of the fleet through the mid 40s.*

1927

Gunmen firing automatic weapons attack Al Capone's Chicago headquarters in broad daylight.

J.C. Penney opens his 500th store and goes public.

Transatlantic telephone service begins between London and New York.

Ford introduces the Model A to replace the Model T and to compete with Chevrolet.

Safety glass is being used in automobile windshields.

This page — *Pulling two trailers has been a popular way to add efficiency and productivity to the company's operation since the early 1930s. These early boxes photographed in Tulsa were 20 feet long and traveled between Oklahoma City and Tulsa. (photo courtesy Oklahoma Historical Society)*

Page 9 — *This round-roof architecture was used for Yellow Cab Dynamic Gasoline stations as well as the company's smaller freight depots. Its second-floor living quarters was part of the desired feature. (photo courtesy Oklahoma Historical Society)*

With Yellow Cab taxis spotted strategically throughout the city, a network of filling stations presented a logical way to lower operating costs, service the cars quickly, and just as important, control the quality of petroleum products they used. The company had already experienced the difficult consequence of using low-cost motor oil and gasoline. Inferior brands, at least in those days, could do serious damage to an automobile's engine.

By starting its own chain of filling stations, Yellow Cab Transit Company developed an excellent alternative. Cleve Harrell claimed that servicing the taxis at wholesale prices saved the company $1,000 per month. Harrell said the savings also kept the operation stable when the rest of the nation was in the midst of a depression.[4]

The stations also gave the company another profit center. Petroleum products were sold to Oklahoma motorists throughout the state under the name Yellow Cab Dynamic Gasoline. At one point, the company operated 18 stations in Oklahoma City alone.

The cabs, buses and filling stations were not the only investments the brothers made. Both Cleve and A.J. bought farms on the outskirts of Oklahoma City. They raised cattle and Cleve even had chickens. Taxi drivers were assigned times to stop by his farm. They picked up eggs produced by his specially fed hens. They took the eggs to the filling stations where they were sold as Yellow Cab Dynamic Eggs.[5]

Family Affair

The 1920s roared with success for A.J. and Cleve Harrell. Their enterprising efforts rewarded them with capital to expand. They were considered excellent employers and earned loyalty from both workers and customers. They paid employees well, kept company equipment clean and reliable, and made friends in the community.

Among employees was a familiar name, Jacob Harrell, father of A.J., Cleve and Marvin Harrell, who worked for the men until his death in 1926. An Oklahoma City Polk Directory listed Jacob as a driver. Oral renditions passed down during the past seven decades indicate Jacob was more of a paternal figurehead. He was granted senior status on account of his family position more so than his company contribution.

The Harrell brothers' sister, Clema, also became an employee, as did her husband, Alex B. (Bliss) Waggoner. Bliss operated one of Yellow Cab's filling stations at 1023 N. Broadway.

1928

Babe Ruth hits 60 home runs in a single season.

Popular songs include: Me and My Shadow, Girl of My Dreams, and I'm Looking Over a Four Leaf Clover.

The Supreme Court rules that income earned illegally is still taxable, giving law enforcers a new weapon in fighting organized crime.

Republican Herbert Hoover becomes president, defeating Alfred E. Smith.

Kellogg' introduces Rice Krispies.

1138
FIRE-CHIEF
CONTAINS LEAD
FIRE-CHIEF
GASOLINE
Sky Chief
STEAM
Cleaned

YELLOW TRANSIT MOTOR FREIGHT LINE
WICHITA - TULSA - OKLA. CITY - DALLAS - FT. WORTH - HOUSTON
YELLOW TRANSIT CO.
YELLOW TRANSIT CO. FREIGHT LINES

Two other Harrell names appeared on the payroll over time. Herbert W. Harrell was a driver for Yellow Cab & Baggage Company in the late 1920s; just a coincidence, not a cousin. And M. Kenneth Harrell drove a truck in the 1930s. Kenneth was Marvin's oldest son.

Marvin, the youngest Harrell brother and a railroad clerk, was reunited with A.J. and Cleve in 1927 when he joined Yellow Cab Transit Company as cashier. He had picked up useful skills and experience with the railroad that A.J. and Cleve could trust.

Marvin's contributions were rewarded with fast promotion. He became bookkeeper the next year, auditor in 1933, general manager in 1934, and eventually he acquired a minority shareholding position and secretary-treasurer of the corporation. Unfortunately, he also had to choose sides when A.J. and Cleve differed over personal matters and decided to divide the company.

Family Divided

Personal accounts of a 1932 dispute between the two founding brothers are somewhat different, but apparently it was not over company policy or how to run the business. Although Cleve took the taxi operation and A.J. the truck line when the personal conflict arose, they initially kept the corporation intact. It remained that way until 1937 when a business issue became the catalyst for a legal restructuring.

Marvin replaced Cleve as an officer of the continuing truck line operation, which changed its name officially to Yellow Transit Company Freight Lines. Meantime, Cleve renamed Yellow Cab & Baggage Company the Yellow Cab Company of Oklahoma City and retained the Yellow Cab Dynamic Gasoline filling stations.

What was the personal dispute over? One account claims the men may have disagreed about profits from investments in oil wells. Another version indicates Cleve's divorce from his first wife, Mae, affected the brother's personal relationship. Neither account is stated with full confidence, casting uncertainty about what really happened. Regardless, the family bond had been fractured.

The more public view was that A.J. and Cleve disagreed about expanding the truck line. In 1936, A.J. wanted the company to acquire Bryan Motor Freight Lines as a way to grow the trucking operation. Bryan had authority to operate from Kansas City, Mo., to Amarillo, Texas, complimenting Yellow Transit's service area in the same states. When Cleve refused, A.J. bought Bryan Motor with personal funds and

This page, top — *Marvin Harrell became general manager of Yellow Transit Company in 1934 after serving as auditor.*

This page, bottom — *With the World War I Liberty Memorial in the background, Yellow Transit Company showed off its powerful set of double trailers, which transported Kansas City products south to Oklahoma and Texas.*

Page 10 — *The first Kansas City terminal was located on Southwest Blvd. near the downtown. Kansas City was the first target for expanding outside of Oklahoma.*

Chrysler Motors introduces the Plymouth to compete with Ford and Chevrolet.

The Amos 'n' Andy comedy radio program begins on WMAQ in Chicago.

Penicillin is discovered to have antibacterial properties and launches the "antibiotic" move in medicine.

This page, top — *Strategically located in the southeast corner of Kansas, Baxter Springs became an important terminal in the early growth period. (photo courtesy Oklahoma Historical Society)*

Page 13 — *Houston was an important addition to Yellow Transit's service network. These unidentified Houston salesmen from 1938 helped produce northbound freight that balanced the system, making the carrier more profitable. (Notice the official executive photos on the far left wall.) (photo courtesy Oklahoma Historical Society)*

operated the company separately while continuing to preside over Yellow Transit. After an official dissolution of the brothers' partnership, monitored by the Interstate Commerce Commission, A.J. was permitted to merge Bryan Motor into Yellow Transit.

Making a Name: Building a Truck line

Credit Cleve Harrell with the name "Yellow," thanks to his hand-painted taxicab. When his personal problem with A.J. caused the two operations to split, Cleve's influence over the truck line ended. A.J. implemented a more aggressive growth plan despite a depressed national economy. He could do it because he had cash.

Although the purchase of the two straight trucks in 1926 gave Yellow Cab Transit Company an entrée into trucking, it was not until 1931 that the operation could stand alone. The Harrell brothers separated the books and allowed the truck line they called Yellow Transit Company to test its independence.

A.J. Harrell wisely created a safe haven from which to learn the trucking trade. The warehouse business – Union Truck Depot – allowed A.J. to observe freight flow patterns. He recognized which cities originated freight and which ones were transfer points. He planned his expansions according to available authority and sought ways to link those cities to his base in Oklahoma City.

Trade from Kansas City and a route to Dallas were A.J. Harrell's two original targets. It was already obvious that more goods moved from the north to the south and from the east to the west, rather than the reverse.

Trucks carrying goods south from Kansas City frequently were routed through Oklahoma. With authority already established between Tulsa and Oklahoma City, it was strategically important to connect Kansas City to Baxter Springs, Kan., in the southeast corner of the state. From there, the freight could be routed onward to Tulsa. Authority was granted connecting Kansas City all the way through to Oklahoma City through Tulsa.

The 145-mile stretch along Route 69 in Kansas was half paved and half graded dirt. The link from Baxter Springs to Tulsa went through Vinita, Okla., on mostly paved sections of Route 66. The connection to Dallas followed Route 77, which was less than half paved. Yellow Transit bought the Oklahoma City to Dallas authority from a company in financial straits. The Harrell's available cash secured the deal for under $1,000.[6]

Routes 66, 69 and 77 offered a single lane of traffic in each direction. Even on paved sections, speeds

1929

- The stock market plummets about 10 percent in one day, setting off a financial crash heard around the world.
- The Ford Motor Company increases the minimum daily wage from $6 to $7.
- Ford introduces the first station wagon.
- Delta Airlines begins passenger service with three six-passenger monoplanes.
- Connie Mack's Philadelphia Athletics win the World Series by defeating the Cubs 4 games to 1.

SOUTHERN PACIFIC LINES

Cleve's Cabs

Cleve Harrell displays his fleet of Yellow Cab taxis in front of the Oklahoma Capitol. (photo courtesy Jan Cooke)

In the mid-30s, Yellow Cab ordered 50 new taxis from a Detroit automaker. The automaker painted the cars yellow and Cleve sent 50 drivers to Detroit to drive them back in a caravan. His picture postcard showed the proud owner with his new fleet in front of the Oklahoma State Capitol. The caption read, "The thinking fellow calls a Yellow." The telephone number shown on the postcard – 2-6161 — was first used in 1930. With the addition of an expanded modern prefix, it's the same number today, still painted on the sides of Oklahoma City's Yellow Cabs.

rarely exceeded 40 mph. The trip was complicated, but not just because of road conditions and routine breakdowns. Each state set its own weight limits and guidelines for total vehicular length. That meant in order to cross state lines, companies had two choices: set up transfer operations or attempt to run illegally.

The biggest challenge for Yellow Transit Company was crossing the border from Oklahoma into Texas. The Lone Star State had extraordinary weight restrictions – 7,000 pounds compared to Oklahoma's 21,000 pounds. It forced A.J. Harrell to create one of the first transfer operations in the industry. The little town of Thackerville, Okla. was chosen for the Pony-Express-like switch. An Oklahoma driver in a large rig arrived at the facility where the freight was unloaded and separated into shipments that fit the Texas-sized units. Three Dallas drivers would be waiting with three trucks to complete the transfer.

Since the company was already in Dallas, the next logical expansion was to Houston. Again, A.J. took advantage of another trucker's failures. He used his cash to buy the Dallas-Houston authority cheaply from an in-debt owner.

Texas Route 75 provided the pathway, which was 244 miles of mostly dirt and gravel. However, the new gateway added a profit dimension that made Texas more appealing. Houston created northbound shipments that balanced the flow of freight. Instead of driving empty trucks to Thackerville, they were now full, producing revenue in both directions.[7]

Trucking Taken Seriously

The Harrells, like hundreds of other pioneers in the trucking industry, learned their trade through trial and error. They had few references for estimating costs and only the railroads against which to compare their prices. As they grew, they faced new challenges due to their broader coverage area.

Roads were primitive. Trucks were prone to break down because of the beating they took. Even a vigilant maintenance program could not prevent problems that arose due to the rough conditions.

Nature caused further complications. A gentle spring rain could create enough mud to stop traffic. And while tires were pneumatic rather than rough-riding solid rubber, the kind mounted on the first trucks, they ruptured easily. The rubber was supported by eight plies of cotton cord. It was rare for a driver to make a trip without changing at least one flat.

Business challenges also came from state legislatures,

Driving a truck in the 1930s was an adventure. Roads presented many obstacles.

1930

Donald Duncan introduces the yo-yo to America.

Popular songs include: Stardust, Honeysuckle Rose, Happy Days Are Here Again, and Tip Toe Through the Tulips.

World depression grows worse as trade declines, production slows and unemployment increases.

U.S. gasoline consumption rises to 16 billion gallons, more than six times the amount consumed a decade earlier.

Page 17 — *Evans A. Nash spent several years as Yellow Cab Transit Company's certified public accountant. A.J. Harrell hired him as an employee in 1932. He soon became an officer of Yellow Transit Company and the person to whom Harrell turned for closest counsel. (photo courtesy Oklahoma Historical Society)*

which were trying to devise ways to regulate and tax an unknown but swiftly expanding service industry. Railroads protested the trucker's seemingly unrestricted freedom and envied the driver's flexibility to go places they could not go. Railroad executives focused their economic leverage on hog-tying the trucking industry. They used their clout to lobby federal and state lawmakers, seeking legal means to undermine newfound competition from the nation's trucks.

Vulnerable because of their political naiveté, a few trucking leaders stepped forward to rally others. Among them was a representative of Yellow Transit Company.

New Ally: An Important Addition

Among his several skills, A.J. Harrell had learned bookkeeping out of necessity. He valued good numbers records because it was a logical way to evaluate his company's performance. After Cleve and he made their corporate pact in 1924, they contracted with Evans A. Nash to audit their books, offer business counsel and account for their earnings.

Nash was like the Harrells; he even looked like them. Somewhat of a free spirit, the college graduate and former newspaperman eventually settled on accounting. In 1932, after working for the company as an independent certified public accountant for several years, A.J. Harrell offered Nash a job as general manager of the company. Nash did not hesitate. He took the job not knowing much about trucking but a lot about running a business profitably. He wasted no time in learning the trade.

The same year he was hired by Harrell, Nash was among a small group of trucking industry executives who met to discuss a critical issue. Railroad lobbyists were working with the Oklahoma state legislature on tougher laws to inhibit the trucking industry's growth. The truckers were tipped off that legislators had plans to raise taxes and stiffen regulations. They knew they needed a stronger voice at the capitol.

Nash placed Yellow Transit employee R.G. Hickox on the committee that petitioned the state for incorporation as Associated Motor Carriers of Oklahoma (AMCO). The group then went to work finding an administrator to run the new organization. They hired Ray G. Atherton.

Atherton was perfect for the job. A good communicator, he understood the battle that needed to be fought and was passionate in his execution of duties. He was so successful, he later served 23 years as general manager

1931

Two air carriers merge to form United Airlines, which cuts flying time between New York and San Francisco to 28 hours.

The amount of paved highways has nearly doubled in nine years to 694,000 miles.

Astronomers at Lowell Observatory in Arizona discover the solar system's ninth planet, Pluto.

Miles Laboratories introduces Alka-Seltzer.

U.S. car sales collapse, causing automakers to lay off 100,000 workers; two of three workers in Detroit are under or unemployed.

THIN

These Oklahoma City drivers ran north and south from Missouri to Texas. Yellow Transit was one of many carriers in Oklahoma that had become a threat to well-established railroads. (photo courtesy Pauline Severs)

for American Trucking Associations (ATA), a national organization formed in 1933 with a similar charter to defend and promote the fledgling industry.

Atherton's first responsibility was to write to every trucking firm and bus operator in Oklahoma soliciting membership in AMCO. The letter aptly expressed what Yellow Transit and others felt had to happen in order to protect their businesses:

Dear Oklahoma Truck & Bus Executive:

As a Certified Operator in this State you cannot fail to appreciate the importance to you personally of the Associated Motor Carriers of Oklahoma, Inc.

You know what the truck and bus men of Oklahoma are facing. You know that the railroads are after YOU, and that YOU are the one who will be hurt most by the unfair, discriminatory and oppressive measures which will be introduced by railroad spokesmen at the next legislature in January.

Now – The Associated Motor Carriers of Oklahoma is the only organized group in Oklahoma that exists solely to fight the battle for the Truck and Bus men....

If we are to have any success at all, and save the thousands of dollars that operators of Oklahoma are in danger of losing through increased taxation and regulation, we must have the support of EVERY Truck and Bus man in Oklahoma.

You cannot afford to wait until the legislature meets to start your defense....

Sincerely,

Ray G. Atherton

AMCO grew from 74 member carriers in 1932 to more than 800 the next year. By 1934, membership reached 1000. Yellow Transit's Hickox was immediately appointed vice president in charge of AMCO's Class A Truck Operators. Nash later became the organization's president in 1941 and served as president again in 1948.[8]

At Yellow Transit Company, Nash quickly stepped in and took over day-to-day operations after making the transition from CPA to general manager of the trucking firm. His financial skills and fixation on detail helped Yellow Transit emerge from the growing pack of trucking tradesmen to become a legitimate corporate business.

Nash managed with many of the same business philosophies the Harrells used to found the company. He preferred dealing in cash and expected price concessions. As the company outgrew its terminal facilities in Dallas and Kansas City, A.J. Harrell and Evans Nash used their financial leverage to acquire new sites for less than one-third the seller's asking price in both locations. They also saved on purchases of items ranging from office supplies to Mack tractors because of their cash policies.[9]

Notre Dame football coach Knoche Rockne is killed in an airplane crash in Kansas.

The Nevada State Legislature legalizes gambling.

Little Orphan Annie debuts over the NBC Blue Network, sponsored by Ovaltine.

Congress makes "The Star Spangled Banner" the U.S. national anthem.

New York's Empire State Building opens.

Further Expansion

After Houston had been added to the service area, A.J. Harrell turned his attention to St. Louis. Yellow Transit purchased Selby Motor Freight Line, Inc., of Rolla, Mo., in 1935. However, Harrell did not get permission to merge the new route into Yellow Transit until 1939. Until then, he operated it under the name Yellow Cab Transit Company of Missouri, with authority to follow Route 66 from Joplin to St. Louis through Springfield and Rolla.

A.J. and Marvin Harrell and Evans Nash were directors of the new carrier, as was James T. Blair, Jr., who had a one-percent stake in the Missouri operation. Blair, a Missouri state legislator from 1928-32, eventually became Governor of Missouri in 1956. It is assumed that Blair's role was to assist the company with state regulatory matters – a lesson learned in Oklahoma when the railroads began to use their political connections to interfere with trucking industry's expansion.[10]

Regulation Begins

Yellow Transit Company grew with the nation. Trade stimulated the economy, produced jobs and generated taxes. Taxes provided the young democracy resources to build a national defense and engage the rest of the world in commercial and civil diplomacy. Active commerce and productive manufacturing gave an upstart nation surprising power at the close of World War I.

Future prosperity depended in large part on a transportation infrastructure that could propel America into the world's marketplace. A planned transportation system could help America grow faster and compete with already-developed European and Asian cultures.

America still had frontiers that needed to be explored. People were concentrated in eastern and western seaboard cities, hugging the Great Lakes and docked against the Mississippi River and its tributaries. The rest of America was agrarian – farmers living off the land in relatively isolated communities, one or two days from the closest major market. Even after motor-driven trucks began replacing horse-drawn wagons, roads were so inadequate, planned treks depended heavily on luck, a good set of tools and plenty of spare parts.

The weakness of this severed society became more obvious following the stock market crash in October 1929. The economy recoiled clumsily when it was

A.J. Harrell is flanked by Evans Nash and Marvin Harrell during a photo taken at a sales meeting in Tulsa. (photo courtesy Pauline Severs)

1932

Franklin D. Roosevelt is elected president.

First-class postage rates increase to 3 cents.

U.S. Route 66 officially opens to link Chicago to Los Angeles with a continuous 2,200-mile highway, dubbed "Main Street of America."

Radio comedy's popular programs include: The Jack Benny Show on NBC and The Fred Allen Show on CBS.

ST. LOUIS
TULSA
848
886
ROSE MFG. CO.
DALLAS
GLASS

clear that credit had been extended too far without enough capital support.

Yellow Cab Transit Company survived because A.J. and Cleve Harrell used cash, not credit. Wall Street's panic and the subsequent depression of the 1930s allowed the Harrells to benefit from the failure of others. It left the company poised for the future because it was capable of treading water until economic stability was restored.

Things were cheap – a 20-oz. loaf of bread was five cents, a pound of bacon was 22 cents, milk was less than 40 cents a gallon and a gas stove sold for $23.95. They were cheap because few people had money to buy from large inventories established during the robust 1920s.

Unemployment was high and those who did have jobs worked for less. A physician was making about $4,000 a year, a schoolteacher less than $1,300 and a construction worker barely $900. On the farm, annual wages were $216. The best place to be was in Congress. A representative earned $8,663, richly rewarding him for representing his district.[11]

Buying anything beyond life's essentials was uncommon in the early 1930s. Demand for transportation slackened. A.J. and Cleve reduced their own executive salaries in order to keep others working. In later years, when Cleve's taxi drivers organized and demanded better wages, he interpreted their actions as ungrateful. It apparently prompted him to sell Yellow Cab Company of Oklahoma City to Y&Y Operating Company in 1940.

Shoring Up the Economy

The nation was going through a transition of its own in the early 1930s. Franklin D. Roosevelt had been elected president. He took bold steps to turn the nation's economy around but not without significant cost to individuals. Personal income taxes increased to finance social welfare programs such as the Civil Work Administration (CWA), Works Progress Administration (WPA) and National Youth Administration (NYA). Public housing also began in this era. A federal gasoline tax also was imposed for the first time – 1-cent per gallon.

Under the National Industrial Recovery Act of 1932, people with jobs were asked to reduce their working hours and income so people without jobs could share the work and wages. Meetings were held at Yellow Cab and Yellow Transit to seek compliance. The act was ruled unconstitutional two years later.

This page — *The Oklahoma Capitol was a favorite backdrop for photos that were meant to demonstrate company pride. A.J. Harrell wanted his drivers and equipment to look their best at all times.(photo coutesy Pauline Severs)*

Page 20 — *The overall appearance of the freight dock has not changed much in 60 years. This Dallas dock scene confirms that fundamental handling procedures at a less-than-truckload facility have stood up well through the years. (photo coutesy Pauline Severs)*

1933

Adolf Hitler becomes dictator of the German Reich.

A National Labor Board appointed by President Roosevelt enforces the right to collective bargaining.

Prohibition ends when Utah, the 36th state to do so, ratifies the 21st Amendment.

Typical prices: Gallon of gasoline, 18¢; quart of milk, 10¢; pound of bacon, 22¢; pound of sugar, 6¢; and a 20-oz. loaf of bread, 5¢.

Douglas Aircraft introduces the DC-1, which can carry 12 passengers at 150 mph; TWA orders 25.

Page 23 — *Military-like uniforms were confidence builders. You could trust a man in uniform and A.J. Harrell used that psychology to his advantage with customers. He insisted that his drivers dress for the image. (photo courtesy Oklahoma Historical Society)*

The government played another role under Roosevelt's leadership that affected Yellow Transit. More business regulation was sought across all industries in an attempt to manage America's push for progress. In some sectors, lack of government control was blamed for the shortsightedness that led to the stock market's crash and later economic depression.

For the trucking industry, regulation came in 1935. Congress passed the Motor Carrier Act, placing the industry under the watchful eye of the Interstate Commerce Commission (ICC). The ICC's first task was to review company routes that existed on June 1, 1935. If a carrier could demonstrate that its routes operated for "public convenience and necessity," the routes would be reauthorized or "grandfathered" by way of certification. The new regulatory agency reviewed nearly 76,000 applications, including Yellow Transit's.

The company's applications were submitted to the ICC in January 1936. Among them was a request for authority to operate Yellow Cab Transit Company of Missouri, acquired just five months earlier.

The overall application featured two established routes connecting Kansas City to Houston, one via Oklahoma City and Dallas, and another via smaller Kansas, Oklahoma and Texas communities along U.S. Routes 69, 54 and 77. St. Louis was linked along many of the same highways.

The commission granted most of what Yellow Transit asked for, keeping the company's principal routes in place. With its overcrowded docket, it took the ICC more than 30 months to rule on Yellow Transit's certification. The delay did not stop expansion. Yellow Transit submitted a new request to the ICC seeking approval for the purchase of a carrier operating in Oklahoma and Texas. That authority would allow Yellow Transit to enter Enid, Okla., and San Antonio, Wichita Falls and Bowie, Texas. It was another drawn-out decision that took nearly four years.

Yellow Transit also submitted a proposal to purchase Kern Motor Express, a carrier operating between St. Louis and Evansville, Ind. In examining the application, the ICC realized that for Yellow Transit to move southbound freight from Evansville through St. Louis to reach Oklahoma City, Dallas or Houston, it had to be interlined with the parent corporation's other subsidiary, Yellow Cab Transit Company of Missouri. The commission recommended that a larger action be considered. It suggested that Kern Motor Express, Yellow Cab Transit Company

1934

Popular movies include: Dinner at Eight with John Barrymore, Duck Soup with the Marx Brothers, Little Women with Katharine Hepburn, She Done Him Wrong and I'm No Angel with Mae West and Cary Grant, Sons of the Desert with Laurel and Hardy, and Tillie and Gus with W.C. Fields.

American Airlines and Continental Air Lines begin carrying passengers.

Men's underwear sales slump after Clark Gable takes off his shirt in a movie to reveal he wears no undershirt.

Bank robber John Dillinger, 32, is killed by FBI agents when he exits a Chicago theater.

ellow Transit Co.
FREIGHT LINES
"Serving the Southwest"
KANSAS

Rapid expansion in Texas added this terminal in Ft. Worth to the Yellow Transit network. (photo courtesy Pauline Severs)

of Missouri and A.J. Harrell's independently owned Bryan Motor Freight Lines be merged with the Yellow Cab Transit Company of Oklahoma, the original carrier, because it was "in line with our policy to encourage corporate simplification."[12]

Unifying all the carriers was approved in 1939. Yellow Transit's service territory covered Evansville, St. Louis and Kansas City across the northern tier; several communities in Missouri, Kansas and Oklahoma in its midsection, including Springfield, Joplin, Wichita, Oklahoma City and Tulsa; and in the south, Dallas and Houston.

A New Order

Yellow Transit took on a more businesslike form as it matured during the 1930s. The same was true for the rest of the motor freight industry. However, there were inconsistencies in related matters that affected business. They required further attention if trucks were going to help the nation move its commerce more effectively. Chief among the issues was America's roads.

Federal officials had enough foresight in 1916 to create rules for proceeding with a structured roadway system. They drafted guidelines for providing federal aid to states and refined them in 1921 with the Federal Highway Act.

In writing laws that established procedures for constructing uniformly paved highways, several things needed to be considered. Utmost was where the roads should go. Secondly, who was going to pay for them and who would maintain them after they were built?

Initially, motor-driven vehicles were luxuries for the affluent and rising middle class. Still, innovative developments were subtly affecting people of every economic stratum. In a system dominated by agriculture and manufacturing, the ability to move goods to market easier and faster was perceived as a big deal. It was obvious, too, that better transportation brought more product choices. More competition meant consumers might expect lower prices. It was a win-win situation in the making.

Railroads demonstrated in the 19th century that dependable transportation between one city and another created a framework for economic growth. What railroads lacked, trucks were now able to supply – door-to-door convenience and flexibility to go places where there were no tracks. Trucks also provided more frequent and flexible schedules, especially for shorter

1935

- The Social Security Act is signed, creating a system of retirement annuities and unemployment benefits.
- The Motor Carrier Act passed by Congress puts interstate truck and bus lines under supervision of the Interstate Commerce Commission.
- Fibber McGee and Molly becomes the newest popular radio program.
- The first major league night game is played in Cincinnati.
- Monopoly is introduced by Parker Brothers, which previously rejected the game because it took too long to play.

lengths of haul, so dependable timeliness of delivery became an additional value in the marketplace.

The federal government took on the responsibility of supplying a missing ingredient – money for reliable highways linking population centers everywhere.

A.J. Harrell captured the essence of the inadequate road issue in a message he sent to more than 150 Yellow Cab Transit Company employees in the company's first employee newsletter called *The Yellow Fleet*, published Aug. 15, 1929.

> Detours, mud holes and bumps, which have long been the bane of Yellow Transit... soon will be a thing of the past on our line to Tulsa. Last of the unpaved gaps on this famous highway (U.S. Route 66) will be closed within the next sixty days, giving us an all weather road. The entire distance will not be hardsurfaced at this time, but never the less, the road will be made passable and serviceable each day of the year regardless of weather conditions.
>
> We have been held back from doing the things we have wanted to because of the condition of this road in the past. It now is possible for us to go forward with our plans, which we intend to do as speedily as conditions will permit. This announcement should be welcomed by all Yellow Transit drivers. It means a great deal to you as well as to ourselves....
>
> In the years we have been struggling to give service on this line we have built up an efficient organization in every department... Good roads and larger equipment means greater volume of business, and increased compensation to our drivers and other employees....

A.J. Harrell later admitted he took other steps to make sure his trucks and buses reached their destination over roads vulnerable to the weather. He said he hired big men, many of them with experience in the oil fields that had the physical capability to get a vehicle out of the mud. "Those boys really knew how to take care of themselves," Harrell said. "They always found a way to get out of their difficulties," he added, downplaying the impact bad roads had on business.[13]

Teamsters Recognized

Yellow Transit Company was among the first trucking firms to make the leap to a full-fledged corporate business. Evans Nash deserved much of the credit. He implemented ways to measure the business revenue and operating costs on a daily basis. Terms such as revenue per hundred weight, revenue per mile and average revenue per day that are still used at Yellow, were tools Nash introduced to gauge the company's ongoing financial ability. Few others in the industry during the 1930s examined their business in this manner.

The check-and-balance system Nash employed enabled him to adjust spending on variables such as labor and equipment purchases. The ultimate goal was to keep the business growing steadily and growing profitably.

EASY TO REMEMBER — Yellow Transit Buses Leave Oklahoma City Daily for Tulsa On Every Even Numbered Hour from 6 A.M. to 4 P.M. and again at 7 P.M.

Yellow Cab Phone 2-6161

The Yellow Fleet

Yellow Cab Phone 2-6161

Vol. 1 — Oklahoma City, Okla., August 15, 1929 — No. 1

Cab Dispatching System Improved

Fifteen Sub Stations Speed Up Service Calls

Of Course He Rode In A Yellow

Washington, D. C.

Directory Reveals Development Facts

Yellow Cab Manual Largest In Company's History

Yellow Fleet was a company newspaper distributed to 150 Yellow Cab Transit Company employees in 1929. Editorial messages from A.J. and Cleve Harrell addressed the important issues of the day.

1936

GM experiences a sit-down strike after firing five workers for wearing union buttons at the Fisher Body plant at Flint, Mich.

Boulder Dam (later Hoover Dam) is completed after 21 months of construction on the Colorado River at the Arizona and Nevada border.

LIFE magazine, a weekly publication, first appears on the newsstand.

Bob Feller signs with the Indians and Joe DiMaggio signs with the Yankees.

1937

Japanese forces invade China.

Oil World Exposition

Growth and success spawned a larger work force at each division of Yellow Cab Transit Company. The number of employees tripled in the 1930s. As it grew, Yellow Transit Company attracted the attention of the Teamsters Union.

The Harrell brothers understood a laborer's point of view. They had been laborers themselves and knew what it took to do physical work. It made them considerate of the men who drove their taxis and trucks, did the mechanical chores and worked in the office. The Harrells also understood what it was like to use a team of horses and a wagon to make a living, just like the men who organized the Teamsters some 30 years earlier.

In the case of Yellow Cab Transit Company, the union had no beef with wages or working conditions. In fact, the trucking division already paid more than union scale and offered group life and accident insurance on top of the wage premium. It also offered vacation time. Few companies could match Yellow Transit's compensation package.

In addition, Harrell instilled pride in his men. He dressed them in uniforms, expected the uniforms to be kept well pressed and demanded their trucks be kept clean and mechanically sound. But the union still wanted in and A.J. Harrell knew it.

Instead of waiting for employees or the Teamsters to take the first step, Harrell and Evans Nash initiated contact with the union. They called on a union representative in Tulsa to discuss organizing Yellow Transit's drivers. They granted the Teamsters the "recognition" the union sought. Harrell and Nash negotiated their first contract without adding any cost. Yellow Transit was unionized.[14]

Triumphs and Tragedies

Policies adopted by A.J. and Cleve Harrell and enforced by Evans Nash and Marvin Harrell preserved Yellow Cab Transit Company during America's darkest hours. Though the company prospered during the economic depression of the 1930s, the World War II years would become a burden to A.J.

His best moments came in the mid-to-late 1930s. Yellow Transit Company set in motion a much more aggressive business agenda and strengthened itself for the trials ahead.

While waiting for the ICC to rule on a number of critical applications, the Harrell-Nash management team forged plans to expand the company further. They also began looking for a new site on which

This page — *The war years idled many pieces of Yellow Transit's equipment because spare parts were hard to find. (photo courtesy Oklahoma Historical Society)*

Page 26 — *Showing off Yellow Transit equipment to prospective shippers was just as common in the 1930s as it is today. Here, a Fruehauf trailer lined with thick oak boards was on display at the Houston Oil World Exhibition. (photo courtesy Oklahoma Historical Society)*

Italy withdraws from the League of Nations after joining the German-Japanese pact.

GM recognizes the United Auto Workers as the sole bargaining agent for workers.

Kerr-McGee Oil is founded in Oklahoma City (KM buys Yellow Cab Dynamic Gasoline stations from Cleve Harrell heirs).

Amelia Earhart disappears July 2.

The Lincoln Tunnel opens to traffic between New York and Weehawken, N.J.

to construct a modern terminal and office facility. They settled on land at the south edge of downtown Oklahoma City near the intersection of Reno and Western Avenue.

Meantime, the ICC examined A.J. and Cleve's application to divide Yellow Cab Transit Company and A.J.'s request to fold all of the various truck lines into one entity. A.J. was confident that he would be operating a single truck line.

The next endeavor was to find new cost-saving opportunities. Fuel was a major expense. Producer margins were thin because dozens of oil entrepreneurs were attempting to survive by selling more volume. A.J. had little room to squeeze more from the refineries. The nation's average gasoline price was 18 cents a gallon. Instead, he created a fuel savings in a little corner of Kansas.

Yellow Transit's north-south route angled near the intersection of Missouri, Kansas and Oklahoma. Missouri tax on gasoline was 3.5 cents per gallon, Oklahoma's was three cents, but Kansas' was only two cents. Fortunately, Route 66 cut off the extreme southeast sliver of Kansas as it wound its way between Missouri and Oklahoma. A.J. took advantage of the penny saving by setting up a major servicing center and repair shop along Route 66 about 17 miles from Missouri and barely two miles from Oklahoma. The spot was Baxter Springs, Kan.

The small Kansas town seemed ideally suited to Yellow Transit for more reasons than its tax savings. It was located about midway between St. Louis and Dallas, and between Kansas City and Oklahoma City – ideal for a refueling stop, a general maintenance shop and relay operations. It was close to Joplin, Mo., and Miami, Okla., good communities to recruit dependable, raw-boned farmhands and oil jobbers, the kind A.J. Harrell liked.

Once established, A.J. met with representatives of Phillips Petroleum, also based in Oklahoma, and chipped another quarter-of-a-cent per gallon from his gasoline prices. In exchange, he granted Phillips exclusive sales to the Baxter Springs facility. About 70 trucks per day stopped at the relay terminal where employees pumped 6,000 gallons into their 90-gallon tanks. The net result: the company saved $125 each day, a sizeable amount in the 30s. The new savings were carefully monitored by A.J.'s chief bean counter, Evans Nash.[15]

1938

The Fair Labor Standards Act is the first attempt to put a floor under wages and ceiling on working hours.

Wall Street's Dow Jones Industrial Average falls to a low of 98.95 (current day DJIA is at 11,000).

The Florida Overseas Highway links Key West to the mainland.

The Yankees sweep the Cubs in the World Series.

A tropical hurricane strikes Long Island and New England killing 680 people and causing $400 million in property damage.

New Friends

A.J. Harrell was just as proud of Yellow Transit's equipment as he was of the men who operated it. He favored Mack tractors and bought only Fruehauf trailers. Whenever A.J. acquired another company, he traded in old trailers for new 20-foot Fruehaufs (later, 26-foot). Again, Harrell used cash when buying the new equipment. When the company did not have the cash, Harrell made personal loans to Yellow Transit at six-percent interest rather than alter his all-cash business policy.

Harvey and Roy Fruehauf enjoyed stopping to see their loyal customer in Oklahoma City. They became personal friends. In later years, A.J. recalled times he visited the Fruehaufs in Detroit when they were just beginning at a blacksmith shop. He was proud that the mutual relationship contributed to the success of both companies.[16]

Harvey Firestone, Jr. also became acquainted with A.J. through a forced business contact that A.J. said "made Firestone a million (dollars)."

One of Firestone's sales engineers was greeted coolly one day when he called on Yellow Transit in Oklahoma City. A.J. had a complaint.

Firestone, like other tire manufacturers, used cotton cords to support its pneumatic rubber tires. As the tires heated in use, they expanded. On axles with two tires side by side, the rubber touched and hastened the wear. It also caused a fire hazard.

Several manufacturers had already experimented with rayon cord, led by Goodrich. However, they had used the experimental cord only on automobile tires, not truck and industrial sizes. A.J. ridiculed Firestone's decision to stick with cotton cord. That prompted an executive visit.

A.J. explained to Harvey Firestone and his sales engineer, Bob Hill, that he kept 3,000 tires in stock because he was using them up at a rate of 200 tires per month. He wanted someone to make a 12-ply rayon cord that would withstand the beating a truck tire took on its intercity treks.

Firestone asked, "If we build a big 12-ply rayon cord tire, how many tires would you buy?"

A.J. committed to buying 600 tires at a time. They made a deal on the spot. Firestone would make the larger, 12-ply rayon-cord tire if Yellow Transit would buy the first production at $48 per tire. Since the trucking firm was paying $68 for eight-ply cotton cord tires, it was a simple decision for A.J.

"The oilfield haulers and people like Haliburton's

A.J. Harrell with his Mack and Fruehauf tractor-trailer combination.

1939

Britain and France declare war on Germany.

Only three percent of Americans make enough income to pay taxes; 670,000 U.S. taxpayers pay 90 percent of the nation's income taxes.

Popular movies include: Gone With the Wind with Clark Gable, Gunga Din with Cary Grant, Mr. Smith Goes to Washington with Gary Cooper, The Hunchback of Notre Dame with Charles Laughton, Stagecoach with John Wayne and The Wizard of Oz with Judy Garland.

The Yankees sweep the Reds to win the World Series after "Iron Horse" Lou Gehrig ends his playing streak due to an illness.

Headquarter Radishes

Yellow Transit's Oklahoma City headquarters and terminal from 1938-1950 covered most of the city block along Western Avenue. To the right is the uniquely designed gasoline station that originally pumped Yellow Cab Dynamic Gasoline. (photo courtesy Pauline Severs)

Employees were quite proud of the new company headquarters on Western Avenue in Oklahoma City. W.L. Stevenson, a longtime secretary to A.J. and contributor to early histories of Yellow, was said to have been a victim of Harrell's playful humor.

Stevenson, who went by the nick-name "Steve," planted expensive grass seed on the terminal grounds. When A.J. learned of his secretary's lavish spending, he scattered radish seed in the lawn. At a time when Stevenson was showing off his lush grass to acquaintances, A.J. walked by, bent over and pulled a weed. He examined its roots in front of Stevenson's guests. "Why, Steve," Harrell said, "this looks like a radish. It smells like a radish, too."

A.J. cleaned off the red root and took a bite. "By golly, it tastes like a radish, Steve," Harrell said. "What kind of grass seed did you plant, anyhow?"

It was a long time before Stevenson and others learned that A.J. had purposely sprinkled the yard with the radish seed.[19]

Cement Company began using them in all their heavy duty equipment," said A.J. Harrell in an interview conducted in 1958. "Also, truck lines all over were delighted to get such big rugged, durable tires. They were the first of the modern, heavy-duty truck tires."[17]

New Headquarters

Operating independent of brother Cleve's taxicab enterprise, A.J. was motivated to build a new home for Yellow Transit Company. It also gave him an excuse to set an example for his management team.

The third level of the three-story terminal built at 311 S. Western Ave. in Oklahoma City housed a plush living quarter. A.J. and his new bride, Julia, moved to the apartment after it was constructed in 1938.

A.J. had set his designs on terminals with living quarters above or attached to the structures. He wanted his terminal managers accessible to the operation even when they were not on duty. Likewise, he figured the manager's wife could perform some of the secretarial chores.

Among the most notable examples of this practice was the terminal in Vinita, Okla., located on Route 66 between Tulsa and Baxter Springs, Kan. Lyle Payne and his wife, Louise, were the first to run the terminal in 1939. It was more than a freight depot and home to the Paynes, it also served as a filling station for motorists and a café for travelers and area residents. Architecturally unique in its round design, it was a memorable oasis along America's Highway.

Payne spent several years with Yellow, most of them in Baxter Springs. Highly regarded by his co-workers, he shared an admirable characteristic with his boss, A.J. Harrell. They were good at remembering names.

Payne and his wife also had a one-year-old son living with them at the Vinita terminal. Bruce Payne, like his father, retired from Yellow after more than 30 years of service to the company. Bruce said that after his father retired in 1980, fellow employees asked how his father was getting along and why he never returned to visit with his former colleagues at Baxter Springs. When Bruce asked that question of Lyle, his father said he was afraid he would embarrass himself by forgetting a friend's name. His ability to recognize employees and call them by name had become such a personal trademark of the elder Payne's, that he did not want to spoil his legacy.

Winonah West remembered Yellow Transit's

This terminal, gasoline station and diner was built in Vinita, Okla., along Route 66 north of Tulsa. The 1930s modern design included second story residential accommodations for the terminal manager.

1940

- The first peacetime U.S. military draft begins.
- The first pressurized cabin airplane takes off in New York en route to Burbank, Calif., via Kansas City.
- B.F. Goodrich unveils the first synthetic rubber tire.
- Popular movies include: The Grapes of Wrath with Henry Fonda, The Philadelphia Story with Katharine Hepburn, and The Mark of Zorro with Tyrone Power.
- Mars makes the first M&M candies as a soldier's ration food.

Page 33 — *A.J. Harrell was a no-nonsense businessman who parlayed a fourth-grade education and hard work into personal fortune. His all-cash purchasing policies enabled him to buy what he wanted when he wanted it despite the nation's worst economic crisis. (photo courtesy Oklahoma Historical Society)*

Western Avenue headquarters. She was hired in 1942 as a clerk when A.J.'s all-male policy changed as a consequence of World War II. Fewer men were available to industry because of the military draft.

West said Julia Harrell occasionally invited female employees to the Harrell's penthouse apartment "for a little visit." West said new girls in the office were sometimes taken on a tour of the apartment. She recalled that the floors were thickly carpeted. It was a beautiful place, she said.

Eventually, the office took over the penthouse when the Harrells moved out. West said her office was located in what was once the den. It had a large fireplace with the head of an elk mounted over the mantel. The wall lamps and thick carpeting were luxuries uncommon to most workplaces.[18]

Life Toughens

Fortune ran well for A.J. Harrell during the 1930s, despite his quarrel with Cleve. He succeeded in shaping the truck line to his liking and building a model headquarters from which to operate his business. He hired Evans Nash, whom he regarded as "the most efficient office man ever in Oklahoma City." And he persuaded his brother Marvin Harrell to stay with Yellow Transit when the family feud caused the founding brothers to break ranks.

In 1939, A.J. was hit hard by the first of three emotional setbacks. Marvin Harrell, 46, died from a heart attack. The father of five had become a close ally to his eldest brother. A.J. had entrusted him with the company's financial supervision.

Marvin left two sons and three daughters. A.J., who never had children of his own, accepted financial responsibility for helping Marvin's family. Among other things, he made sure Leroy, Marvin's youngest son, received an excellent education. Leroy and his sister, Pauline, stayed in contact with A.J. throughout their lives.[20]

Then, the second tragic event occurred. In 1942, three years after Marvin's death, Cleve Harrell died from a stroke. Janet Cooke, Cleve's stepdaughter, remembered A.J. stopping by the church at Cleve's funeral. He never came into the church, said Cooke, then 17. She recalled "Uncle Art" sadly expressing his sympathy to her and her sister Susan through the rolled-down window of his car.

Cleve Harrell, 58, left a significant mark on Oklahoma City. He also left a name and tradition for Yellow. His hand-painted Model-T Ford created

1941

World War II expands as Germany invades Russia and Japan bombs Pearl Harbor.

U.S. truck production is 4.85 million compared to 3.5 million in 1931.

President Roosevelt establishes the Office of Defense Transportation.

Stan Musial, 22, hits .426 for the Cardinals when called up late in the season to start a 22-year career in St. Louis.

1942

Japanese forces take Manila.

a taxicab marketing image copied throughout the United States. Among those who envied the idea was John Hertz, who later built Yellow Cab automobiles, which Cleve bought. Hertz, of rental-car fame, founded Yellow Cab of Chicago and copyrighted the name. He used the Yellow name on a coach and truck manufacturing firm he later sold to General Motors.

Cleve's contributions to his Oklahoma community included prominent civic accomplishments. As a school board member, he chaired the building committee and was given credit for leading the construction of numerous schools built during the 1930s. Still, he never forgot his friends from the early days in Oklahoma City. When he visited the schools he helped build he stopped by to say hello to the janitors with whom he worked for 10 years starting in 1906.

Distraught by the loss of his brothers, A.J. faced another emotional hardship. The United States began drafting his men – the drivers, mechanics, clerks and salesmen who helped him build his company. The country was at war and A.J. felt like one of its victims.

A.J. regarded his employees as "the best in the country." He knew his workers by name and had a paternal instinct to keep them in his fold for as long as he could. That was impossible when they were needed on the battlefield. It wore him down.

Operating Yellow Transit Company became even more difficult because World War II consumed America's resources. Tractors, tires, trailers and fuel became scarce. Sixty-five Yellow Transit trailers were put up on blocks at one point, because the company couldn't get tires. Fourteen tractors sat idle because parts were unavailable. On occasion, in order to keep the freight moving, tires were taken off of incoming trailers and mounted on loaded outgoing trailers so they could depart.

The stress of these events caused A.J. to weaken. He became ill and made up his mind to sell Yellow Transit if an offer came along.[21]

The last new auto built for three war years rolls off the Ford assembly line.

Nationwide gasoline rationing is ordered.

1943

Freshman Congressman J. William Fullbright drafts a resolution to create the United Nations.

1944

Allied forces invade Normandy, France, June 6, D-Day.

A Federal Highway Act establishes a U.S. National System of Interstate Highways.

The War and Weary Years

Nash Makes His Mark

A.J. Harrell leaned heavily on Evans Nash to keep the company sound. Nash had a well-earned reputation for resourcefulness and attention to detail. A certified public accountant by training, Nash had developed an avid interest in the company and industry while auditing company records.

After acquiring Selby truck line in 1936, Harrell learned first hand how helpful his accountant could be during a trip to St. Louis. Their goal was to find a new terminal. Yellow Transit had been sharing facilities with Viking, another carrier, but the space was inadequate.

Harrell and Nash found what they wanted at 6th and Poplar Streets, now a parking lot at the current site of Busch Stadium. Though the asking price was much higher, they discovered they could buy the property for $26,000 cash. Problem was, they did not bring money with them.

"How are we going to buy this property?" Harrell asked Nash.

"Let's get a cashier's check," was Nash's answer. To Harrell's surprise, it was that easy. A nearby St. Louis bank wrote them a check for $26,000 almost on the spot. Nash had planted the seed for such an occasion when several months earlier he had filed a financial report with Dun & Bradstreet. The bank reviewed Dun & Bradstreet reports as a common practice when investigating companies seeking loans. It was clear to the bank that Yellow Cab Transit Company was a well run, financially sound company and presented no risk based on the report prepared and filed by Nash.

As the two executives left the bank, Harrell reportedly said to Nash, "You know, that was so easy, I think we should have asked for more."[1]

Between Nash and Harrell, they kept Yellow Transit on the move, buying other carriers and expanding the operation. They established Yellow Transit as a carrier specializing in less-than-truckload service. A relatively new innovation at the time, LTL service was rapidly accepted as a way to ship smaller quantities and keep inventory mobile. LTL was a value worthy of premium pricing.

Among the company's acquisitions during the Harrell-Nash era were the purchases of four carriers

The parking lot south of Busch Stadium in downtown St. Louis once was the ground for Yellow Transit's terminal. A.J. Harrell and Evans Nash bought the terminal with $26,000 cash, although it was listed for more than twice that amount.

1945

- President Roosevelt dies and is succeeded by Vice President Harry Truman.
- Two atomic bombs are dropped on Japanese cities Hiroshima and Nagasaki.
- World War II ends in Europe May 8 and in the Pacific August 14.
- U.S. gasoline and fuel oil rationing ends.
- Henry Ford, 82, steps down as president of Ford Motor Com., relinquishing control to 28-year-old grandson Henry Ford II.

Lawsuit in Louisville

Louisville's terminal allowed Yellow Transit to enter a new state and extend its Midwestern service to the south.

In 1943, a taxi firm, Louisville Taxicab and Transfer Company, filed a civil action against Yellow Transit Company claiming it had rights to the name. The taxi company did not want to compete with Yellow Transit Company's advertising and operations in Louisville and Jefferson County, Kentucky. The Kentucky courts ruled in favor of the local company. However, the lower court decision was overturned by the Circuit Court of Appeals, and Yellow Transit was allowed to continue operating in Louisville.[2]

in Illinois and Indiana. They enabled Yellow Transit to extend its service to several important markets, most notably Chicago and Louisville. But the motive behind acquiring two of the carriers, Kern Motor Express and Holsapple Truck Lines, stemmed from Harrell's early contacts with oil explorers.

Oil was being discovered in east central Illinois. Fields were rumored to cover a patch of land 100 miles wide. Harrell heard that producers would eventually be moving equipment to the area for drilling. He wanted to link his Texas and Oklahoma routes to the area so he could benefit from anticipated freight traffic. He expected that oil companies already operating in the two southwestern states would be supplying the Illinois site.

Harrell kept his thoughts quiet and bought all four companies for around $50,000.

The acquisitions proved to be quite lucrative. The routes provided access to important commercial centers and resulted in significant growth. Expansion between 1937 and 1943 tripled the company's revenue ($2.7 million) and assets ($1.8 million) and quadrupled profits ($171,899). Employment doubled from 280 to 560.

Missouri Gap Filled

Kansas City and St. Louis were important cities in Yellow Transit's formative years. They had become key manufacturing centers in the Midwest and originated much of the traffic that flowed to Texas through Oklahoma. With the additional connections to Chicago and Louisville, they also became important consumer markets, but Yellow Transit did not have the authority to directly link the two Missouri communities.

Freight sent via Yellow Transit between St. Louis and Kansas City had to go through Springfield, Mo., which added more than 200 miles to the trip. That changed when Harrell acquired authority along U.S. Route 40 through Boonville. He bought the authority from Kansas City-Illinois Motor Express. In addition to the savings created by eliminating 200 miles of travel, the new route cut 10 hours of service time.

Time was a critical competitive factor. With more freight flowing from Chicago and Louisville, Harrell wanted southbound trucks leaving St. Louis on the hour. The objective was to get them to arrive in Kansas City and Dallas precisely and spaced for optimum dock efficiency.

Experience had taught Yellow Transit management that following exact schedules helped them control

Springfield, Mo., served as a turning point between St. Louis and Kansas City until Yellow Transit secured authority along U.S. Route 40, a direct route saving nearly 200 miles of travel and 10 hours.

Penicillin and streptomycin are introduced as commercial antibiotics.

Popular songs include: It's Been a Long, Long Time, For Sentimental Reasons, Let It Snow! Let It Snow! Let It Snow!, and He's Got the Whole World In His Hands.

Products developed during wartime that have become commercial successes include frozen orange juice and Swanson's frozen poultry meals.

Page 39 — *These unidentified Dallas employees from 1944 operated an important Yellow Transit terminal under adverse conditions. World War II consumed the nation's resources. They often kept freight moving with ingenuity. (photo courtesy Oklahoma Historical Society)*

their loading and unloading processes at the terminals. It also maximized labor productivity.

Real Estate Profits

Either very intuitive or very lucky, Harrell and Evans Nash successfully speculated on land that they thought would make good sites for Yellow Transit terminals. In a few cases, land values rose so quickly they sold for the profits before they could build a terminal. One such case was in Dallas.

Harrell found a lumberyard in the southwest part of the city. He thought the site would make a good terminal. He bought the property for $60,000, which was more than he usually paid for a terminal site and, of course, he used cash. Within two years he was offered an irresistible amount. He sold the lumberyard for $120,000.

In a later and related Dallas deal, Nash was the buyer. He had to find a new terminal since Harrell had sold his prospective property. Nash settled on vacant ground nearly 20 miles west of downtown Dallas, almost as close to downtown Ft. Worth. Critics thought Nash was crazy for buying property in the sticks. There were no factories, warehouses or department stores nearby, only open fields and a crossroads between cities.

"We were already on rubber," Nash said as he recalled his logic for the decision. "Dallas was beginning to spread out," he said. "It did not make much difference whether we would have to go downtown to pick up freight and bring it back out to the terminal, or go out from a downtown location to pick up freight in an outlying location."

Furthermore, he said he picked a spot where road drivers could make their relay transfer without getting tangled up in city traffic. Nash said he considered the safety factor.

Nash was correct in his assumptions. Dallas spread quickly. Soon the terminal was surrounded by other businesses. It made the property worth several times more than the $38,000 he paid. Even after outgrowing the Harry Hines Boulevard terminal, the company moved to a site close by because of the general conveniences Nash anticipated when he made his original purchase.[3]

Property Attracts Important Offer

In early 1944, Harrell, 61, was weary of the daily toll extracted by running a growing freight company. He shared his concern with Evans Nash. What would he think about selling the company?

1946

The United Nations opens its first session.

Inflation surges as demand for post-war consumer goods and housing drive prices upward.

Nationwide strikes idle 4.6 million workers.

U.S. troops are used in strikes against the nation's rail and soft coal industries.

Popular movies include: It's a Wonderful Life with James Stewart, The Postman Always Rings Twice with Lana Turner, and The Razor's Edge with Tyrone Power.

Dallas Tex
10-10-44
UNDERWOOD
SUNDSTRAND

TOR FREIGHT Inc.
CLARKS GARAGE
BRYAN
LLOW TRANSIT Co.
FREIGHT LINES

Nash told Harrell to pursue what was best for him. "It sounds OK to me if you can get enough money for it," Nash said. "I'll operate the business while you're doing the talking."[4]

Other interests occupied Harrell. He had investments in oil, his farm and raising cattle and hogs. He had purchased property at the southern edge of Oklahoma City and was building a new home. He wanted to sell Yellow Transit Company, but it was not an obsession. The company was running well under Nash's supervision. It was doing well enough, in fact, that Harrell had to think about expanding his Oklahoma City terminal once again after being at Reno and Western Avenue for only five years.

His search for a new location began in earnest early in 1944. He soon made an offer on property well suited for a new terminal. The deal brought a New York investor to Oklahoma City to negotiate with Harrell. He was so impressed with Yellow Transit, he inquired about buying stock in the company. Harrell informed him that he had no interest in taking on a financial partner.

Not willing to take no for an answer, the investor came back to A.J. with a bigger offer. He wanted to buy the whole company. Because all assets were owned free and clear, the investor planned to use the terminals and trucks as collateral in securing financing for the purchase. However, he still did not have enough to meet Harrell's price. After asking for more time to put the deal together, Harrell gave him 60 days.

Later, while touring terminals in Louisville and Vincennes, Ind., Harrell received word that a man was desperately trying to find him. Harrell relayed a message to have the man contact him at his hotel.

"I'm in shape to close the deal," said a familiar voice over the telephone. The response was not what the man wanted to hear.

"Your contract is already up," Harrell told him. "The 60 days are gone."

Harrell pointed out that Yellow Transit Company had made $42,000 profit in the short time since the offer was originally made. If the investor was serious about buying the company, he now needed to come up with the additional money.

Shortly after returning to Oklahoma City, and not unexpectedly, Harrell had a visitor. It was Arlington W. Porter, the investor. He had the extra $42,000 and was ready to buy Yellow Transit Company.

Recalling the transaction nearly 15 years after the

Page 40 — *This elevated view of Yellow Transit's headquarters terminal at 311 S. Western Ave. in Oklahoma City revealed much about the company and the times. From the oil well towers in the background, the Bryan trailer in the yard and the Lee Way terminal across the street (upper left), this was a clear picture of the unique circumstances in the 1940s. (photo courtesy Oklahoma Historical Society)*

1947

Popular songs include: Get Your Kicks On Route 66, Tenderly, Stella by Starlight and The Christmas Song (Chestnuts Roasting on an Open Fire).

AMF introduces the automatic Pinspotter at a bowling tournament in Buffalo.

The grandiose Flamingo Hotel begins a Las Vegas frenzy to build similar gambling resorts.

The Truman Doctrine announces plans to aid Greece and Turkey and others threatened by Communist takeover.

Page 43 — *Swamp Holly orange not yellow was the official color of Yellow Transit Company. A.J. Harrell, the legend reveals, chose the color for its safety features.*

deal closed, Harrell said he could have gotten more for the company if he had parceled out the routes and authority. But his health was failing and he did not want to be troubled by the detail. He sold his company to Porter and walked away.

With Yellow Transit Company under new ownership, A.J. Harrell focused his time on his farm, livestock and oil interests. He lived a long life, although terribly overweight and in ill health for many years. He died in 1972 in Oklahoma City, a few weeks short of his 90th birthday.

The Harrell Legacy: Swamp Holly Orange

It has been more than half a century since A.J. Harrell ran the company, but he left a legacy and more than a few legends. Perhaps the most notable is the mystery that surrounds the apparent contradiction between the company's name and color. It is the question asked most by motorists, customers and especially curious and confused children. "If your name is Yellow, why are your trucks orange?"

The unconfirmed story passed down for 50 years is that Harrell was especially concerned about the safety of his employees and equipment on the road. Travel between cities from 1924 to 1944 was nearly all on two lanes. Trucks and cars shared the same narrow and poorly marked pathways. Even the most sophisticated highway in Yellow Transit territory – Route 66 – was never more than three lanes, the center lane for passing.

The highway shoulders were dirt. If a truck was forced off of narrow pavement to avoid a collision, it often meant getting stuck in mud. Or worse still, it meant overturning because of a sudden shift and imbalance inside the trailer. The risks would be minimized if the trucks were easily seen.

Harrell reportedly contacted E.I. DuPont's paint division and asked the company to recommend a color that could be seen the farthest regardless of weather conditions or time of day. The chemical and paint company supposedly tested a variety of colors according to specifications. The result was a color that DuPont called "swamp holly orange."

Since that time – presumably early in the company's founding years – every vehicle has been painted the bright orange color while sporting the name Yellow.

Pauline Harrell Severs, one of Marvin Harrell's five children and a resident of Oklahoma City, confirmed that her uncle A.J.'s trucks were orange for as long as she could remember.

The Central Intelligence Agency is formed to combat the growth of Communism mostly in Western Europe.

The Taft-Hartley Act restricts organized labor's power to strike and prohibits closed shops and the use of union funds for political purposes.

B.F. Goodrich introduces the first tubeless automobile tires which seal themselves when punctured.

Jackie Robinson becomes the first black major league baseball player after signing with the Brooklyn Dodgers.

The Yankees win the World Series by defeating the Dodgers 4 games to 3.

Yellow Transit Co.
FREIGHT LINES
"Serving the Southwest"
KENTUCKY INDIANA ILLINOIS
MISSOURI KANSAS OKLAHOMA
TEXAS NEW MEXICO
NO.
438
FRUEHAUF
NO PASSENGERS
NO.
Mack

Translucent roofs allow additional light to illuminate working conditions, a safety and efficiency bonus. Yellow Transit Company experimented with translucent trailer roofs 60 years ago.

Vehicle color was not the only lasting innovation. Translucent panels were installed in the roofs of trailers to allow more light for stackers and checkers. Today a common practice, translucent panels were an innovative safety solution during the industry's adolescence.

Yellow Transit also installed teletype machines in each of its terminals. When a truck was dispatched, a message was sent to the destination terminal advising of the truck's contents and time of departure. It allowed the receiving terminal to anticipate and prepare for the arrival of its inbound freight. The relatively simple communications process gave Yellow Transit a significant competitive edge in servicing its customers better. It was a long time before other carriers caught up to the technology.[5]

Intangibles

A.J. often recounted that he and his brother Cleve were pioneers. They explored business opportunities courageously without the benefit of experience or knowledge, because it was all new. They took a fledgling trade that many others operated poorly – and that railroad executives attempted to sabotage – and gave it legs to stand on. They demonstrated that financial discipline and sound operating practices could make trucking a viable and highly profitable business. Long before the terms "logistics" and "supply chain management" came into vogue, they proved that transportation flexibility and speed could greatly benefit manufacturing and retailing.

The Harrells were well known for hiring people who were as resourceful as they were. A.J. Harrell admitted in 1958 that he struggled to find managers who shared his vision and work ethic before finally putting his brother Marvin and Evans Nash in charge. The others had no imagination, A.J. confessed. They were former railroad operators who doubted the company's potential.

Harrell's insistence that solutions be found – rather than excuses – was a trait Evans Nash shared. Nash kept it alive for six of the eight tumultuous years after the company was sold. He knew it was a trait that needed to be preserved for the company to do well. Nash stayed with Yellow Transit Company when A.J. Harrell departed, but the years ahead would test his mettle.

Enter A.W. Porter

Arlington W. Porter, the financial investor who first met A.J. Harrell during a property deal in Oklahoma

1948

President Truman wins re-election defeating Thomas E. Dewey.

The president puts the Army in charge of the nation's railroads to prevent a nationwide strike; control lasts four years.

The first automobile air conditioner is manufactured.

Michelin makes the first radial tire.

One million U.S. homes have TV sets, up from 5,000 in 1945.

City, took over Yellow Transit Company in the fourth quarter of 1944. President Roosevelt had just won re-election to a fourth term in office. The Supreme Court had just ruled that an American citizen could not be denied the right to vote based on color. The Battle of the Bulge was about to inflict heavy casualties on American troops in Europe, and Congress was passing the GI Bill of Rights, which in part financed a college education for returning servicemen and women.

It was also the year Congress passed the Federal Highway Act that established a new U.S. National System of Interstate Highways. It authorized a plan to build a network of roadways stretching 40,000 miles and linking 182 of 199 U.S. cities above populations of 50,000, including 42 state capitals. Unfortunately for the trucking industry and other motorists, it would take 12 more years before another act of Congress would finance a revised plan.

Porter bought Yellow Transit because he recognized it was a well-run company. The first 20 years of profits had been poured back into the company. Assets were owned, not mortgaged. Operating disciplines were sharp and managed astutely by employees. And one of the key architects of the company's soundness, Evans Nash, was willing to stay on as president. Porter had purchased a gem.

He had loyal customers, 562 professional employees and 142 vehicles, which were driven more than nine million miles the year before. During 1943, the business had generated $2.7 million in revenue and $170,899 in net income, with an operating ratio of 87.0. Revenue and profits were going to be better in 1944.

New Financial Policies

Arlington Porter and Evans Nash got along well during their honeymoon. They met frequently. Porter traveled to Oklahoma City to tour Yellow Transit terminals with Nash and get better acquainted with his company. Nash, meantime, made several trips east for meetings at the U.S. Chamber of Commerce and Office of Defense Transportation. He served as a committee participant on both. While there, he would also meet with Porter.

Porter and Nash came from very different backgrounds and not surprisingly had business philosophies that were almost diametrically opposed. Nash measured success by the amount of working capital available to expand operations when opportunities permitted. Porter appeared to measure success solely

Still a new industry with regulations and procedures changing routinely, it was smart for a driver to carry his rules-of-the-road booklet with him at all times.

Popular movies include: Oliver Twist with Alec Guinness, Red River with John Wayne, The Treasure of the Sierra Madre and Key Largo with Humphrey Bogart, and The Snake Pit with Olivia de Havilland.

Popular songs include: Tennesse Waltz, It's a Most Unusual Day, Red Roses for a Blue Lady, Buttons and Bows, Sleigh Ride and I'll Be Home for Christmas.

New consumer products include Dial soap, V-8 vegetable juice and Baskin-Robbins ice cream.

OFFICIAL
WEIGHT STATI
RELIABLE
Yellow Transit Co.
FREIGHT LINES
"Serving the Southwest"
KENTUCKY INDIANA ILLINOIS
MISSOURI KANSAS OKLAHOMA
TEXAS NEW & OLD MEXICO
492
427

through rapid return on investment.

The Harrell brothers' financial policy had been crystal clear – cash ruled. If there was no cash in the kitty, nothing was purchased. With cash purchases the company expected price concessions from vendors, suppliers and property owners as a way to keep operating and capital expenses at their lowest.

Porter's strategy was based on mortgaging assets to their maximum. Either he or those advising him saw in Yellow a debt-free business that could be fully leveraged.

Still, Porter and Nash worked through their differences, with Nash becoming a highly valued business associate in the early going.

In the first full year Porter owned Yellow Transit Company – 1945 – Yellow Transit's revenue grew by 5.7 percent and net income grew by 6.3 percent. During the year, Porter divided the company into subsidiary units, including Yellow Terminals, Inc., a Delaware corporation, and Yellow Equipment Company, an Illinois corporation. He moved the terminal assets to Yellow Terminals and the equipment assets to Yellow Equipment. Then each of the subsidiaries charged the parent organization a fee to lease the terminals and equipment in order to operate Yellow Transit.

Porter was able to gain tax benefits under this scenario. He assumed an appreciation in the value of his terminal assets of 65 percent and an even bolder gain of 154 percent in the value of his equipment when the assets were transferred to their respective subsidiaries. That gave him a much higher base in which to depreciate both assets, and thus, additional tax benefits and a much better cash flow.

One particularly lucrative opportunity came as a result of the establishment of Yellow Equipment Company. Porter received a check for $375,000 when he mortgaged the trucks for which A.J. Harrell had paid cash. He did this by selling shares in Yellow Transit to Yellow Equipment Company, his own subsidiary. He lost no control this way and still got his hands on a large amount of money that the Harrells had put into the company.

Nash Objects

Evans Nash, the conservative CPA and president of Yellow Transit during the Porter ownership, objected to the methods that were used to appraise property and equipment during their transfer to subsidiaries. His concern was that the liberal accounting practice could eventually hurt the company.

Page 46 — *Missouri Highway Patrolmen inspect Yellow Transit equipment traveling between St. Louis and Tulsa, Okla., along U.S. Route 66. This inspection station was located near Washington, Mo. Speed limits rarely exceeded 45 miles per hour. (Missouri Highway Patrol photo)*

1949

NATO is formed as a strategic military alliance in the North Atlantic.

Germany's post-war east and west republics are created.

A Minimum Wage act amends previous laws by raising the minimum hourly wage from 40 cents to 75 cents.

This page — *A.J. Harrell paid cash for Yellow Transit tractors and trailers. If the company was short of cash, A.J. lent Yellow Transit personal funds in order to get the best deal for the company. A.W. Porter mortgaged the equipment to finance his acquisition of the company. (photo courtesy Oklahoma Historical Society)*

Page 49 — *It was easy to keep the Dallas parts room and shop spotless during the war years. Parts were unavailable. Trucks remained road worthy by borrowing from other vehicles idled by shortages. (photo courtesy Oklahoma Historical Society)*

With the assets heavily leveraged, he needed to operate even more effectively. The company had to grow in order to pay down the newly acquired debt.

To complicate Nash's task further, the trucking industry was still reeling from consequences of World War II. Parts and equipment were in short supply, especially in 1945-46. It took until 1948 for the nation's economy to adjust to peacetime – to retool and produce adequate amounts of industrial goods. But by then Porter's financial maneuvers had Nash at a complete disadvantage. Instead of having cash reserves to replace old and worn equipment as the company had done in the 1930s, Yellow Transit was cash poor in 1948. Income was eaten up by the high cost of dividend payments and servicing company debts. The company was caught woefully unprepared for opportunities.

Nevertheless, Yellow Transit operated reasonably well until 1950, although not at par with the industry. Evans Nash found ways to grow the company under adverse conditions.

Thanks to a good, although costly, maintenance program, aging equipment continued to travel the highways safely. Nash managed the equipment problem in part by sticking to the same long-time vendors. That way, mechanics remained familiar with vehicles and shop management could inventory parts and supplies with some efficiency.

Nash also apparently did a good job of keeping customers happy during this period. Revenue increased from $2.8 million to $5.1 million between 1945 and 1948.

Post-war inflation certainly aided the rapid revenue growth. That was evident because freight volume did not increase proportionately. While revenue jumped 82 percent, tonnage grew by only 44 percent. Meantime, Yellow Transit's operating expenses also jumped sharply. In 1947 alone, labor expenses went up 29 percent.

Faster transit times and better operating efficiencies enabled Yellow Transit to offset some of the labor increase. Porter and his advisers were content as long as the company's revenue growth kept pace with rising expenses. Cash flow continued without disruption and dividends were satisfactory. The bottom line – aided by aggressive tax-avoidance strategies – looked robust.

Yellow Transit also became more efficient when Yellow Terminals, the subsidiary from which Yellow Transit leased its facilities, added a few key structures.

Perhaps most important was the new 42-door terminal on Harry Hines Boulevard in Dallas. Dallas had long

1950

Popular movies include: Adam's Rib with Spencer Tracy, The Third Man with Orson Welles, Twelve O'Clock High with Gregory Peck, It Happens Every Spring with Ray Milland and On the Town with Gene Kelly.

Ad man Peter Hodgson introduces Silly Putty.

Communist North Korean forces invade South Korea.

PARTS
ROOM
631
FREIGHT LINES

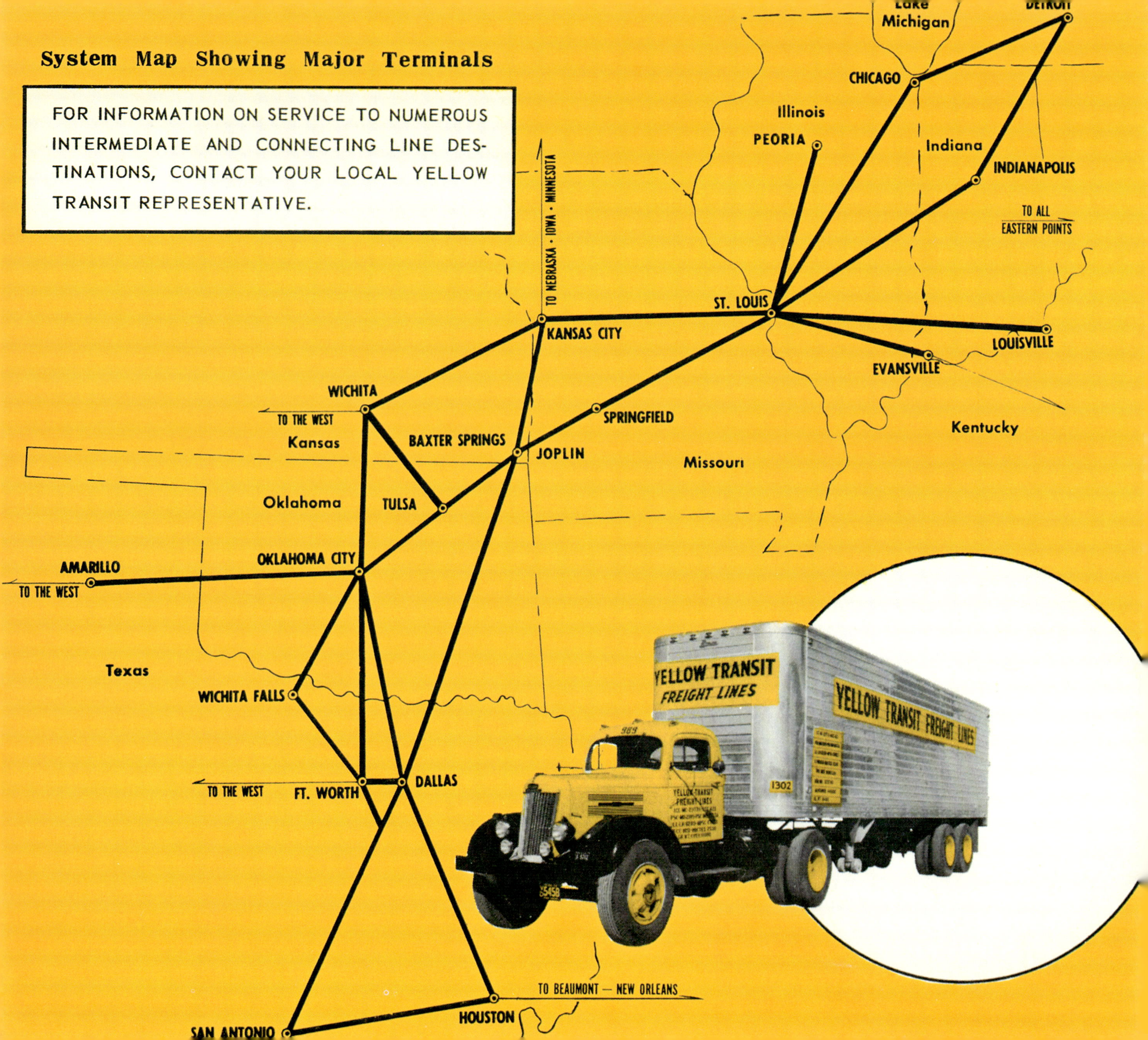
System Map Showing Major Terminals
FOR INFORMATION ON SERVICE TO NUMEROUS INTERMEDIATE AND CONNECTING LINE DESTINATIONS, CONTACT YOUR LOCAL YELLOW TRANSIT REPRESENTATIVE.
Lake Michigan
CHICAGO
Illinois
PEORIA
Indiana
INDIANAPOLIS
TO ALL EASTERN POINTS
TO NEBRASKA • IOWA • MINNESOTA
ST. LOUIS
KANSAS CITY
LOUISVILLE
EVANSVILLE
WICHITA
TO THE WEST
Kansas
BAXTER SPRINGS
SPRINGFIELD
JOPLIN
Kentucky
Missouri
Oklahoma
TULSA
OKLAHOMA CITY
AMARILLO
TO THE WEST
Texas
WICHITA FALLS
TO THE WEST
FT. WORTH
DALLAS
TO BEAUMONT — NEW ORLEANS
HOUSTON
SAN ANTONIO
YELLOW TRANSIT FREIGHT LINES
YELLOW TRANSIT FREIGHT LINES
1302

been one of the most important inbound cities in the Yellow Transit Company network. Operations improved throughout the system when Dallas ran without congestion.

At about the same time, a similar 42-door terminal with a garage facility went up in St. Louis on Chouteau Avenue. The additional space improved the consolidation and transfer operation in St. Louis, a key location in the flow of products destined for Missouri, Kansas, Oklahoma and Texas.[6]

By the mid 1940s, Chicago had become an important center in the overall operation as well. In fact, several other carriers had been using Yellow Transit's St. Louis terminal as an interline point, connecting Chicago shippers to the fast-growing consumer markets in Texas. After Yellow Transit purchased and improved a 36-door terminal in the Windy City, the company became more aggressive, going after the same freight that was being interlined. Yellow Transit offered a superior service unencumbered by the paper delays inherent with interlining processes.

Taking the business upset former interline partners. But, the vastly improved Chicago-Dallas lane was much more profitable. Even more important, the service made customers happy. Still, there was some concern about freight imbalance.

Chicago shipped 34 percent more loads of freight than it received. One truck in three came back to Chicago empty.

One solution considered was to offer shippers in the southern part of Yellow Transit's service authority a chance to send full truckloads of goods at a reduced rate. For the most part this plan was rejected because northbound freight in the 1940s tended to be mostly raw materials that were already rated among the cheapest to haul. Evans Nash opted to endure the imbalance rather than start a trend of carrying low-return freight, the antithesis of his business philosophy.

As Chicago business grew and post-war supply shortages evaporated, Nash plotted eastward expansion. Yellow Transit bought Brashear Freight Lines. The acquisition gave Yellow Transit access to Indianapolis along U.S. Route 40. The company already had both interstate and intrastate authority along Route 40 in Illinois, but adding the Indiana extension created an important shipping lane between Indianapolis and St. Louis. Once that lane was opened, it created another critical link from an industrial center to the southwest markets. Indeed,

Page 50 — *Post-war expansion boosted revenue. This is what the Yellow Transit system looked like in 1949.*

Sen. Joseph McCarthy claims to possess a list of "known Communists" and begins his famous attempts to expose them all.

GM has new record high profits among all U.S. corporations and signs a 5-year deal with the UAW.

There are 1.68 million miles of surfaced roads in the U.S. compared to 1.34 million in 1940.

The U.S. population has doubled since 1900.

"Serving the Southwest" became Yellow Transit's marketing slogan to entice Midwest shippers.

Losing Ground

Arlington Porter died unexpectedly in September 1948. He was 59. Trained as a chemical engineer, Porter's aptitude for making money guided him to Wall Street. After nine years as a broker, he opened his own firm at 30 Broad Street in 1931.

Porter's death was especially disheartening for Nash because it was the beginning of the end of his relationship with Yellow Transit Company, a company he had sustained through weary times.

Before Porter died, Nash had attempted to enlighten the owner and his advisers about problems he saw arising from Porter's more liberal and aggressive financial strategies. Nash claimed that the company's service was being compromised by the use of operating capital to expand the company through construction and purchases. Nash wanted to expand only when it was justified by revenue opportunities. He also continued to object to the fractured corporate structure. To his way of thinking, the tax benefits gained were offset by the additional expense of running subsidiary companies that produced no income except for what the parent organization paid in leases.

Disagreements widened after Porter's death. Uninterested in Yellow Transit Company, Porter's widow turned business matters over to her husband's advisers and other heirs. They proceeded to make even more outrageous changes, at least to Nash's way of thinking. They created a new parent organization in the state of Delaware, called Yellow Transit Systems, Inc. Yellow Transit Company, organized under Oklahoma law, became a subsidiary.

The most troubling concern for Nash and his operating group at Yellow Transit was that the company was not keeping up with competition. Since Porter – and then his heirs – burdened Yellow Transit by siphoning income without providing sufficient operating funds, the company was failing to match the progress enjoyed by other carriers. The company outperformed the industry in 1945, turning in a better operating ratio and generating more revenue per mile driven. But in 1947, 48 and 49, the company fell behind these key industry averages.

Nash vs. Board

Instead of deferring to Evans Nash after Arlington Porter's death, the board of directors took the

1951

Julius and Ethel Rosenberg are found guilty of selling atomic secrets to the Soviet Union.

The first war games using atomic weapons and troops is conducted in Nevada.

The U.S. has 8.62 million trucks, nearly double the amount from 10 years earlier.

Chrysler installs power steering in 10,000 new cars.

Local telephone calls jump from 5 to 10 cents.

Railroad Influence

Yellow Transit tractors await drivers and their route assignments at the Dallas terminal.

Yellow Transit Company attempted to make a point about its regular freight service between cities during the Arlington W. Porter regime. As a marketing ploy, the company named its high-profile longhaul routes. It was a tactic used by passenger railroad lines. The thought being that promoting the "Longhorn," a St. Louis to Dallas direct route, for instance, made it more enticing advertising material. It was a short-lived idea.

Nevertheless, these names were used to market routes: "Plainsman" (St. Louis to Oklahoma City), "Exporter" (Houston to St. Louis), "K.C. Flyer" (Kansas City to Oklahoma City), "Friendship" (Kansas City to Dallas), and "Jayhawker" (Wichita to Houston).[7]

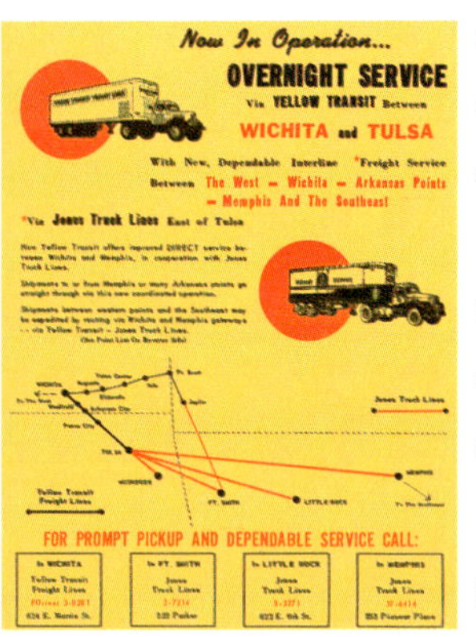

This page — *Overnight service is by no means a new convenience. Yellow Transit Company promoted its overnight capabilities during the 1950s.*

Page 55 — *The new 42-door Dallas terminal on Harry Hines Boulevard, built in the mid 1940s, was the first experiment with suburban convenience. It took advantage of less traffic congestion and sacrificed proximity to downtown customers.(photo courtesy Oklahoma Historical Society)*

opposite tack. They discredited Nash and focused on ways to set up additional tax loopholes and more executive luxuries.

Ironically, when Arlington Porter died in 1948, the board of directors gave Nash a raise and five-year contract. While it appeared to be a strong vote of confidence, it proved to be a smoke screen.

Nash plodded through 1949 as though things were going to work out. Shipping rates had jumped 15 percent the year before, producing better than average income for the company and giving the board a false sense of security. Nash had asked that some of the income funnel back into the operation, but the board, led by Chairman Robert C. Hardy, determined that a large dividend was due investors.

Setbacks in the first quarter of 1949 because of weather conditions prompted discussion of rescue tactics. A large rate increase was proposed. Nash resisted, believing the risks were too great. Price increases, he feared, could chase shippers back to the railroads. Even more threatening was the chance that they would cause larger shippers to create their own private fleets. That was a customer reaction Nash definitely wanted to avoid. He held prices firm.

The solution Nash settled on was an echo from the past – increased revenue through expanded service and better yields through controlled costs and improved efficiencies. Yellow Transit acquired authority from Motor City Express to run between Chicago and Detroit along U.S. Route 12, with stops in Kalamazoo, Battle Creek and Jackson. That step helped generate more revenue.

On the cost front, overtime had been the biggest drain, so belts were tightened. Nash insisted that freight get handled and moved during regular working hours. Part of the problem was solved with a modest investment in new trucks. There were fewer breakdowns, so fewer drivers were getting paid while waiting on repairs. The year ended much better than it started.

The next year began on solid footing. The first quarter of 1950 did so well that the inexperienced directors of the board started feeling their oats. They ordered new trucks and a new fleet of cars for the sales force. They began improving terminal properties beyond the modest requests sought by Evans Nash. They even proposed a bold move of the corporate headquarters from Oklahoma City to the more prestigious setting of Dallas. The one thing they felt they did not need was an experienced trucking executive. Evans Nash was fired.

1952

- Popular movies include: The African Queen with Katharine Hepburn and A Streetcar Named Desire with Marlon Brando.
- Baseball's newest players include Mickey Mantle, 19, and Willie Mays, 20.
- The Yankees win the World Series in 6 games against the Giants.
- Gen. Dwight Eisenhower is elected President of the United States.
- Britains George VI dies of lung cancer at age 56; Queen Elizabeth II replaces him on the throne.

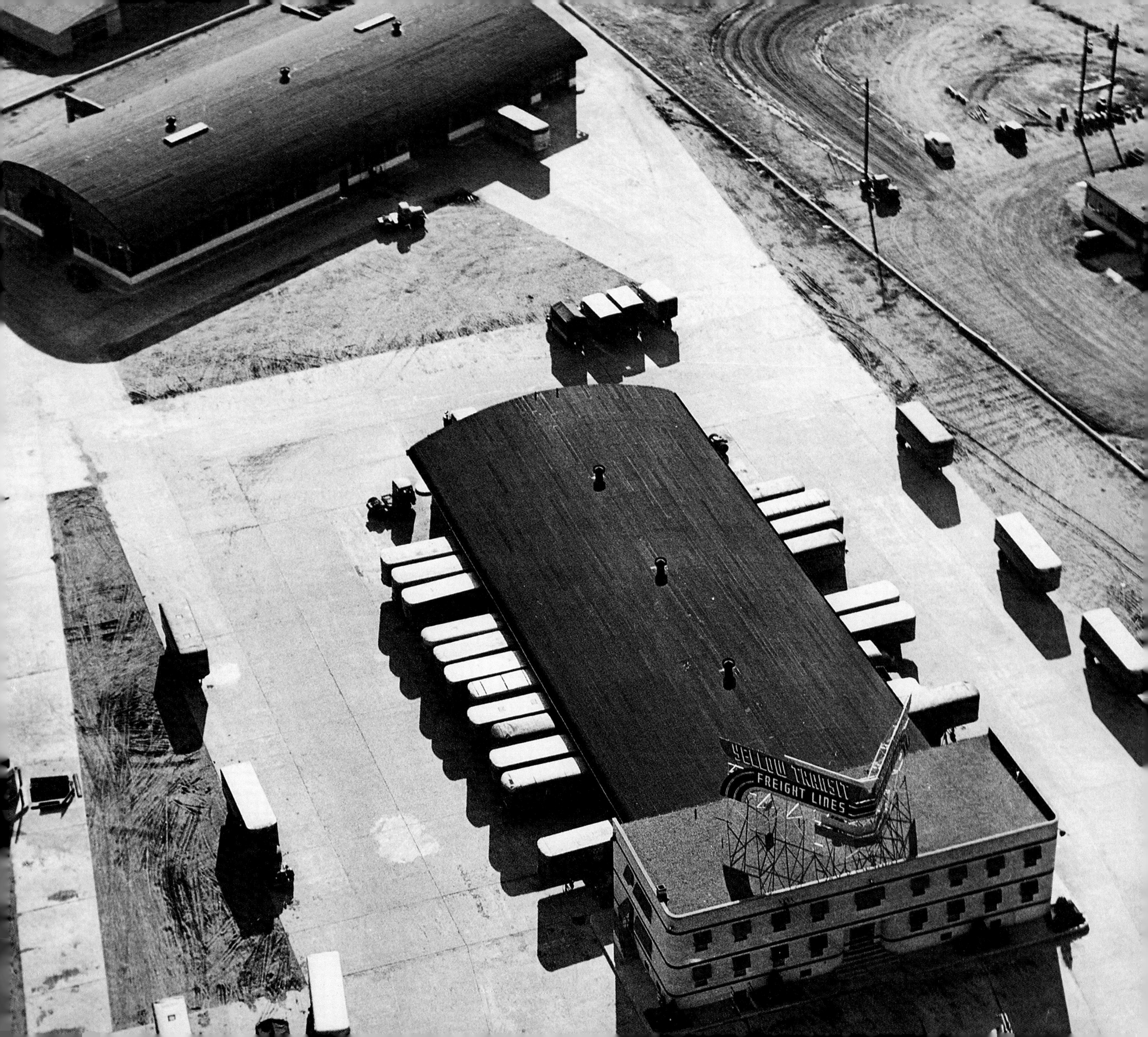
YELLOW TRANSIT
FREIGHT LINES

Driving Safely

This page, top — *Safety pins and badges honored Yellow Transit drivers who drove accident free each year, with special recognition going to those drivers who had accumulated a million miles. Most full time drivers could achieve the million-mile goal in 10 years.*

This page, bottom— *An over, short and damaged (OS&D) manual helped employees manage one of the most frustrating aspects of the freight transportation business.*

In 1944, Sam Kimmey wanted to drive a big rig on the highway. He was driving a local furniture truck when Yellow Transit Company hired him to operate a city unit in a small Oklahoma community. He met Yellow Transit's road drivers and let it be known that he wanted a job like theirs. He learned from his new co-workers that if he intended to drive for Yellow Transit or any of the other major carriers, he had better obtain five years of accident-free highway experience.

Kimmey spent less than a year with Yellow Transit as a pick-up and delivery man. He took to heart the advice he received from Yellow Transit's road drivers. He set his goal to drive over the road for five years without an accident before re-applying for the job he really wanted.

...fter successfully reaching his goal ...late 1949, spending five years driving ...uel tanker without a safety blem-..., Kimmey went to the major truck-... carriers in Oklahoma City. Instead ...Yellow Transit, though, he ended up ...Lee Way Motor Freight, which coin-...lentally was directly opposite Yellow ...nsit Company at the intersection of ...no and Western Avenue. Although ...mpetitors, Kimmey said there were occasions when the two companies were quite compatible. If one carrier were in a pinch because it needed a tractor or trailer to complete a delivery, the other carrier would lend the equipment to help out.

Sam Kimmey drove for Lee Way until the company closed its doors in 1984. He was moved seven times by his former employer and drove under every condition imaginable. Within a short time after Lee Way shut down, Kimmey was back working for the company that started his career journey, only by then it was known as Yellow Freight System.

The most amazing part of his sojourn is that he continues to drive for Yellow without an accident. He has been on the road in a truck more than 50 years, traveling more than five million miles. Accident free.

Lawsuit Trial

Board chairman Hardy took over the company and began the move to Dallas in September 1950. Meantime, Nash sued his former bosses for breach of contract. It eventually led to a weeklong trial in Oklahoma City. The board claimed that Nash had failed to perform his duties according to their agreement and resisted its attempt to modernize the company.

One employee who was called to testify at the trial was Lloyd C. Brandt. Starting with Yellow Transit in 1946 as a clerk at the Kansas City terminal, Brandt rose quickly. By Nash's trial date in 1951, Brandt was branch manager in Kansas City. He said he remembers receiving a curious teletype message from the general office prior to the trial, requesting information about any recent lost business. He dutifully collected and sent the data. Then he got a call to come and testify.

Brandt, who would later become a corporate executive and board member at Yellow in the 1970s and 80s, said it became clear at the trial that the board was trying to prove that Nash was incompetent, or a least insubordinate.

Brandt said following Porter's death, the board was obviously on a course of rapid growth, but their lack of experience in the trucking industry had them executing a poorly thought-out game plan. They aggressively secured more freight, so they needed more trucks. They bought more trucks, so they needed more terminal space to handle the equipment and freight. They acquired more terminal space with borrowed money and added to their debt. Revenue rose, said Brandt, but expenses rose faster.

Nash wanted to grow more slowly and plan the company's expansion based on the company's prior experience. The disagreement over strategy notwithstanding, the Oklahoma court was not convinced that Nash should be fired. He won his lawsuit and $87,500.[8]

Image Changes

Paying off Evans Nash seemed to be just a minor hiccup. With the trial done, Hardy and his supporters were free to set up well-appointed offices in Dallas and create a new Yellow Transit image. They fiddled with the company logo, creating at least two different banners that were painted on the trucks. They even changed the corporate name again, this time to Yellow Transit Freight Lines, Inc., an Indiana corporation. They merged the Oklahoma company into Yellow Terminals as one of approximately 50 subsidiaries,

U.S. steelworkers start a 53-day strike after the Supreme Court rules that President Truman's seizure order is illegal.

Social Security benefits are raised by 12.5 percent.

The first pocket-sized transistor radios are introduced.

Jet aircraft begin flying passengers between London and Johannesburg.

American Bandstand debuts on TV with host Dick Clark, 22.

including 24 terminal subsidiaries and 24 equipment subsidiaries. Operating leases grew from $258,868 in 1950 to $1,021,245 in 1951.[9]

Creditors began to get nervous. Revenue was certainly growing, jumping nearly 35 percent in 1951. Unfortunately, employment grew by 42 percent and overall expenses by 50 percent. Spending brakes were applied later that year, but it was too late.

In an attempt to salvage some respect from creditors, Hardy's team shut down general offices in Dallas and set up more austere space in Indianapolis. The salvage mission failed.

Creditors seized control of the board and eventually petitioned bankruptcy courts to restructure Yellow Transit in an attempt to correct its financial imbalance. A court appointed referee took over supervision of the company in March 1952. Robert Hardy resigned as chairman and president and for the next eight months Yellow Transit operated under the guidance of the court.

Petitioners, including Fruehauf, the trailer manufacturer with whom A.J. Harrell proudly did cash business when both companies were startups some 20 years earlier, claimed a complete lack of confidence in Yellow Transit's board of directors. Upon examining company books to understand if creditors had cause to feel as they did about the board, the courts stated that the complex corporate structure contributed to sloppy record keeping and mismanagement.

The creditors were not the only ones upset. Porter's widow and her children also felt victimized. Expecting a nest egg, they had nothing. Arlington Porter's company owed $3.3 million in delinquent taxes and secured and unsecured debts.

Inexperience took its toll. The men who expected it would be easy to run a truck line were out, two years after firing Evans Nash. Waiting in the wings were several well-known truckers, hoping to snare a bargain in distress. Each came with a plan and an offer to take over the once heralded Yellow Transit operation. Among them were Roadway Express, Navajo Freight Lines, Interstate Motor Freight and Associated Transport, but none of them would win the bidding war. That victory – and its challenges – belonged to a group from Kansas City.[10]

Yellow Transit searched for a new marketing identity in the late 1940s, revising its truck logo at least twice before settling on a basic name banner.

Popular movies include: High Noon with Gary Cooper, The Quiet Man with John Wayne, Come Back, Little Sheba with Burt Lancaster, The Greatest Show on Earth with Betty Hutton, The Red Badge of Courage with Audie Murphy, and Singin' In the Rain with Gene Kelly.

Popular songs include: Lullaby of Birdland, Takes Two to Tango, Do Not Forsake Me, Don't Let the Stars Get In Your Eyes, Your Cheatin' Heart and Blue Tango.

Kellogg's Sugar Frosted Flakes and Gleem toothpaste are new products and the first Holiday Inn opens in Memphis.

YELLOW TRANSIT CO

Reclaiming Yellow's Pride

A Surprising Pursuer

Kansas City was still recovering from the worst flood in U.S. history when 1952 began. A series of summer rain storms six months earlier drove the Missouri and Kansas Rivers over their banks and into the city and surrounding areas, causing $1 billion in property damage and claiming 41 lives. Two hundred thousand people were left homeless.

Later in the year, a Kansan would be elected President of the United States, replacing Harry Truman, a native of Missouri who had served since 1945. The metropolitan area was at the center of national attention. In the midst of the drama and excitement, a former Kansas City banker, who for the previous five years presided over a trucking company, was quietly assembling a leadership team and finances to buy Yellow Transit Freight Lines.

Like A.J. Harrell, that former banker, George Everett Powell, had carved out his own path to success. After attending Chillicothe Business College near his family's farm in North Central Missouri, Powell had an opportunity to replace his older brother as assistant cashier at Traders National Bank of Kansas City. He received the news when a horseman delivered a telegram to the wheat field where he and his father were working.

At age 20, Powell was all set to start a new life. In his new suit and dapper straw hat, Powell quietly became a man of the city. His salary was $50 a month, a respectable income for 1917. Like many other young rural men leaving farm life for urban opportunities, Powell first took up residence at the downtown YMCA. Studious and unpretentious, he worked his way up the banking ladder, quickly acquiring officer status and developing a reputation as an astute businessman and leader.

In late 1946, when Evans Nash was struggling to find parts and supplies to keep Yellow Transit Company mobile, George Powell received an unusual offer. Richard Riss, owner of Riss & Company, a Kansas City-based trucking firm that specialized in franchising arrangements, asked Powell to become president of his organization. The timing was right. Powell had viewed the business world from a banker's perspective long enough. He was eager to test his financial acumen in the industrial

Page 60 — *An unidentified Kansas City shop employee wades through 1951 flood waters at the terminal. Inundation from the Kansas and Missouri Rivers caused property damage and extraordinary cost in 1951.*

1953

Josef Stalin dies at age 73.

U.S. planes bomb North Korea dams, flooding rice fields.

U.S. Unemployment drops to its lowest point since the end of World War II.

New York's double-decker bus service ends because the city can't afford to pay for a fare collector on each bus.

Popular movies include: The Robe with Richard Burton, Julius Caesar with Marlon Brando, and Roman Holiday with Audrey Hepburn.

Page 63 — *George Powell, Sr. (right, 1st seat, 3rd row) presided over Riss & Company from 1946-1951. His son, George Powell, Jr. (standing next to easel in background) was part of the staff, as was Mark Robeson (4th sitting row, 3rd from back). The three men worked together at Riss and Yellow for 30 years.*

sector – an environment quite different from the white-collar world he had known.

Working for Riss was an eye-opener. Riss was a gambler, the antithesis of Powell, whose lifelong personal and business philosophy reflected the twin principals of thrift and hard work. Legend has it that Riss won an expansive trucking authority in a crap game. The authority stretched from the Midwest to New York and Boston. Under regulated rules, in order to keep the authority, he had to use it, so he developed his unique franchise structure. Later, the franchise scheme was challenged by the Interstate Commerce Commission, which said it was not legal. Under Powell's watch, Riss & Company had to quickly restructure the organization, which it did by offering its franchisees a compensation package to amass full ownership.

When Powell's five-year contract expired with Riss & Company on Jan. 1, 1952, he was ready for another adventure. Again, timing was perfect. He had learned from an acquaintance that Yellow Transit Freight Lines was having serious financial problems. The acquaintance knew firsthand about Yellow Transit's circumstances, because his company was a principal creditor. The acquaintance was Roy Fruehauf. George Powell had befriended Fruehauf when he lived in Kansas City and conducted business with Trader's Bank, Powell's former employer.

Fruehauf Corporation, the Detroit trailer builder that A.J. Harrell proudly claimed as an entrepreneurial kinsman, had a huge stake in Yellow Transit's survival. Yellow Transit owed Fruehauf money. Just as important, the Fruehaufs had more than a 20-year business relationship with Yellow Transit that the firm valued and wanted to see continue. In contacting Powell, Fruehauf was hopefully planting a seed for the future. It was a calculated move to tempt an experienced and trusted businessman like Powell to take over a good trucking company in a bad situation. Powell had the right skills and Fruehauf knew it.

Powell had other allies as he discretely began to investigate buying Yellow Transit Freight Lines. The most obvious among them was his 26-year-old son, George Powell, Jr. At the suggestion of his father, the younger Powell also acquired hands-on trucking experience at Riss & Company. He started in 1947 as a part-time accountant at one of five franchise offices in Chicago while attending Northwestern University in nearby Evanston. By the time his father's management contract expired, George Jr.,

Popular songs include: I Believe, Rags to Riches, Oh! My Pa-pa, Hi-Lili, Hi-Lo, That's Amoré, and That Doggie in the Window.

New products include Sugar Smacks, Schweppes Tonic Water, TV Dinners, and Treyton cigarettes.

Comic actor Charlie Chaplin is denied re-entry into the U.S. because he is determined to have Communist sympathies and "subversive, un-American" opinions.

IBM introduces the "701," its first computer.

RISS
Service at Freight
OUTBOUND L.T.L. LOAD ANALYSIS
REVENUE
EXPENSES

George Powell, Sr. and George Powell, Jr. worked effectively as a father-son team at Riss & Company before buying Yellow Transit Company in 1952. George Jr. said that his father expected him to manage operating details while he devoted time to financial and industry issues.

as he was commonly known, had become secretary-treasurer at Riss. The two Powells worked well together as a father-son team, but neither knew just how critical their partnership would be until 1952.

Neighborly Counsel

Leading up to his bailout offer to buy Yellow Transit, George Powell, Sr. researched the carrier's financial predicament. Time was a factor. He knew others were vying to take over the truck line, so he had to quickly demonstrate both trucking competence and a financial plan that appeared feasible to the Interstate Commerce Commission and bankruptcy courts. It also had to appease creditors.

According to family accounts, Powell was nervously stewing over details on Sunday morning, uncertain how and whether to proceed. He called his neighbor Ken Midgley, an attorney, and asked if he would come visit with him for 10 to 15 minutes before Midgley went to church. Midgley obliged, but said instead of 15 minutes, the conversation lasted 25 years. That is how long Midgley provided Powell and the company legal counsel.[1]

With the benefit of Midgley's expertise, Powell finalized his plan to get Yellow Transit Freight Lines out of bankruptcy in relatively short order. After assembling a handful of investors, including Fruehauf, Powell offered to lend Yellow Transit $750,000 in order to pay off the carrier's debts. In exchange, Powell expected the courts to name him general manager of the company and to create 100,000 shares of common stock and 4,900 shares of preferred stock that would be controlled by the new investors. All parties agreed to Powell's initial plan. The Powell team took over operation of the company on May 1, 1952, although it remained under the supervision of the bankruptcy court.

For the next four months Yellow Transit continued to operate in the red, but in September the company turned the corner, breaking even for the month. "In October, we were profitable and never looked back," said George Powell, Jr.

The Interstate Commerce Commission was satisfied. It gave its approval for Powell's group to take over ownership. Creditors approved the takeover on Oct. 7, and on Oct. 27, 1952, the bankruptcy court released Yellow Transit to Powell and his new management team.

To get a clearer picture of the character of the team that was taking over Yellow Transit Freight Lines,

1954

- Former WAC commander Oveta Culp Hobby is named the first secretary of Health, Education and Welfare established by Congress.
- Liggett & Myers introduces a filtered cigarette, L&M, which it promotes as "just what the doctor ordered."
- Moscow rejects a plan to re-unify Germany.
- South Vietnam gains complete independence from France.
- Sen. Joseph McCarthy is condemned for misconduct demonstrated in his anti-Communist drive.

there is this footnote: When Arlington W. Porter died in 1948, his widow relinquished control of her husband's company to Robert Hardy, who was secretary-treasurer of the board and who then became chairman. Many observers felt that the board treated Mrs. Porter abominably. During settlement of the acquisition, the Powell ownership group offered to pay Mrs. Porter $500 per month for a period George Powell, Jr. estimated to range between two and five years. By today's standards the income was small, but in 1952 a $6,000 annual salary was a reasonable amount, especially since it was given without being required.

People who had been in command during the Porter-Hardy era were officially terminated. In their place were Powell, his son and an eclectic mix of leaders, including a 25-year veteran of the airline industry, a frozen-food distributor, an engineer from a truck manufacturer and a terminal operator who had spent most of his 11 years with another carrier. Powell suspected others in the industry would look askance at his selection, but he placed young people like his son in key positions to capitalize on their energy. He knew the work ahead demanded long hours, travel and rigorous attention to detail.

Two experienced Yellow Transit employees were asked to stay. They remained with the company several more years: rate man L.E. Tomlinson, who had been with Yellow Transit since A.J. Harrell ran the company, and Harold H. Edwards, the company's young treasurer.

"Tomlinson was a highly respected rate man in the industry," said George Powell, Jr. Individuals like Tomlinson had developed such specialized skills that the job nearly became a cottage industry.

The rate man's task was to determine the fairest price to charge the customer for carrying each of hundreds of different commodities, so that the company earned a fair profit for its service. In justifying a rate to the Interstate Commerce Commission, which had governmental oversight responsibilities, the individual had to know about handling costs, transit risks and other less obvious factors that could affect the true shipping expense.

In truth, old-time Midwestern truckers doubted that Powell had much of a chance of pulling off his bailout plans. Employees and associates close to the situation recalled being around those men who joked about the new team's lack of experience in trucking. In retrospect, it was the Powells who had the last laugh.

Popular movies include: The Caine Mutiny with Humphrey Bogart, On the Waterfront with Marlon Brando, Rear Window with James Stewart, 20,000 Leagues Under the Sea with Kirk Douglas and The High and the Mighty with John Wayne.

Gasoline prices average 29 cents per gallon.

The New York State Thruway opens.

Pittsburgh school children are the first group to be vaccinated against polio.

Page 67— *Yellow Transit's first permanent home in Kansas City was at 1626 Walnut Street. The two-story structure was first leased then purchased from Evans Electric Company. It was the headquarters from late 1952 until 1960.*

Goin' to Kansas City

Once he had the green light, Powell consolidated Yellow Transit's offices in Kansas City. Again, some industry observers questioned the choice. They said Kansas City was the wrong place. St. Louis, Dallas and even Baxter Springs saw more of the company's traffic and already employed a large percentage of the company's work force.

Powell recognized the importance of the other cities. As further evidence that he intended to push more authority for operating decisions away from the general office, he established St. Louis and Dallas as headquarters for north and south operating divisions. But Kansas City was home, centrally located and an important rail and trucking center, so it was quite suitable for the general office. Reflecting on the decision in more recent times, George Powell, Jr. said that even in the early 1950s technology had made it possible to operate businesses from a distance as indicated by the large number of companies that were becoming national in scope.

One issue George Sr. wanted to avoid was the demonstration of favoritism toward any one terminal, so the company leased office space at 18 E. 17th Street rather than joining the Kansas City terminal. It was one of 18 facilities operated by Yellow Transit when the Powell team took over in 1952. In fact, Hardy's management group converted most of the 18 terminals to extremely long-term leases in his final year. It was another desperate move to shore up finances. The Kansas City terminal lease was the longest by far at 40 years.[2]

Separating the general office from the freight-handling chores was a difficult concept for the more seasoned trucking employees to embrace in 1952. The common practice in the industry had been for owners to control every detail of the business, including the daily operation, and therefore, they set up their general office at one of the terminals, usually in the center of the operating authority.

Powell had acquired a different perspective after observing the way Richard Riss had creatively structured his franchises to give operators maximum autonomy. At Riss, Powell ran a general office and sales organization that generated freight for franchise operators who essentially operated small businesses within a larger network. He saw that centralized management, separated from day-to-day freight movement, could still direct operations. So, it was not surprising for Powell to delegate responsibility

RCA begins selling color television sets although color reception is unreliable.

The St. Louis Browns become the Baltimore Orioles.

Hank Aaron, 20, joins the Milwaukee Braves.

France grants South Vietnam independence.

The Soviet Union rejects a proposal from the U.S., France and England to re-unify Germany.

YELLOW TRANSIT FREIGHT LINES
ONE WAY

George Powell, Sr.

for operations and sales, and to expect local managers to be accountable for terminal performance.

Recalling their plans from nearly 50 years ago, George Powell, Jr. said his father did not want to learn the nuts and bolts of the operation at age 53. That chore was assigned to him, George Jr. Moreover, the assignment was not to learn how to operate each terminal, but to understand how the network of terminals created a dynamic operation, and once understood, to be able to monitor the network's performance continuously. Each day the goal was optimum efficiency and profitability.

Was there an early vision to create a national carrier that would become the largest in the industry?

"No," said George Jr. "Our first objective was to get Yellow turned around, profitable and with a sound balance sheet. Then we began to think about a next step."

He added that he, his father and the rest of the young team that took over Yellow Transit knew that they were not going to be able to "play the same game forever." He said they expected to establish a systematic acquisition program once they had their footing.

"We knew we had to," Powell said.

Establishing a New Structure

When the Powells, their advisors and investors met in Kansas City after officially being told by the courts that they could take over Yellow Transit Freight Lines, George Sr. was elected president and George Jr. was elected controller.

"We had enough money to operate the company for 10 months," said George Jr.

Their due diligence led them to believe that if they undid the strange moves of the Hardy group, such as sheltering taxes with layers of subsidiaries, they could recreate the excellent operation established by A.J. Harrell and continued by Evans Nash. That was their mission with very specific objectives.

Things That Changed

Eliminated subsidiaries

Yellow Transit began its streamlining by reducing the number of subsidiaries. In the previous two years, three subsidiaries had become 50. Under the Powell management group the former structure was restored. Within a year the company had been shrunk to six subsidiaries.

1955

A 2-year study concludes that cigarette smoking is a serious health hazard.

Milkshake-machine salesman Raymond A. Kroc buys franchise rights from McDonald brothers in California and begins his golden-arch hamburger stands.

The U.S. minimum wage rises from 75 cents to $1.00 per hour.

The AF of L and CIO merge under Walter Reuther and George Meany.

General Motors introduces the first Chevy V-8 engine.

Established maintenance discipline

Half of the rolling stock was purchased after 1950, so it was relatively free of major repairs. The charge given was to set up a maintenance discipline to protect the relatively new investments. Similarly, older equipment had to be well maintained in order to prolong its usefulness for the lowest possible cost.

Restored precise schedules

The Powells subscribed to the same scheduling philosophies designed by Harrell and enforced by Nash, but abandoned under Hardy. They felt that both customer service and operating expenses improved when freight moved on schedule. They revived operating precision, making the company more dependable. The change also lowered operating costs by keeping dockworkers and drivers consistently busy and not overburdened with unpredicted surges in freight volume. Surges often compounded costs, especially when freight arrived at the end of a dock shift, causing overtime.

Chose freight more selectively

Another operating practice used by Harrell and Nash, but forsaken by Hardy, was selectively choosing freight for system balance and handling economies. In fact, under Hardy's growth plan, sales agents were soliciting all possible freight to increase revenue. The plan succeeded exceptionally well. Top-line revenue jumped, but costs exceeded the revenue gain, so profits turned to losses. By instituting more planned sales and marketing efforts the Powell team regained freight-flow balance and handling efficiencies that led to profitability.

Among the critical decisions was the termination of approximately 100 sales agency agreements whereby an independent contractor could solicit freight shipped via Yellow Transit Freight Lines. The previous administration fostered the relationships, which did generate additional freight. Unwittingly, the agents were rewarded for producing revenue, but suffered no consequence for overburdening operations with hard-to-handle freight or system imbalance.

Prioritized longhaul traffic

Moving both interstate and intrastate shipments meant the company had to maintain two different operating procedures, one for longhaul and another for shorthaul. The new leadership team saw more opportunity in longhaul and interstate authorities,

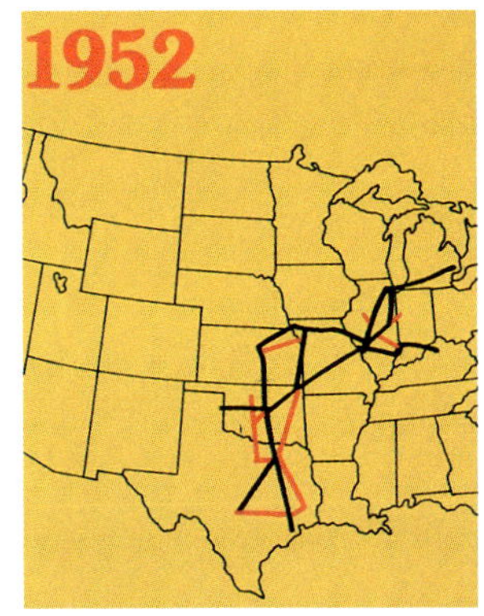

This system map shows Yellow Transit's service authority when the company was acquired by George Powell, Sr. and his investment group in 1952.

Ford introduces the Thunderbird, a 2-seat sports car.

New York's Long Island Expressway opens, but is inadequate for the volume of traffic.

New York installs "walk/don't walk" signals on busy street corners.

Popular movies include: Mister Roberts with Henry Fonda, Rebel Without a Cause with Natalie Wood, Marty with Ernest Borgnine, Oklahoma! With Gordon MacRae, and Picnic with William Holden.

MICHIGAN MO
FREIGHT LINES INC.
YELLOW TRANS
YELLOW
TRANSIT

and therefore sold many of the intrastate routes. It helped the company focus on a core service and eliminated conflicting procedures, and thus, led to more profitable efforts.

Implemented departmental budgets

When investigating the previous administration's accounting practices, the bankruptcy court made several disparaging comments about the condition of records and data, calling them faulty and incomplete. Corporate minutes, the court-appointed referee said, were in a "deplorable state." Attempting to avoid similar pitfalls, the Powells demanded that each department of the organization submit a budget for approval, and that spending stay within the budgeted amounts so finances could be monitored and balanced.

Wrote strategic plans

With departmental budgets came controls that stimulated planning. Knowing that growth was an essential part of future prosperity, the new management team set revenue goals and overall spending limits aimed at creating profit targets. It was a process that observers found missing from previous administrative practices.

Fast Turnaround

By the end of the first 18 months of operation, Yellow Transit Freight Lines, under the Powells' leadership, had met its short-term objective. Taxes and secured debts were paid off and a monthly schedule was being followed to repay unsecured debts. In addition, the Powells were able to repay themselves and their investors 90 percent of the funds put up for operating the company – the $750,000. The remaining 10 percent became the cost of stock ownership, valued at $1 per share.

The Powells owned 15,000 shares jointly, and George Sr. had an option that he exercised for an additional 25,000 shares. The Fruehauf Corporation owned 30,000 shares, Lester Brinkman and George Williams each owned 10,000 shares and each became board members, and Jack Merriman also owned 10,000 shares, accounting for all of the common stock.

Revived Ingenuity

Looking back at Yellow Transit's bankruptcy ordeal and the Powell team's rescue of the ailing carrier, it all happened rather quickly. It took less than two years to create the financial dilemma and less than two years to fix it. By 1954, the company was ready to move on

This page — *The Waco, Texas, terminal.*

Page 70 — *This Michigan Motor Freight Lines terminal later became one of Yellow Transit's expansion facilities after the regional carrier was acquired in 1957.*

Popular songs include: Rock Around the Clock, Roll Over, Beethoven, Something's Gotta Give, Love Is a Many-Splendored Thing, Cry Me a River, and Love and Marriage.

The Brooklyn Dodgers win their first World Series 4 games to 3 over the Yankees.

The Philadelphia Athletics become the Kansas City Athletics.

Disneyland opens 25 miles south of Los Angeles.

Driving the routes traveled by Yellow Transit trucks was one way to learn about safety concerns and route preferences between terminals. In the 1950s, George Powell, Jr. rode with managers in the company's Plymouth safety vehicle to inspect conditions.

to new matters, and at the head of the list were items that once more called for creative thinking.

In for the Long Haul

The decision to sell Yellow Transit's intrastate authorities was initially prompted by the need to simplify operations. The authorities also gave the company a revenue source when cash was needed. Later, though, at a point that George Powell, Jr. described as "one of the most trying times I ever remember," the company had to examine its operating practices very closely.

People were working hard to reduce the company's expense and restore the kind of prosperity Yellow Transit had enjoyed under A.J. Harrell and Evans Nash. Powell said he was frustrated because the company struggled for small gains, but the gains were nothing like what he knew could be achieved. He recognized that the people managing the terminals, driving the trucks and handling the freight were doing excellent work, so he assumed there was a flaw in senior management's strategy that needed to be resolved.

Powell admitted he was the one with operating responsibility, so it was his problem to figure out. At the time, he was president of the company.

With a chuckle, he said the answer came at a moment of exasperation, although the solution was quite simple and purely mathematical. The company had not gone far enough to limit shorthaul coverage. Indeed, the officers had done just the opposite when Yellow Transit made its first and very daring acquisition of Michigan Motor Freight Lines in 1957. That carrier served several important industrial centers in northern Indiana and Ohio as well as in Michigan. The added authority gave Yellow Transit excellent connections that complimented existing routes, but Michigan Motor had operated primarily as a shorthaul carrier. Rather than adapt the acquired system to Yellow Transit's longhaul processes, management attempted to convert to shorthaul.

By their nature, shorthaul shipments are smaller but more frequent. The advantage of regional shipping to customers is speed of delivery. Because they are moving short distances, products can easily move overnight.

The issue, though, said Powell, was that distance did not matter when it came to the cartage operation. The cost of pick-up and delivery was about the same whether it was to pick up 400 pounds or 800 pounds. Those were the approximate weights of the average

1956

Argentine dictator Juan Perón is overthrown in a coup; Perón had created Latin America's first and only labor movement.

H&R Block is founded by Kansas City tax accountants Henry and Richard Bloch; the firm will be doing 10 percent of all annual U.S. tax returns within 20 years.

The Guinness Book of World Records first appears, written by sportswriter Ross McWhirter and his twin brother Norris.

Captain Kangaroo and The Mickey Mouse Club first appear on television.

President Eisenhower wins re-election.

shorthaul and longhaul shipments, respectively, in Yellow Transit's system. So, sending a 400-pound shipment from Tulsa to Wichita – a 200-mile trip – cost the company about as much for cartage services as sending an 800-pound shipment between Chicago and Dallas – a 1000-mile trip. There was a huge penalty, however, in what Yellow Transit was allowed to charge its customers for making the shorter of the two hauls.

According to Powell, Yellow Transit and other carriers tried to get the Interstate Commerce Commission to recognize the muddled pricing issue that discouraged shorter runs. Over time, he said, adjustments occurred.

Powell's insights led to further changes. More effort was put behind marketing and selling longer routes. Thoughts about acquiring additional companies to gain shorthaul authority were abandoned. After changing the former Michigan Motor operation and returning to the longhaul focus, the average length of haul grew and so did profits. It was an important strategic decision and one that set a course for the next 30 years.

Diesel Power

Refocusing on longhaul LTL drove other decisions very logically. Better profits prompted talk about investments in new tractors and trailers. That led to the critical debate about the type of tractor to buy. The question asked most frequently in the executive corridors was whether this was a good time to convert to diesel tractors? Truck manufacturers had been saying that diesel technology was ready. They said tractors were more powerful, more fuel efficient and with fewer parts, more cost effective to maintain.

The deliberation stemmed from the fact that it was an all-or-nothing choice. Slowly transitioning to diesel meant mechanics would have to work on both kinds of linehaul tractors for several years. Not very practical. Converting quickly would be very expensive. And either way, intense training would be required for drivers and mechanics.

It came down to this: What makes the most sense if the company is really committed to be a longhaul LTL carrier? The answer was obvious. All diesel.

With that question answered, the next challenge was to find the best equipment for the right price.

George Powell, Jr. began assessing several vehicles with assistance from Superintendent of Maintenance William R. Riley, formerly an engineer with a truck manufacturer, and Superintendent of Transportation Robert J. Leary, who had experience in the food

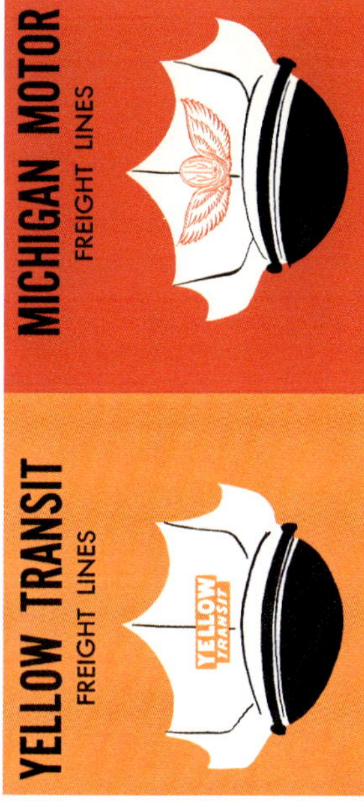

Yellow Transit introduced its new service territory with this brochure promoting the acquisition of Michigan Motor Freight Lines.

The Supreme Court outlaws racial segregation in intrastate public transportation.

The world's first containership port opens in Elizabeth, N.J.

The S.S. Andrea Doria collides with Swedish liner S.S. Stockholm and sinks near Nantucket Island, Mass.

Popular movies include: Anastasia with Ingrid Bergman, Friendly Persuasion with Gary Cooper, Giant with Rock Hudson, The Searchers with John Wayne, Bus Stop with Marilyn Monroe, The Teahouse of the August Moon with Marlon Brando.

Interstate Highway Impact

The transition to interstate travel was gradual, beginning with the opening of short stretches of multiple lane sections in several states. Many states claimed to be the first to open a part of the new interstate soon after Congress approved funding.

In 1954, a 559-mile state toll road – the New York State Thruway – opened between New York City and Buffalo. The toll road exceeded revenue and traffic estimates 10 years ahead of schedule.

It was a sign from motorists that they wanted better highways and were willing to pay for them.

The Federal Highway Act of 1916 was the first legislation to officially declare a national stake in highway interests. In subsequent years the government moved slowly until a wake-up call came in 1944. Germany's army was swiftly motoring across the autobahn, by far a superior roadway to anything built in the United States.

The Nazi's incredible mobility jolted American lawmakers into designing a sophisticated national highway system. That year, 1944, Congress drafted legislation to create a 40,000-mile U.S. National System of Interstate Highways. However, lawmakers failed to finance the bill and kept the legislation useless for 12 more years.

President Dwight Eisenhower was commander of operations in Europe during World War II. Once elected in 1952, he became directly involved in the highway issue, drafting a five-man advisory committee, including David Beck, president o the Teamsters. He asked another former military man to head the committee, General Lucius Clay.

The Clay Committee spent several weeks in 1954 conducting interviews and holding committee hearings at which dozens of interested groups testified. The committee drafted a report for President Eisenhower that was shared with a less receptive Congress.

Concurrent with the Clay Committee's efforts, George Powell, Sr. and Dr. L.L. Waters were members of a larger exploratory group established by the Commerce Department, which at the tim had administrative responsibilities for national transportation interests. The Transportation Council of the Commerce Department wrestled with numerous issues, and as Dr. Waters described it, generated a cacophony of simultaneous discussions within its meeting chambers Waters said it was the carefully analytica observations from Powell, representing one of the smallest companies participatir on the panel, which often quieted the group, steering members to more productiv conclusions.

War gave us a pretty dramatic reaction the need for (better) highways," said Dr. ters. He said the nation learned that rail-ds could not move people and freight t enough nor with the necessary flexible eduling, especially in times of crises. hways had to be improved.

he discussion moved to a new venue, U.S. Senate. Tennessee Senator Albert e (father of Vice President Albert Gore) gan hearings in a subcommittee to sort the various issues.[6]

enator Gore admitted after the grueling rings that he had turned 180 degrees. or to gathering opinions and data, he s opposed to using federal tax dollars highways, but after listening to arguments, said he was persuaded to support fund- and passage of the bill.

owever, since the House had previously fted legislation pertaining to transporta-, U.S. Representatives had their noses of place over the matter. The so-called e bill was defeated and the general nion was that the issue would not sur- again until a new Congress came into ver, which was more than a year away. hen the second session of the 79th ngress convened, despite being an ction year, the public was demanding that Congress do something fast about interstate highways.

The new proposals originated this time in the House of Representatives. The final bill assessed the entire cost of the program on its users. Title I authorized construction of new highways and incorporation of several thousand miles of state-chartered toll roads into a free federal highway system. Title II established procedures for raising funds to build and support the system as it grew.

Work began immediately. Gasoline taxes and other user fees generated the first round of payments. The trucking industry took the sticker shock in stride.

The government's plan was to have the roads built by 1975. Construction lasted well beyond the projected date. In total, 42,500 miles of multiple-lane highways made up the officially titled Dwight D. Eisenhower System of Interstate and Defense Highways. The project included construction of more than 55,000 bridges.

To put it all into perspective, interstate highways today make up just one percent of the nation's road network but move 23 percent of all vehicular traffic. Travel time between the nation's major metropolitan areas has been reduced on average by 20 percent since the interstates were built. Cross-town travel time inside a metropolitan area has been cut by as much as 60 percent.[7]

The commitment to build modern transcontinental highways in the United States was one of the most expensive national endeavors ever undertaken, and one that is unprecedented in its impact on a nation's economy. In the trucking industry alone, the additional speed and convenience provided by interstate highways lowered tractor-trailer-operating expenses by an estimated 17 percent, savings that have been enjoyed by everyone in America. In the first 40 years of existence, the highways are credited with saving consumers $1 trillion, which is more than three times the gross investment in building the interstates.

As a bonus to these economic benefits, interstate highways also have been credited with saving 187,000 lives during the first 40 years. Nearly 12 million injuries have been avoided. Improved safety features were part of overall interstate highway strategy and design.[8]

This page, top — *Don McMorris rejoined the Powells at Yellow Transit Company in 1954. He had worked with them at Riss & Company in Kansas City.*

This page, bottom — *The cab-beside-engine (CBE) tractor, built by Kenworth in 1955, was a unique design that caught the attention of all motorists. It also was watched closely by the industry because Yellow Transit was taking a bold risk with this vehicle in converting its entire over-the-road fleet to diesel power.*

storage and distribution industry. Their choice was to go with a bizarre looking cab-beside-engine (CBE) tractor built by Kenworth and powered by a Cummins diesel engine.

The tractor looked like a rolling telephone booth. The driver's enclosure was a rectangle that wrapped directly around his single seat. The design gave drivers great visibility but an unusual perspective compared to the traditional tractor. It was extremely light, shorter than other tractors, and yet the Cummins engine increased horsepower over Yellow Transit's gasoline tractors by 40 percent.

Buying the unusual tractor was a major event not only for Yellow Transit, but also for Kenworth, Cummins and the trucking industry. It became a story followed closely in trade publications. Other truckers wanted to know if a company like Yellow Transit, a mid-sized operation at the time, could convert to diesel. The industry watched to see what impact it would have on its operating efficiencies.

Watching for Results

Don McMorris joined Yellow Transit in 1954 as controller. He was one of two key former Riss & Company employees who followed the Powells to Yellow Transit. The other was Mark Robeson. At Riss, McMorris had been an auditor, controller and eventually, treasurer. His transition to Yellow Transit came at the time when debate was heating over the diesel decision. Once the Kenworth-Cummins tractor was picked as the best option, McMorris recalled the intensity of negotiations.

There was enormous concern, he said, even after the Kenworth was selected. Managers stewed over whether diesel power was the right decision. Yellow Transit wanted guarantees that the manufacturers would stand behind their performance claims.

"When Yellow Transit bought the Kenworth cab-beside-engine tractors, the manufacturer gave a written assurance that Yellow would get a certain fuel mileage," McMorris said. He added it was a "very rosy figure," indicating that Kenworth and Cummins were willing to reimburse Yellow if their savings were not met. It was not needed, McMorris said. The tractor performed as promised.

In 1955, Yellow Transit Freight Lines bought 200 Kenworth CBE tractors. Over time, the number increased to 350. It was a huge business risk that proved to be one of the key turning points in the company's development. It laid the foundation for the

Popular songs include: Love Me Tender, Hound Dog, Heartbreak Hotel, I Walk the Line, Folsom Prison Blues, Around the World in 80 Days, and Que Será, Será.

Don Larsen pitches the first World Series perfect game in game 5 for the Yankees.

The Federal Aid Highway Act authorizes construction of 42,500 miles of highways linking U.S. cities; 90 percent of the cost to be borne by the federal government.

company's later growth and success. But at the time it was simply a leap of faith for everyone concerned.

Yellow Transit received the fuel efficiency, durability, safety and reliable power it sought, and the Kenworth-Cummins team grabbed an important lead in the diesel production race with its competitors.

The company drove the odd-looking tractors for about six years. A few units stayed in service well into the 1960s. In an unusual way, the telephone-booth tractors helped the company get noticed in the marketplace.

Carl Sheets, an Oklahoma City road driver, who started with Yellow Transit in Baxter Springs in 1965, remembered driving a couple of the Kenworth CBEs. He said he used to see them on the highway when he was younger and driving for his father. There was a strange attraction about the vehicle, he said. In a peculiar way, it was one of the reasons he wanted to work for Yellow Transit. The tractor fascinated him.

Sheets said he knew the CBE made a lot of money for Yellow Transit. In his critical view, the tractor drove kind of hard. It carried a tremendous amount of weight on the drive axle, which presented some disadvantages to the driver and vehicle maintenance. The other unusual sensation, said Sheets, was having the "fifth wheel" sitting so close to the cab. The fifth wheel is the name given to the huge center-drilled steel plate that sits at a slight angle on the heavy framework over the back axle of a tractor and onto which the trailer locks into place.

McMorris concurs, the Kenworth CBE provided Yellow Transit the economy it sought, but it was not perfect. While other potential buyers analyzed Yellow Transit's experience with the CBE, Kenworth and Cummins had time to improve their engineering. Regardless of the few flaws, the diesel tractor gave Yellow Transit the impetus it needed to charge forward with confidence.

Trailers Enlarged

The cab-beside-engine design was selected for three reasons: one, its low weight; two, it had an easy access to its engine so there was faster maintenance speed and therefore, lower labor costs; and three, it was shorter. Being shorter, it gave Yellow Transit another critical advantage – an opportunity to expand the length of its trailers, which in turn created more volume to carry more freight over strategically longer routes.

Although state regulations had become more uniform since the days when A.J. Harrell had to build a relay

Chicago mechanic John Purvis services one of Yellow Transit's 350 Kenworth CBE tractors with its Cummins diesel engine.

1957

- Miss Clairol hair coloring introduces the famous marketing slogan, "Does she or doesn't she?"
- Anheuser-Busch introduces Busch Bavarian beer; Budweiser has been around 80 years and Michelob 60.
- Federal troops quell riots in Little Rock during attempts to desegregate schools.
- Congress creates a Civil Rights Commission to provide voting rights safeguards.
- Soviet launch Sputnik is the first manmade satellite to circle the Earth.

This page — *The handoff of freight bills to a Yellow linehaul driver has been an important and long-standing first step in the delivery process.*

Page 79 — *One of the first safety lessons for dockworkers is that a clean dock is a safe dock. The Chicago dock was kept safe based on this 1957 photo.*

system to transfer freight at the Oklahoma-Texas border, there were still rules that governed the length of the tractor-trailer combination. In the mid 1950s, trailer lengths had to be less than 32 feet in order for the combination to meet most state total-length limits. With a shorter tractor, Yellow commissioned Fruehauf Corporation to build 35-foot trailers. The new boxes were constructed with aluminum bodies, making them even lighter to accommodate additional freight and still stay under the regulated highway weight limits.

Yellow Transit replaced its entire trailer fleet with a purchase of 400 new 35-foot Fruehaufs. Trailer volume expanded by 30 percent, adding still more efficiency to the company's strategy of focusing on longer hauls. Combined with the tractor purchase, the equipment order was among the most impressive one-time expenditures ever made in the industry.[3]

Behind the Wheel

In the A.J. Harrell era, drivers were personally responsible for their own tractors. They were motivated to treat their tractors as though they were their own vehicles. Many even spent personal time after their runs polishing fenders, bumpers and doors.

According to one legend, there was a certain tobacco-chewing driver who took great pride in his tractor, but, to A.J.'s great displeasure, did not have the same respect for the company's trailers. While tooling down the highway, the driver would spit his tobacco juices out his window and inevitably they landed on the box he was pulling. One day when the driver was polishing his tractor, A.J. walked up to the truck and spit his own tobacco wad against the shiny fender when the driver was polishing it. While protesting, the driver learned A.J. expected his trailer to receive the same respect the driver displayed for the company's tractor.

The policy of assigning tractors to individual drivers fell by the wayside as Yellow implemented its long-haul strategy.

The problem lay with regulations that called for an individual to rest for eight hours after driving 10. In an industry that was operating every hour of nearly every day of the year, the company could not afford to have the tractor sit idle for eight hours or more.

With its purchase of an all-new fleet, the company adopted what is known as a "slip seat" relay plan. A fully loaded trailer in Indianapolis destined for Houston, for instance, could feasibly make the entire trip behind the same tractor. At the company's relay

The last Atchison, Topeka and Santa Fe steam locomotive retires as diesel power eclipses steam on U.S. railroads.

The world's longest suspension bridge (3,691 feet) opens at Mackinaw City, Mich.

Jimmy Hoffa takes control of the IBT, which is ousted from the AFL-CIO on charges of corruption.

Popular movies include: Paths Of Glory with Kirk Douglas, 12 Angry Men with Henry Fonda, Man of a Thousand Faces with James Cagney, Peyton Place with Lana Turner, and The Pajama Game with Doris Day.

20
21
19
7
6
5

YELLOW
TRANSIT
SYSTEM MAP
CANADA
MICHIGAN
WISCONSIN
LAKE HURON
LAKE MICHIGAN
LAKE ERIE
ILLINOIS
IOWA
NEBRASKA
MISSOURI
INDIANA
OHIO
KENTUCKY
KANSAS
KANSAS TURNPIKE
OKLAHOMA
TENNESSEE
ARKANSAS
LOUISIANA
TEXAS
MEXICO
N
S
E
W
YELLOW TRANSIT
YELLOW TRANSIT
FREIGHT LINES
General Office: 1626 Walnut Street, Kansas City 8, Missouri

points along the authorized routes, a new driver would slip into the seat rather than hook up his or her permanently assigned tractor. The relay system maximized the use of revenue-producing equipment and fit much better into the longhaul strategy.

Inventive Thinking

The acquisition of Michigan Motor Freight Lines was an important learning experience. The shorthaul character of the new coverage area inspired a number of changes that would be especially important years later when Yellow created its innovative "hub and spoke" national network.

The line of cities along old U.S. Route 12 in Michigan, which is now mostly covered by Interstate 94, created a corridor of important manufacturers. However, each city alone did not produce enough longhaul freight to justify establishing a terminal in its community. Instead, Yellow Transit set up a consolidation center in one of the communities, Marshall, which was about midpoint between Kalamazoo to the west and Jackson to the east. Trucks would make the longer-than-usual pick-up runs to adjacent towns and return to Marshall where the freight would be broken down and consolidated into trailers going to destinations like Kansas City, Dallas or Houston.

When old-time truckers heard that Yellow Transit was going to pick up freight, move it east for breaking and consolidation and then move it back west again across the same roads, they said the process would never work, that it was too expensive to back-track freight.

They were wrong. The savings created by consolidating for the region more than made up for the added cartage costs. The process added a new dimension. It enabled carriers to look at possible ways to optimize the system by sub-optimizing a portion, or in this case, a small regional pick-up and delivery operation.

Interlining Experiences

Prior to the Michigan Motor acquisition, Yellow Transit was able to move freight east of its operating authority using interlining partners. Still used today, it was a necessary practice in a regulated environment. Nearly half of the tonnage Yellow Transit handled during the 1950s was moved in partnership with one or more other carriers. It had its drawbacks, though.

If an interlining carrier operated poorly, failing to deliver freight in a timely manner, it reflected badly on Yellow Transit. There also were inequities associated

Page 80 — *Expansion in the 1950s took Yellow Transit east to new communities in Indiana, Michigan and Ohio. The move eliminated the need for some interline partners.*

The Frisbee is marketed by Wham-O Manufacturing.

U.S. births hit a record 4.3 million.

Seventy-one world cities have more than 1 million people compared to only 10 cities in 1914.

Ford invests $250 million to introduce the Edsel to compete with GM's Oldsmobile; it's a failure and raises doubts about the effectiveness of market research.

Berry Gordy, Jr., 30, invests $700 to start Motown Corp., a music recording company in Detroit.

Uniforms continued to be a source of pride as Yellow Transit Company grew. The emblems, stripes, hat badge and safety pins on the uniform of this unidentified Detroit driver reveals his length of service and years of safe driving.

with billing processes that often caused friction between carriers and sometimes their customers.

One interlining partnership that did work effectively for about two years was between Yellow Transit and Federal Express. In mid 1954, the two carriers linked together Ohio manufacturing cities from Cleveland to Youngstown with Yellow Transit's markets in the central states and southwest. They promoted the routes together and exchanged trailers in Indianapolis. When Federal Express acquired rights into St. Louis in March 1956, the partnership ended. Yellow Transit de-emphasized interlining partnerships after 1956. By 1957, 60 percent of the company's freight moved within its own authorized routes. By 1960, the percentage increased to 70.[4]

Safe Handling Expected

The marketplace has changed dramatically since the 1950s, but the fundamental customer expecta tions were the same then as they are today. They wanted freight delivered as promised – on time and intact.

In 1952, eight percent of Yellow Transit's revenue was spent repaying customers for damages or lost freight, or for safety issues involving drivers and freight handlers. It was an embarrassingly large sum that implied that the company was doing a poor job of taking care of its customers' products. The new management team had to quickly address customer dissatisfaction, which it did by reinforcing a coding system for the terminals aimed at improving routing accuracy and updating freight-handling techniques.

Stacking issues that led to damaged freight were resolved then much the same way as they are today. Portable freight tables were designed to insert into the trailers to prevent heavy top freight from crushing items below it.

Concurrently, the company initiated a safety campaign designed to heighten awareness. It, too, was credited with changing behaviors. For one, terminal docks were kept cleaner to avoid mishaps due to slips and trips over debris and freight stacked in unexpected places.

The results produced by closer attention to details were remarkable. By 1960, payments made on freight claims had been lowered to less than one percent of revenue, and safety claims filed by employees and continuing safety programs all cost less than three percent of revenue. The improvement caused the company to take another leap of faith that year. It set

1958

New York's last trolley car crossing the Queensboro Bridge is retired.

Nikita Krushchev is named chairman of the Soviet Council of Ministers.

U.S. unemployment reaches a post-war record of 5.1 million.

First class postal rates increase from 3 cents to 4 cents per ounce, the first increase since 1932.

up a self-insurance program, except in states where self-insuring was prohibited. That meant that instead of paying premiums to a third-party insurance provider to protect Yellow from financial risks due to accidents or freight claims, the company set aside part of its revenue. The amount it set aside was based on its claims experience. The reserves were then used to pay for mishaps if and when they occurred.[5]

Service Salesmanship

With the operation stabilized by the mid 1950s, Yellow Transit's senior management began to move more aggressively toward expansion, both through acquisition and by setting up a stronger sales organization within its established authority. Hugh Coburn had spent 25 years in the airline industry. He had been the man George Powell, Sr. tapped for leading the company's sales and traffic departments.

Initially, all terminal sales managers reported directly to Coburn, vice-president – traffic and sales. In many cases, a terminal had only one person with sales responsibilities. Even at the larger facilities there were only a few salesmen with one city sales manager. That changed shortly after Coburn had set up his organization. He created district sales offices and set up northern and southern sales regions headed by regional sales managers.

The sales organization grew, but just as A.J. Harrell had problems keeping employees during World War II, young salesmen were difficult to hire and keep because of the Korean conflict.

It was through an emerging sales organization that many of the marketing concepts were tested. Senior management relied on the sales force to be the eyes and ears of the company. Constantly considered were ways to differentiate Yellow Transit from a wide range of carriers attempting to do business.

Avoiding Dull

Conferences and meetings became the accepted channels for dialogue with the sales organization. In April 1957, the company chose a resort site as a relaxing venue to conduct an important motivational and fact-finding session with its sales force. An extraordinary amount of fanfare surrounded the event that took place in Galveston, Texas. Spouses were invited and participated in several social outings as the salesmen cloistered for brainstorming sessions. In the evenings they reunited for banquets, dancing and even a country hayride.

Meetings like the one in Galveston became a means

The Chicago sales staff in 1959 included (back row, left to right) John Czerney, William Walsh, Homer Fowler, C. Megary, (front row, left to right) Earl Hanna, Jr. and Al Rosene.

The median U.S. family income has climbed from $3,187 in 1948 to $5,087.

The U.S. atomic submarine Nautilus successfully navigates under the North Pole.

Popular movies include: The Defiant Ones with Tony Curtis, Separate Tables with Rita Hayworth, Vertigo with James Stewart, Cat On a Hot Tin Roof with Elizabeth Taylor, Curse of the Demon with Dana Andrews, and Look Back in Anger with Richard Burton.

Boeing's 707 jet begins flying passengers.

This page, top — *Among the dinner guests at the Galveston sales meeting were (left to right) Gale Fitzwater, Mrs. Fitzwater, Mrs. Shelley, and Prentiss Shelley.*

Page 85 — *Sales meeting photo May 5, 1957.*

From left to right: Seated 1st row: H.W. Coburn, executive vice president; P. Schunk, Evansville, P. Shelley, Tulsa; B. Thompson, St. Louis; C. Davenport, Sherman; G. Fitzwater, Beaumont; R. Young, regional sales manager-South; N. Secrest, assist. regional sales manager-South; G. Powell, Jr., president. 2nd row: A. Rosene, Chicago; B. Glenn, advertising manager; H. Johnson, Detroit; H. Op'tHolt, Marshall; R. Ozee, Mattoon; F. Rys, Springfield; L. Payne, Baxter Springs; D. Ellis, Waco; E. Albritton, Detroit; J. Jones, Ft. Worth; F. Green, Indianapolis; B. Braun, Detroit; L.E. Tomlinson, general traffic manager. 3rd row: B. Heider, sales manager-national accounts; C.R. Megary, sales manager-Chicago national accounts; J. Francis, Kansas City; B. Garrison, Peoria; T. Newby, Houston; T. Wood, San Antonio; L.D. Luper, Oklahoma City; J. Garner, Amarillo; H.C. Hoerter, Louisville; M. Martin, Austin; B. Stauffer, regional sales manager-North. 4th row: W. Younts, Wichita; M. Robeson, vice presidnet-personnel; L. Brandt, assistant regional sales manager-North; A. Pryor, Wichita Falls; D. Sable, vice president-sales & traffic; D. McMorris, vice president-finance; B. Bush, Dallas.

of setting the tone for customer contacts. The festive atmosphere helped unify an organization that needed to succeed over broad and very diverse geographic sections of the country.

The Talent Pool

Yellow Transit took on a personality during the 1950s. It contrasted sharply with other truck lines of that era. Rather than an assertive, hard-nosed image, Yellow was quietly calculating. The new breed that George Powell, Sr. assembled was a mixture of different backgrounds. The common thread was that Powell wanted each individual to experience the full range of the business – operations, sales, traffic and rating, personnel management and labor negotiations, asset management and government regulations. He recognized leaders among the group and from the start groomed those who demonstrated both an aptitude and willingness to be in charge. Native abilities rather than specific training attracted him more.

Powell's handpicked team developed extreme loyalties to him and to Yellow. Individuals like George Powell, Jr., Don McMorris, Mark Robeson, Hugh Coburn, L.E. Tomlinson, David Padgett, Don Sable, William Riley, Harold Edwards, Lloyd Brandt and Forrest Burm were men who spent years together following Powell's executive model.

Dr. L.L. Waters remembers these and others in the Yellow family vividly. He, too, became a close adviser to George Sr. after the two served together on the Transportation Council of the U.S. Department of Commerce. Waters, a highly respected professor of transportation at Indiana University, and before that, professor of finance and director of the Bureau of Business Research at the University of Kansas, said Powell "surrounded himself with young, highly energized and well-educated men when he took over Yellow."

Most amazing to Waters was the relationship among George Jr., McMorris and Robeson. He said the three men were uncanny in their ability to think and act as one. He described them as a "triumvirate that worked with uncommon harmony." Eventually, all of them – Waters, too – served on Yellow's board of directors.

Over his academic tenure, Waters would see more than 100 of his former students go to work for Yellow in varying capacities. Mark Robeson was one of his first.

Waters' expertise was in high demand. He served as a board director for numerous transportation companies in addition to Yellow. He once wrote that he had

The U.S. launches its first satellite to circle the Earth.

Popular songs include: Diana, Satin Doll, Volare, Arrivederci Roma, Splish Splash, Sugartime, Twilight Time, Catch a Falling Star and The Chipmunk Song.

The New York Giants becomes the San Francisco Giants; the Brooklyn Dodgers become the Los Angeles Dodgers.

Americans buy 100 million Hula Hoops.

YELLOW
TRANSIT
3438
YELLOW
TRANSIT
2189

delivered approximately 3,000 speeches, which he said meant that he either had an important business message or companies were hard up for programs.

To this day Waters is effusive with his praise for the elder Powell. Like others who remember Powell's manner during this period, Waters said Powell would begin every serious conversation by stating that he did not know much about the topic, but he had some thoughts he wanted to share and then wanted to know what others were thinking. When he spoke, Waters said, he had a calming and homespun directness.

Public Ownership

George Sr. had done what he intended, rescued Yellow Transit Freight Lines with his son at his side. George Jr. became president of the company by the mid 1950s, but George Sr. remained active as chairman of the board. He stayed engaged in industry activities and devoted significant time to Kansas City civic endeavors. By 1959, together, they had the company ready to go public. Their inexperienced management team had matured and had grown the company's revenue from $7.5 million in 1952 to $31.3 million in 1959.

Two hundred six thousand shares were issued in October at $11 per share. The goal was to raise working capital and increase the capital structure. There was plenty of risk.

Only 10 truck lines had gone public since 1939. Investors, perhaps doubtful of an industry that seemed rooted in family-owned operations with limited professional business skills, shied away from trucking stocks. That would change, but meantime, Powell had already moved Yellow beyond the stereotype.

The decade of the 50s ended with Yellow Transit a much stronger and much wiser organization. In place was one of the strongest management teams in the industry. They would stay together and grow the organization nearly 30 fold in 20 years. And then they would face the most revolutionary challenge of their collective careers.

This page — *Yellow Transit Company sold stock in the company for $11 per share starting in 1959. The sale helped raise capital for expansion.*

Page 86 — *When the Kenworth diesel cab-beside-engine (CBE) tractor was introduced in 1955, it drew both curiosity and fanfare. Here, the curious get their up-close glimpse at the "telephone booth" vehicle.*

1959

Fidel Castro assumes leadership in Cuba after engineering a 2-year revolutionary overthrow of dictator Batista.

Alaska and Hawaii become the 49th and 50th states.

The Landrum-Griffin Act requires unions to file annual financial reports with the Department of Labor.

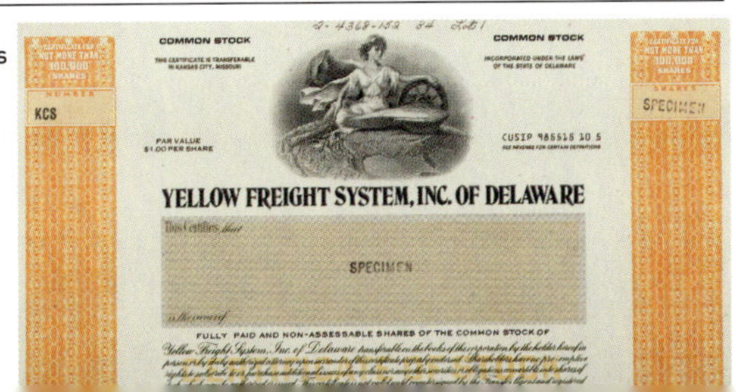

Those Who Remember

Kansas City terminal manager Bill Saylor congratulates Yellow Transit driver Glen Woodroof for his safe driving record during the late 1930s.

Only a handful of active Yellow drivers fully appreciate how significant the differences are today from what it was like steering a truck from one city to another or one customer to another prior to interstate highway construction.

Oklahoma City linehaul driver Sam Kimmey remembers that he had to ask what an interstate highway was the day when a manager held a meeting to announce the start of construction in the Oklahoma City area.

Wally Smith, an Atlanta linehaul driver with 51 years of experience, is another who remembers the days of driving before interstates. He began his career driving for Adley Express between Hartford, Connecticut, and New York. The trip was two lanes all the way. His first encounter with multiple-lane highways was when he got inside New York City. It was a harrowing new experience, vehicles passing on the ht side of the truck. Some truckers d never even thought of mounting rrors on the right side of their ctors, so drivers were severely ndicapped on multiple lane high- ys. It put other motorists at risk well.

etting to New York, said Smith, k up to five hours. He covered t 120 miles, averaging 24 miles r hour. He made similar trips to iladelphia, a 211-mile trip. It k eight hours, so it meant he had to spend the mandatory eight hours of resting time in Philadelphia before he could return with a load for Hartford.

Jim Porto and Smith were driving colleagues at Adley in the 1940s and 1950s. Porto, a linehaul driver in Nashville, said his father began driving the same northeast routes in 1925, so he knew what he was getting himself into when he climbed behind the wheel at age 16.

"These people today don't know how lucky they are," said Porto. "We carried tool boxes for when we broke down."

And break down they did. Flat tires, fender-benders, engine or transmission failures; any number of problems could interfere with schedules, so arriving at destination without spending time along the roadside was a very satisfying occurrence.

Central Conference of Teamsters
JAMES R. HOFFA
DETROIT, MICH.
CCT
CONVENTION
INTERNATIONAL
BROTHERHOOD
OF TEAMSTERS

Turbulence, Triumphs & Teamsters

Growing Pains in the 60s

The 1960s were as eventful for the trucking industry as they were for the nation at large. The White House was transformed into Camelot. The president declared America would land on the moon, and it did. A little country in Southeast Asia would dominate world news and suck America into the most controversial and extended international conflict of its short history. Assassins would snuff out the lives of beloved national leaders. The Beatles and Elvis would remake the recording industry and an innocuous street corner in San Francisco would become the epicenter of a cultural revolution.

The trucking industry had grown up. The nation was spending twice as much to move products between cities via trucks as it was to move products by railroads. A few years earlier railroads dominated freight transportation, and in 1960 they still carried slightly more tonnage than the trucking industry. But those tons were mostly bulk commodities like coal, grain and ore. Truckers were taking an increasing share of the revenue pie by moving smaller shipments requiring more labor-intensive handling, flexible pickup and precise delivery. Higher rates were the result.[1]

The industry was coming of age on Wall Street. But investors moved cautiously. Most recognized that it took more than experienced operators, aggressive salesmen and discerning accountants to make the transition to a large publicly traded corporation. While the operators, salesmen and accountants would always be the backbone of the business, a different and perhaps more visionary style of management was required to take a company to the next level of success.

The investment community was concerned about one thing in particular, the company's relationship with the Teamsters. Was the carrier with a union contract capable of successfully negotiating reasonable and competitive wages and benefits? Or, would there be uncooperative wrangling leading to strikes and service disruptions? These were questions financial analysts asked when they reviewed Yellow's 1959 initial public offering of 206,000 shares.[2]

There was another far more macro-economic issue at work. A more conservative investment philosophy ruled the day, creating a much smaller pool of equity investors. Most small investors stayed the course with

Page 90 — *James R. Hoffa (right) and Dave Beck talk backstage at the 1957 Teamsters Convention in Florida. Beck was retiring as president of the union and Hoffa, a vice president, was the leading candidate to replace him. Hoffa won and was installed in 1958. (AP/Wide World Photos)*

1960

John F. Kennedy, 43, is elected president, defeating Vice President Richard Nixon.

Political pundits credit the first live television debates for Kennedy's edge over Nixon.

Electricity generating atomic power plants begin to operate; the first is at Dresden, Ill., south of Chicago.

The U.S. has 2.17 million miles of paved highways, up from 1.68 million ten years earlier.

OPEC meets for the first time in Baghdad to shape its oil producing strategies.

The International Brotherhood of Teamsters headquarters in Washington, D.C., located near the Capitol and busy Union (train) Station.

savings bonds and bank accounts. The general population depended heavily on company retirement systems and social security for their futures and spent their income on homes, cars, vacations and new luxuries that emerged in the 1960s. Unlike millions of Americans today, they were not investing in stocks and mutual funds for retirement security.

Companies like Yellow that sold stock to raise capital appealed to a comparatively small group of buyers and fund managers. For their willingness to gamble on industries and companies with no track records, higher returns were required. But could a company operating in a regulated industry grow its profits well enough to appease investors?

Before Wall Street would embrace Yellow Transit, company leaders had to demonstrate considerable finesse in working with labor and political leaders while establishing a track record of good business judgment. Those investors who took the chance were extremely gratified in fewer than five years.

Teamsters and Truckers

By 1960, the International Brotherhood of Teamsters was a labor force to be reckoned with. Formed in 1903 in a merger of two small unions, Teamster membership had grown to 1.1 million. James Riddle Hoffa, an intense young labor organizer from Detroit, who had been elected to the general presidency in 1958, was about to grab national headlines.

Ever since the A.J. Harrell era, Yellow Transit had operated with numerous contracts. Each local negotiated separately. To a degree, this worked in the company's favor. It certainly limited the company's exposure to expensive national health, welfare and retirement reforms that were implemented in the 1950s.

The issue confounding the entire industry was one stemming from the way labor contracts were set up. Teamster locals bargained on the strength of employee demands and the skill of area negotiators. The contracts established "cartage" rules and procedures.

When linehaul drivers went from one city to another, they entered new contract territory where rules changed and preferential treatment was given to the driver from the local union. A driver needing to return to his domicile with a load often was forced to wait, frustrating him and his company. The solution was obvious, but also a risk.

By the mid 1950s, companies like Roadway, Consolidated Freightways, Denver-Chicago, Garrett,

The U.S. launches the first communications satellite, Echo I.

Popular movies include: The Apartment with Jack Lemmon, Psycho with Anthony Perkins, Elmer Gantry with Burt Lancaster, The Entertainer with Laurence Olivier, Inherit the Wind with Spencer Tracy and The Magnificent Seven with Yul Brynner.

and Transcon, among others, were spreading out and dealing with more and more Teamster locals. Hoffa, who worked tirelessly during the 1940s and 50s recruiting more members and preaching solidarity as the way to get better contracts with management, believed that the union needed to seize the opportunity to write one contract that put an umbrella over the entire industry. It could solve the problem for over-the-road operations.

Hoffa's concept was to have a master agreement that covered over-the-road issues and built uniform procedures into local negotiations. He also wanted each local and area contract to settle at the same time the national agreement was reached. Hoffa sold the concept to other union leaders. In return for their commitment, he promised that no area would sacrifice work rules or other benefits they had fought to build into their local contracts.

In preparing to negotiate a nationwide contract, Hoffa spent long hours coaching more than 350 local union leaders. His mission was to prepare them for a clause that said the next contract would be negotiated as a master agreement with a single expiration.

He started with the smaller geographic areas in the Northeast. He took their signed agreements to Chicago in 1960 and convinced the powerful Central States Conference that momentum was building for a national agreement. With the Central States Conference behind him, and others lining up behind it, Hoffa entered negotiations on the 1961 contract exactly where he wanted to be, cued up for a master contract in 1964. He was prepared to put all carriers under the same general financial package and working conditions.

At the time, Ray Beagle was a young Kansas City lawyer specializing in labor law. He represented a 200-member Missouri-Kansas trucking employer group. Beagle was asked to take on more duties. Specifically, he was recruited to represent the industry in the Central States, the most populated Teamster territory in the nation from which Hoffa and several international union leaders had risen. Later, he would be appointed to a critical role in national contract negotiations.

Beagle said he and the industry raced against time to bring 41 employer groups together in 1963, representing hundreds of trucking firms. Hoffa, meantime, had power of attorney from 350 local unions.

From his law office in Kansas City and using a post office box in Washington, D.C., to make it look

A dockworker identified only as Opry handles freight in Dallas. Dockworker wages grew steadily in the 1960s while payments to health, welfare and pension benefits increased rapidly.

1961

Popular songs include: The Twist, Itsy Bitsy Teenie Weenie Yellow Polka Dot Bikini, Only the Lonely, and Cathy's Clown.

Aluminum cans are used commercially for the first time.

A failed coup against Fidel Castro known as the Bay of Pigs invasion places Cuban and U.S. relations in peril.

The Berlin Wall is erected to halt a mass exodus of East Berliners to the West.

The U.S. has 11.7 million trucks or 26 percent more than 10 years earlier.

James R. Hoffa (right) talks with Robert Kennedy (left) between formal sessions of a Senate Investigating Committee. Hoffa and Kennedy, counsel for the committee, made headlines at the 1957 proceedings because of their heated exchange. (AP/Wide World Photos – individual in center of photo unidentified)

more official, Ray Beagle successfully organized the employers from across the nation under one banner, Trucking Employers, Inc. (TEI), a Missouri corporation. To the surprise of the union and Secretary of Labor, watching the spectacle closely because of the national media attention it was drawing, TEI was ready to negotiate with Hoffa and his conference leaders when the action began in Chicago during the fall of 1963.

Successfully rallying more than a thousand carriers into a cohesive bargaining group was a masterful accomplishment. Beagle credits many strong industry leaders at the time for enabling all of the companies to muster a strong negotiating effort.

When bargaining began, Beagle and a large group of trucking executives elected by all the carriers, sat across the table from Hoffa, a man who was known worldwide. His reputation was primarily the result of his public discourse with Bobby Kennedy in U.S. Senate chambers.

Kennedy was a young prosecuting attorney working for the Senate in 1957. His brother, John, was a U.S. Senator who was already considered a good presidential prospect. It was Bobby Kennedy who questioned Hoffa accusingly in 1957 about his association with organized crime figures, a charge that continued to nag Hoffa even during this critical bargaining period in 1963. It became more fodder for the media. The negotiations drew so much attention that it was difficult to get anything done, so negotiators agreed to move talks to Miami.

Though removed from network television cameras, talks had to be suspended in November, while a shocked nation recovered from the assassination of its president, John F. Kennedy.

Negotiations resumed in Chicago early in 1964 with Hoffa facing criminal racketeering charges. Despite the circus-like atmosphere fueled mostly by the news media, TEI and the Teamsters reached a settlement. The carriers were successful in getting a "thin" master agreement that avoided a national wage and benefit scale, which would have put an instant financial burden on many companies.

Later in 1964, Hoffa was convicted in Chattanooga and Chicago in two different criminal trials. He appealed both convictions. The appeals process dragged on for three years, extending into the second National Master Freight Agreement negotiations, which turned out to be just as dramatic as the first.

Negotiations on the second NMFA began in

1962

Popular songs include: Moon River, It Was a Very Good Year, Crying, What Kind of Fool Am I?, and Blowin' In the Wind.

Roger Maris hits 61 home runs breaking Babe Ruth's record of 60.

The Cuban missile crisis causes a major confrontation between the U.S. and Soviet Union.

President Kennedy embargoes trade with Cuba.

Marilyn Monroe, 36, dies after taking an overdose of sleeping pills at her Hollywood home.

late 1966. This time, there were 1,165 carriers on the TEI roster and more than 243,000 Teamster members employed by those member carriers.

Three weeks before the old contract was to expire, March 31, 1967, Jimmy Hoffa's legal appeals on his racketeering convictions from 1964 ran out. He was sent to jail and talks between TEI and the union were put into a tailspin. Several locals threatened to strike in protest of Hoffa's incarceration, and indeed some did in the South.

Part of the purpose behind organizing TEI was to manage these types of situations – a regional strike directly affecting part of the membership. The trucking firms put their organizational charter to test. The dare imposed on company members, including Yellow, was to implement a defensive lockout in order to force the striking locals back to the bargaining table.

Unity prevailed. The companies shut down their operations and parked their vehicles. Employee paychecks stopped. The nation's highways were suddenly emptied of Teamster-driven trucks.

En route to jail, Hoffa assigned responsibility for the union to Frank Fitzsimmons, his long-time Detroit associate. Fitzsimmons went to Washington, D.C., to restart talks with TEI. With government officials looking over their shoulders, an agreement was reached within three days, averting a prolonged battle between TEI carrier members and their employees.[3]

The NMFA Impact

Yellow and other unionized carriers were alarmed about the prospects of a national labor agreement. They feared the union would use the carriers' geographic and operating differences to divide and conquer. Their concerns notwithstanding, many industry leaders also recognized an advantage in negotiating one national contract. With it, growth-oriented companies could acquire other operations and merge them using a single change of operations rather than a complex layer of changes filed with each local union that would be affected. It was a critical advantage to Yellow in the 1960s because it meant faster and more cost effective large-scale operating changes. It continues to provide the same benefits even today.

Fate's Hand

Ironically, government regulation of the trucking industry made it possible for the union to grow stronger during the 1960s and 1970s. The Teamsters

Marine pilot John Glenn orbits the Earth in Mercury capsule Friendship 7.

Ross Perot, 32, founds Electronic Data Systems, which will make him a billionaire.

Popular movies include: Lawrence of Arabia with Peter O'Toole, and To Kill a Mockingbird with Gregory Peck.

The New York Mets and Houston Colt 45s (later Astros) play their first season.

Sam Walton opens his first Wal-Mart store after retail employer, Ben Franklin, dismissed his idea.

Wage scale During the 60s

Year	Teamster wages/hour	Weekly health, welfare & pension contributions
1964	$ 3.12	$12.30
1965	$ 3.21	$13.80
1966	$ 3.31	$16.50
1967	$ 3.56	$17.50
1968	$ 3.74	$18.50

faced little resistance from the industry in bargaining for higher wages and benefit contributions because the companies could easily pass along their inflationary costs to the shipping public and their consumers.

Hoffa shrewdly understood that the government would serve as his ally if he could centralize the union's power. He knew that well-managed trucking firms were sheltered from costs driven by labor. As long as the economy grew and products needed to be moved, Hoffa could boast and almost guarantee that his membership would earn better wages and benefits with each new national contract.

After absorbing the resulting rate hikes, shippers caught on, too, and improved organizational efforts to protect their interests during ICC hearings where rate increases were proposed. The maneuvering put Yellow and its shareholders in a regulated vice between its Teamster-represented employees and its customers.

Regulation also made it cost prohibitive for startup nonunion carriers to acquire route authority. Moreover, if the union wanted to drive an uncooperative trucker out of business, it could do so with very little impact on industry jobs because regulation would fill vacated service by allowing another established, probably unionized, carrier to acquire the routes.

By the 1960s, trucking firms had been under the watchful eye of the ICC for 30 years and were entrenched in doing business by rules, regulations and classifications.

The industry had an attitude. Circumstances had turned freight transportation into a utility rather than a free-enterprise industry. Companies performed their responsibilities dutifully, and in Yellow's case, remained inventive in creating tools to assist its operation. But overall, the industry fell short in satisfying customers.

Raising the Stakes

By 1960, economic growth had made Yellow Transit's operating capacity inadequate. Interstate highways were already causing transportation planners to think differently about how they would achieve greater efficiency in the future.

As George Powell, Jr. reset the company's course on longhaul transportation, the transition required a radical change of operations. While disruptive, it was one of those key turning-point decisions that kept the company on a path of growth and increasing success.

In 1960, Yellow management held a series of

1963

John F. Kennedy is assassinated while visiting Dallas.

Martin Luther King, Jr. tells celebrants at the Lincoln Memorial, "I have a dream..."

NAACP leader Medgar Evers, 37, is murdered at his home in Jackson, Miss.

U.S. factory workers make $100 per week for the first time in history.

meetings with Teamster employees from Texas to Michigan and Ohio. The company explained that Yellow needed to make dramatic alterations that would result in layoffs, though they would not be permanent. The union was receptive and supported the long-range plan.

According to Powell, Jimmy Hoffa protégé Roy Williams, a Kansas City labor leader who would later rise to prominence in the Teamster organization, was one who understood Yellow's strategy best. The company kept its word, eventually putting affected employees back to work.

Some in the management ranks, however, found the changes unnerving and were not willing to stick around, a move they may have regretted later. Although financial analysts were generally skeptical at first, they praised the changes implemented in 1960 when profits began to improve.

Compared to Others

A few other trucking companies went public about the same time as Yellow. Those names included Consolidated Freightways, Ryder and Specter. Despite enormous revenue growth in 1961, these three carriers in particular saw profits suffer, driving their stock prices downward to approximately one-third of their initial offering price in 1960. Yellow Transit, meantime, improved profits by 47 percent in 1961 despite 15 percent less revenue due to the operating change. The next year revenue began to grow again, up nine percent. Profits, meantime, more than doubled. It earned the relatively small Kansas City-based carrier the attention of *Forbes* magazine, which called Yellow Transit a "new breed" of trucker because of its astute profit management.[4]

There were several factors that kept Yellow's ship upright and steady during the 1960s. They were the same factors that had put the company back on course during the 1950s. Foremost, Yellow had established a professional team of business leaders that remained true to its objective of growing the company profitably by offering customers a high quality service. Management was also intent on creating a desirable place to work.

Another factor was the firm growth of the American economy. Quality carriers kept pace with the growing demand. As manufacturers, retailers and other key users of for-hire trucking became stronger and more efficient, they urged the better carriers to target national coverage as a motivation to gain more of their freight.

Night dispatcher Jim Bickness kept the lights burning and the freight moving around Chicago.

The U.S. budget is $100 billion, almost half going to military expenditures.

Two-thirds of the world's autos are in the U.S., which has 6 percent of the population.

Popular songs include: Fly Me to the Moon, Blame It on the Bossa Nova, Falling, Blue Bayou, and I Wanna Hold Your Hand.

The Los Angeles Dodgers win the World Series in 4 games against the Yankees.

Eastman Kodak introduces the Instamatic camera.

46
47
CISCO MFG CO.
HOUSTON, TEXAS
LIBERTY
4

Although regulation presented occasional roadblocks, a few carriers were bearing down on coast-to-coast and border-to-border authority. Yellow Transit was not among this elite group as the decade began. The company was less than half the size of current-day rivals Roadway Express and Consolidated Freightways.

In 1960, Yellow Transit employed 2,000 people and generated $32 million in revenue, serving eight states: Michigan, Indiana, Illinois, Kentucky, Missouri, Kansas, Oklahoma and Texas. Its special hauling division, which concentrated on moving steel primarily for the auto industry, also served Ohio.

As the decade unfolded, Yellow Transit made three strategic purchases and other minor acquisitions that aided the company's double-digit annual revenue growth for the next 10 years.

Years of Growth and Prosperity

Yellow Transit Freight Lines was one of 1,200 Class I regulated freight carriers in 1960, which meant simply that it had revenue in excess of $1 million per year. There were 16,000 Class II and III carriers with less than a million in revenue, which were also regulated by the Interstate Commerce Commission. To its 30,000 shipping customers, Yellow Transit was an important company, but it was relatively small and mostly unnoticed, with the exception that its management team was very involved in industry activities and eager to take leading roles in industry projects.

For the previous eight years, Yellow Transit had been quietly creating a platform for success from its hidden bunker in Kansas City. The company's extraordinary growth began with a rather modest purchase of Central States Freight Service, a freight forwarder with a small cartage subsidiary, A&G Transport.

Forwarding Freight "Piggyback"

By buying Central States Freight Service, Yellow Transit acquired a relatively inexpensive direct link to the East Coast, connecting key manufacturing centers with its service area in the Midwest and Southwest. Freight was transported by over-the-road trucks and by rail. The railroads had started to capitalize on the trucking industry's growth by creating more reliable flatcar service on which truck trailers could "piggyback." The purchase of Central States Freight Service gave Yellow Transit an entrée into the emerging intermodal service market, protecting the company against any revenue losses the company

This page — *Drivers in Yellow Transit Company's founding state were strongly competitive from the onset; Oklahoma driver Robert B. Snider kept the tradition active with his selection as state driver of the year in 1965.*

Page 98 — *Dallas dock-worker D.W. Watson uses a forklift to handle his loading and unloading chores. The forklift became a critical tool in improving freight-handling efficiencies.*

1964

President Johnson is re-elected with the largest popular vote plurality in U.S. history.

Leonid Brezhnev replaces Nikita Khrushchev as leader of the Soviet Union.

The Warren Commission tells America Lee Harvey Oswald acted alone in assassinating President Kennedy.

Studebaker-Packard is the first automaker to offer seat belts as standard equipment.

The Medicare Act creates the first government-operated health insurance program.

This page, top — *"Piggyback" operations lowered linehaul costs and reduced risks due to transfer errors.*

This page, bottom — *Expansion into freight forwarding prompted Yellow Transit to recast its image, creating a new company logo and unofficial name, Yellow Freight Lines.*

Page 101 — *General office employees moved into a new facility in 1960 that was built at 92nd and State Line in Kansas City, Mo. The structure drew accolades for its beauty, but rapid company growth made its space inadequate within the decade.*

might suffer if intermodal transportation began to displace traditional LTL longhaul traffic.

Initially, freight forwarding was used to send exportable products from the Midwest to ocean harbors in New York. Yellow reversed the freight flow direction after observing that the service was not as profitable as using New York and Boston as originators for domestic traffic moving west. Once those products reached Chicago and St. Louis, they were broken and reloaded for distribution throughout Yellow Transit's territory. When the forwarding process started to contribute to the bottom line, Philadelphia and Baltimore were added as points of origin. At that point, the freight-forwarding subsidiary became known as Yellow Forwarding Company. It also prompted senior management to cast about for a new image for the corporation, although unofficially.

As a marketing tactic, the company designed a new logo – a broad T-shaped shield in which the word "Yellow" stood alone and underneath the shield were the words "Freight Lines." It was a new umbrella image for all of the subsidiaries, including Yellow Transit Freight Lines, Yellow Forwarding and Yellow Transit Steel Division, formerly known as the special hauling division.[5]

There were no other purchases until 1965. Instead, the company focused on revitalizing its network of terminals, building new ones where they were needed and expanding established terminals where land permitted. The company also moved headquarters into a modern office building in south Kansas City at 92nd and State Line, the road that serves as the border between Missouri and Kansas.

In midyear 1961, Yellow Transit instituted an equipment replacement policy that put one of the best looking fleets on the highways. It sold 247 older road tractors – the unique "telephone booth" tractors – and replaced them with 200 new leased diesels. It bought 100 more tractors in the first quarter of 1962 and replaced more than 775 trailers. By 1964, the average age of the company's tractors was less than one year and the average age of trailers was less than two years.

It took a profitable carrier to do this, especially considering that Teamster wages were increasing four percent per year as stipulated in the first National Master Freight Agreement ratified in 1964. But profits were good and getting better. In 1964, Yellow Transit reported earnings per share of $2.83, up from $.42 per share in 1960.

New consumer products include Pop-Tarts, Lucky Charms and G.I. Joe dolls for boys.

President Johnson orders bombing attacks on North Vietnam.

The president announces a doubling of draft calls.

Malcom X, leader of Afro-American Unity, is gunned down as he prepares to address a multi-racial audience in Harlem.

YELLOW
FREIGHT SYSTEM

Everything's up to date in Kansas City, where changes are constant and quite obvious when comparing nearly 40 years of progress, including an interstate highway system encircling the downtown. (new photo by Ron Coppock-King)

Purchase Doubles Carrier Size

Yellow Transit Freight Lines, Inc., under the preferred but unofficial banner Yellow Freight System, was operating well in 1965. Revenue was growing steadily by 20 percent per year and profits were jumping by more than 25 percent per year. The company was ready for its next venture, one that would rock the industry.

In February 1965, Yellow offered to buy Watson-Wilson Transportation System, a carrier bigger than Yellow in coverage and one that had already established a transcontinental route from Charleston, S.C., to San Francisco, Calif.

The 1962 merger of two older carriers had created Watson-Wilson, both with pasts similar to Yellow. Three brothers in Nebraska had started Watson Brothers Transportation Company in the 1920s. Brothers H.C. and Jesse Wilson founded Wilson Trucking Company in Tennessee in 1933.

Oddly enough, the opportunity to buy Watson-Wilson was the indirect result of the 1960s business trend of creating corporate conglomerates spanning multiple industries and multiple business lines within an industry.

The complicated story began in 1959 when a company named Walnut Grove Products bought Watson Brothers Transportation from the family heirs of the original founders. Three years later, in 1962, the company added Wilson Trucking to its portfolio of assets and combined the two operations into Watson-Wilson Trucking. Walnut Grove Products also owned freight forwarding companies and an air forwarder by that time.

Then W.R. Grace & Company bought Walnut Grove Products and put Watson-Wilson on the for-sale block. Everett A. Kelloway, the president of Walnut Grove Products who had built the mini-empire, talked Gilbert Swanson of Swanson Foods into buying the truck line. But that marriage lasted only five months. Swanson went looking for a new buyer and found Yellow.[6]

After several months of negotiation, Yellow formally offered to buy Watson-Wilson for 15 shares of Yellow and $175 in cash for 100 shares of Watson-Wilson. The offer was not well received by a small group of Watson-Wilson shareholders that had bought the stock on speculation after Yellow announced its intention. The protesting shareholders claimed that Yellow's offer was inadequate. Other carriers also protested the merger.

President Johnson describes the "Great Society" where poverty is eliminated in America.

Ralph Nader publishes Unsafe at Any Speed, a book critical of the lack of safety on America's highways.

Lady Bird Johnson urges the removal of billboards along Interstate Highways.

Popular songs include: Satisfaction, Yesterday, Michelle, Sounds of Silence, I Got You Babe, and What the World Needs Now Is Love.

Home delivered milk now accounts for 25 percent of sales, down from 50 percent before World War II.

It was three years before the legal and regulatory tangle was unsnarled. Meantime, the ICC had granted Yellow temporary control of Watson-Wilson to operate separately. This was actually Yellow's preference all along. The management team wanted time to merge the different organizations slowly. The two former carriers, Watson Brothers and Wilson Truck Company, had never fully integrated their operations and were quite different employment cultures. After Watson-Wilson was merged in 1962 as part of the Walnut Grove Products conglomerate, on-time service slipped to below industry standards and was far below Yellow's. Immediate work was needed to improve fundamental operating processes.

Yellow achieved fast results by applying longstanding quality controls and eliminating duplication in sales and administrative functions. Offices in Omaha were closed and work was moved to Kansas City. Watson-Wilson's sleeper operation was converted to slip-seat relays like Yellow's. Pleased that Yellow was stepping in to rescue a venerable union carrier, Teamster locals throughout the Watson-Wilson network were cooperative.

Yellow and Watson-Wilson gained a mutual competitive advantage through access to each other's service territory and by marketing their broader coverage to their separate customer lists. Shippers liked the convenience of using the two carriers, particularly in the three major overlapping markets of Chicago, St. Louis and Kansas City. There was some inefficiency related to freight exchanges between terminals in these three cities, but that was a minor inconvenience compared to the savings and business gains that developed.

The ICC granted Yellow permanent authority to control Watson-Wilson in May 1966 and by September, Yellow owned all but less than two percent of Watson-Wilson's stock. Yellow provided Watson-Wilson nearly $2.5 million to buy new trucks and build new terminals.

Although the two carriers had to operate independently until the ICC gave final approval, Yellow set up five service divisions to manage both companies, including general commodities, steel transport, defense transport, thermo transport and international forwarding. Domestic forwarding remained part of general commodities. It allowed Yellow's managers to integrate the companies well in advance of the merger, which was officially granted in December 1968.

In St. Louis, the two companies were coping with tensions resulting from the dovetailing of Watson-

An unidentified mechanic adjusts headlights on Yellow Transit's unusual "telephone booth" CBE tractor.

1966

University of Mississippi's first black graduate, James Meredith, is shot during a march from Memphis to Jackson, Miss.

The National Organization for Women (NOW) is founded.

New York makes Fifth Ave. and Madison Ave. one way streets to ease congestion.

Congress passes a Fair Packaging and Labeling Act that calls for clear labels of net weight and imposes other controls.

Popular songs include: Yellow Submarine, Eleanor Rigby, Mellow Yellow, Scarborough Fair, Monday, Monday, and What Now My Love.

Lawsuit Attempts to Stop Merger

Tony Theler, a St. Louis linehaul hostler, went to work for Yellow Transit Freight Lines in 1965, the same year Yellow purchased Watson-Wilson.

Anthony (Tony) Theler and Rosemary Donley started work at Yellow's St. Louis terminal in 1965. Tensions were high. City drivers were upset that Watson-Wilson employees were going to be dovetailed into Yellow's seniority list. They fought the company and their own union local over the matter, said Theler. The local union sided with Yellow.

Dovetailing meant everyone's seniority was based on his or her starting date with either company. Many of the former Watson-Wilson employees had longer tenure and therefore bumped Yellow employees further down the seniority list, causing them to move to less desirable working hours, and in some cases, threatened lay off. Donley said even office employees were affected.

"I dropped 35 notches in one day," said Theler. "I was on the 3:30 to midnight shift for 2-and-a-half years, but I still had a job." Theler

id the union told protesting mem-
rs that as long as Yellow's purchase
Watson-Wilson was considered a
erger, it meant dovetailing was the
oper method of combining the
rk forces. Still, Yellow drivers
ed an attorney and filed an
tion to stop the merger.
ccording to Theler, Yellow officer
rl Cotton visited the terminal and
plained that Yellow needed
tson-Wilson's West Coast rights
d facilities to expand. Cotton said Yellow could not risk waiting for the carrier to close due to financial problems because other competitors would challenge Yellow for the Watson-Wilson route authority.

Harvey Williamson had worked for Watson-Wilson since 1958. He retired from Yellow in 1999. He said local union leaders had assured the Watson-Wilson employees that there was no threat from the lawsuit. As long as Yellow accepted a package of pencils from Watson Wilson during the merger, union employees had to be dovetailed. Nevertheless, Williamson said bad blood between the two work groups lasted a couple of years. However, there was no problem between employees and management. "Management at that time was really good down there," Williamson said.

Yellow Freight System operated Watson-Wilson trucks from 1965 until 1968 when final government approval was granted to merge the two carriers. Watson and Wilson were two carriers that had merged in 1962 to form a company larger than Yellow.

Wilson and Yellow seniority lists. Management had decided that individuals with the longest union tenure would maintain their seniority regardless of which company they started with. In some aquisitions, unionized employees of the acquired company were moved as a block to the end of the seniority list, called endtailing.

The carriers combined their St. Louis operations into one terminal in January 1967, right during the time of contract negotiations for the second NMFA and corresponding wildcat strikes and resulting industry-wide lockout. Two groups of union workers were dovetailed and 22 employees were laid off, but only for three weeks. By the time the merger was approved several months later, new employees had been hired behind all the workers who had protested dovetailing, so they were securely entrenched and their protest was moot.

Still Growing

The three-year merger process did not slow business nor stop Yellow from looking for additional acquisitions. When Pacific Express Transportation, a carrier with authority to serve California, became available in September 1967, Yellow bought it and added the rights to Watson-Wilson. It was a good fit for the carrier because both Watson-Wilson and Pacific Express had authority and contracts with the federal government to move military explosives.

In 1966, thanks to the addition of Watson-Wilson, Yellow surpassed the $100 million revenue milestone. Furthermore, in 1968, the company's stock split 5-for-2. Added to Yellow's portfolio was air forwarding, which came with Watson-Wilson's subsidiary, Star Forwarders, Inc.

As the nearly four-year merger process with Watson-Wilson concluded in late 1968, Yellow was moving to fill in small pockets of authority that enhanced its expanded service capacity. Two smaller carriers in the Chicago area were purchased. They were Race Motor Service and its subsidiary, Fleet Services, which gave Yellow blanket coverage for a 50-mile radius around Chicago.

About the same time, Red Arrow Transportation Company, which was founded as Missouri-Arkansas Transportation Company, was acquired, giving Yellow access to additional markets in southern Missouri and Kansas and northern Arkansas and Oklahoma. Lang Transit Company of Lubbock was bought to expand the Texas service area, and American

1967

The Arab-Israeli "Six-Day" War occurs in June.

U.S. bombers attempt to disrupt supply routes around Hanoi.

Martin Luther King, Jr. calls for massive disobedience to apply pressure on Washington to meet African-American demands.

Cartage Company and Scott Transportation gave Yellow authority in the San Joaquin Valley and south central California.

Yellow had suddenly become far more diverse than in previous years. In fact, some among Yellow's management were concerned that the diversity was reminiscent of the 1950-52 period in which the company became entangled in a web of complex layers of subsidiaries, leading to its financial woes. A number of Watson-Wilson's subsidiaries that Walnut Grove Products' Kelloway had developed were shed to eliminate those concerns. They were companies too unlike the core business.

One company kept was the air forwarding subsidiary that reported through Star Forwarders – Global Air Cargo, Ltd. Yellow applied to the Civil Aeronautics Board to own the company's stock outright, stating in its 1966 annual report that it felt Global Air had potential to grow.

Final 60s Addition – Norwalk

As the decade of the 1960s was coming to a close, Yellow began another aggressive move to expand its operations. Norwalk Truck Lines, another carrier dating back to the 1920s, was for sale. Founded in Ohio, Norwalk had expanded eastward when it purchased Shirks Motor Express, serving among others, Baltimore, Lancaster, Philadelphia, New York, Buffalo and Rochester, west to Cleveland.

Norwalk had been on a financial roller-coaster ride since its founder's death in 1953. The company operated two units; the original Ohio company and the old Shirks line that had been renamed Norwalk Truck Lines of Delaware. The company restructured itself in 1965 under the new corporate name Nortruk, Inc. Still failing to make ends meet, it was acquired by United-Buckingham Freight, another well-established and highly recognized carrier. But Norwalk had deteriorated too far. Rather than being a boost, Norwalk actually took United-Buckingham down.

A short while later, Yellow received a call from Ringsby Truck Lines. Ringsby was interested in buying parts of the United-Buckingham/Norwalk authority but not all of it. Representatives from Ringsby solicited Yellow's interest in acquiring the authority it did not want in hopes of completing a desirable transaction. Yellow bit.

The authority Ringsby wanted Yellow to buy was mostly the old Shirks operation, which had been renamed Norwalk of Delaware. The authority was

United Auto Workers' 1.6 million members quit the AFL-CIO.

New York's Adirondack Northway opens from Albany to the Canadian border.

Popular movies include: The Graduate with Dustin Hoffman, In Cold Blood with Robert Blake, In the Heat of the Night with Rod Steiger, Cool Hand Luke with Paul Newman, The Dirty Dozen with Lee Marvin, The Taming of the Shrew with Elizabeth Taylor, and To Sir with Love with Sidney Poitier.

Popular songs include: Ode to Billy Joe, Up, Up and Away, All You Need Is Love, Penny Lane, Lucy in the Sky with Diamonds and Release Me.

Lancaster Connection

An unidentified Norwalk employee and child, presumed to be his son. The old Norwalk of Delaware division became part of Yellow Freight System in 1969.

An important Norwalk of Delaware terminal was located in Lancaster, Pa., about 75 miles west of Philadelphia on U.S. Route 30. The man running the terminal in 1969 was Al Evans. Evans retired from Yellow in 1996 as regional manager after making the Lancaster terminal his office for 30 years.

Already a seasoned trucker when Norwalk hired him in 1966, Evans had begun his career in the 1950s in Akron, Ohio, which he called the trucking capital of the world at that time. He estimated he had about 100 employees at the terminal and a hefty number of linehaul sleeper teams domiciled in Lancaster when Yellow entered the picture. Today there are 875 employees at the terminal.

Norwalk had hired Curvin Snellbecker and Ralph Bollinger the same day, March 27, 1964. John Deichert was hired two weeks after that and T.J. Mehaffey six weeks after Deichert. Snellbecker, Bollinger and Mehaffey continue to man the road while Deichert moves trailers around the yard. An impromptu reunion at the author's request triggered memories.

"Would you want to go back to two lane highways, Ralphie?" Snellbecker asked Bollinger. "No, I don't think so," said Bollinger. "You should have seen the roads we drove in the 60s…"

"I drove on some cow paths not fit for a truck," Snellbecker quickly inserted. The four men said they had ven together when Norwalk and ited-Buckingham ran sleepers.

eichert, the hostler, had the most id recollection of what that was e, recalling a specific incident that vealed the labor climate of the late s. He and his driving partner were urning from a trip to Milwaukee, lling a "ragtop trailer." Deichert d it was during a steelworker ike. Union members forced their ck off the road.

weighed 250 pounds and they lled me out of my truck and threw to the ground," he said. The other ver was in the bunk and got roust- too. Deichert said his interrogators nted to know if they were carrying steel.

"We told them we didn't know what we were carrying."

Fortunately, a Pennsylvania Highway Patrolman stopped. He settled nerves and escorted Deichert and his fellow driver to a nearby diner as all three of them watched the strikers rifle through the back of the trailer.

Deichert said they remained in the diner for 24 hours before they were permitted to get back into their truck and return to Lancaster. When they got home and saw the trailer unloaded, they were more shocked. Deichert said buried beneath other freight was 20,000 pounds of steel rods. He said the strikers "would have burned our truck and probably roughed us up a bit if they found it."

"My dad was a truck driver for 42 years," Mehaffey said proudly. "My brother retired from New Penn after 42 years also. (He) was most senior employee." Mehaffey needs just seven years to match their trucking stamina.

He recalled his very first trip, driving to North Bergen, N.J., in a Mack tractor. "It was number 1466," Mehaffey said.

"I never had a good job like that before. I wanted to do a good job."

With so much experience at the table, was there any thought about retiring? "I always enjoyed driving," said Snellbecker, 72, who implied he had no intentions of stopping.

NORWALK
NORWALK
8048
8048

ideal for expanding into familiar markets served by Yellow Forwarding Company and added a lot more operating flexibility. The purchase opened several markets that still have Yellow Freight System terminals: Albany and Syracuse, N.Y.; Edison, N.J.; Erie, Pittsburgh, and Scranton, Pa.; Springfield, Mass.; and Wilmington, Del.

One of the few drawbacks was that the Norwalk of Delaware territory had a reputation for being a low-profit zone. It was one of the things that plagued all of the previous owners of the authority, including Shirks, Norwalk and United-Buckingham. On the flip side, Yellow was adding exposure to several thousand customers through Yellow Forwarding – customers who represented steady business and the potential for even more growth.

Despite the fears, Yellow went ahead with the transaction. It took about a year for the ICC to give its final approval and by that time, Yellow had the Norwalk routes operating in the black. It had also built new facilities in Baltimore, Philadelphia and Springfield, Mass.

Long-time Yellow employee Bill Wisniewski remembers the transaction vividly. He had been a linehaul dispatcher with Norwalk for about a year when Yellow entered the picture. Like many Norwalk employees, he had an option – stay and work for Ringsby, the carrier buying the western half of the company, or move to Yellow. He decided to play both sides against the middle.

Knowing that he still had a job as linehaul dispatcher where he was, he interviewed with Yellow, which was looking for supervisors. He was offered a job and a salary of $600 per month.

"I told them I couldn't take the job for less than $650," Wisniewski said. He was shocked when his interviewer said OK.

"God was watching out for Woj," Wisniewski added, "because all but one guy who stayed with Ringsby was let go within six months." Ringsby, a truckload carrier was only interested in the Norwalk authority so it could get to Cleveland and other Ohio cities from the west and had no real interest in Norwalk's facilities, equipment or people.

Changes at the GO

When the decade of the 60s began, a new general office building at 92nd and State Line was considered a corporate headquarters showcase for the industry. By the end of the decade, even after major expansion

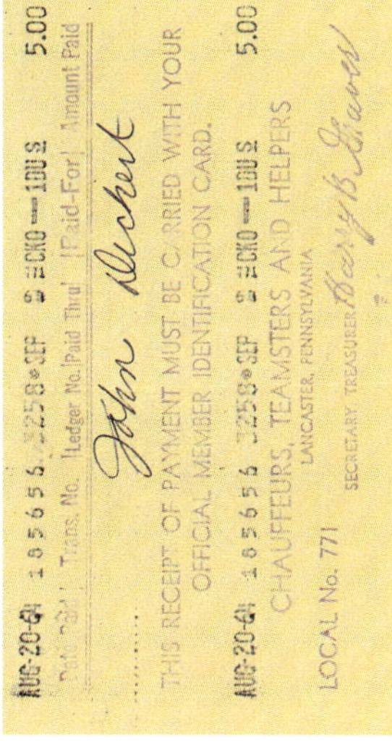
5.00
John Weckert
THIS RECEIPT OF PAYMENT MUST BE CARRIED WITH YOUR OFFICIAL MEMBER IDENTIFICATION CARD.
5.00
CHAUFFEURS, TEAMSTERS AND HELPERS
LANCASTER, PENNSYLVANIA
LOCAL No. 771
SECRETARY TREASURER

This page — *A driver's union dues receipt was evidence that he was in good standing with the Teamsters.*

Page 110 — *Yellow Freight System bought Norwalk Truck Lines of Delaware in 1969, rights that once belonged to Shirks Motor Express and which were later owned by United-Buckingham. Norwalk operated two divisions. Ringsby Truck Lines, a truckload carrier, purchased the western division, Norwalk of Ohio.*

1968

The Green Bay Packers defeat the Kansas City Chiefs in Super Bowl I.

The U.S. population passes 200 million, having doubled in 50 years.

The Tet Offensive begins as North Vietnamese forces attack 30 cities.

Nine Catholic priests burn draft cards outside a Catonsville, Md., selective service office in protest of Vietnam involvement.

Sen. Robert Kennedy is assassinated while campaigning for the presidency.

This page — *Accuracy and a steady pace were virtues sought in Yellow's terminal offices throughout the system. Shirlee Pergler, Joliet, Ill., was one of many cashiers that kept paperwork and billings up to date so the company could collect its revenue.*

Page 113 — *Virgil R. (Ray) Alderson (foreground) tracks the movement of linehaul units along a Plexiglass wall constructed for that purpose. Alderson was instrumental in advancing the concept of strategically managed linehaul operations.*

of the facility, the company had run out of room.

Karen McQuitty and Carol Kirchhoff started working at the general office in May and June 1965 – McQuitty in payroll and Kirchhoff in freight claims. They recalled how different the pace was at the general office on State Line and how quickly it changed when Yellow purchased Watson-Wilson Transportation.

"It doubled the company's size, but it didn't quite double the payroll," said McQuitty, who has become the company's expert on Teamster employee payroll matters.

McQuitty said she learned fast that the industry is much more complex than people on the outside realize. Part of the complexity was reporting to so many government agencies – the ICC, and after they were created, the Department of Transportation and OSHA. All of them have had an impact on Yellow and its employees, McQuitty said.

Kirchhoff was hired away from another carrier in the Kansas City area. She already had experience handling cargo claims. The carriers she worked for have all gone out of business, which made her move to Yellow fortunate, she said.

"Everything was done manually on typewriters," Kirchhoff said. "We handled claims for all three subsidiaries, Yellow Transit, Watson-Wilson and Yellow Forwarding."

She said being a smaller size in 1965 allowed people to get to know each other better. "It was good pay, good benefits, no reason to look for something else," Kirchhoff said. "Now it's a pressure cooker... We have three fax machines constantly receiving messages, " she said. "We can process much faster today, too, and pay faster if we have all the necessary documents. That speed raises expectations."

The Executives

Despite the growth, the executive team changed very little during the 1960s. But tasks assigned to the individuals did change as part of the management philosophy. The Powells wanted their executives to be versatile and to understand the entire operation, especially those groomed for corporate leadership.

In mid 1968, George Powell, Sr. retired as chairman of the board, but kept the title as honorary chairman. It triggered a major reshuffling of executive positions. Principally, George Powell, Jr. moved to board chairman and remained chief executive officer. Don McMorris, whom George Jr. characterized as his "right-arm man," became president and chief

Bloody riots in Chicago mark an emotional Democratic convention.

Richard Nixon defeats Hubert Humphrey and George Wallace to become president.

Martin Luther King, Jr. is shot dead while stepping out to his motel balcony in Memphis

Popular movies include: The Lion in Winter with Peter O'Toole, Rosemary's Baby with Mia Farrow, 2001: A Space Odyssey with Keir Dullea, Planet of the Apes with Charlton Heston, and The Producers with Zero Mostel.

SOUTHBOUND
RELAY

INDIANAPOLIS
VINCENNES
ST. LOUIS
LOUISVILLE
EVANSVILLE
WICHITA
OKLAHOMA CITY
WICHITA FALLS
FORT WORTH

administrative officer, and Mark Robeson became executive vice president and a new member of the board.

Robeson and McMorris had been with the Powells since their days at Riss & Company in the late 1940s. McMorris, in fact, said he first met George Sr. in 1941 when he applied for a job at the bank where Powell was an officer. He said Powell bluntly but gently rejected his application because McMorris was "draft material" at the time. Now, 27 years later, it was Powell who was drafting McMorris for an important role with the company.

Robeson's contribution became quite specialized. A soft-spoken diplomat, Robeson was intensely involved in industry affairs. He was elected president of the American Trucking Associations (ATA) in 1968, a prestigious position in Washington's political circles because of its enormous responsibility for the industry. He served as chairman or held other key posts on at least a half dozen industry associations.

Ray Alderson, who eventually held a variety of executive positions, became known for his innovations in establishing a tightly run linehaul operation. Coordinating the efforts of Central Dispatch Operations (CDO) starting in the 1950s, Alderson was one of the CDO leaders who led the installation and use of a Plexiglas wall on which pegs were inserted to track linehaul movement.

Later, Yellow was one of the first to use computers to enhance the basic tracking principal in the Plexiglas design. Computer enhancements so enriched the tracking system, that Yellow became one of the first carriers during the 1970s to use visual display.

Page 114 — *In 1968, George Powell, Sr. ended his active involvement in the company. He retired as chairman of the board although he remained honorary chairman.*

1969

Penn Central is formed in a merger prompted by competition from trucks and automobiles.

Man walks on the moon; Neil Armstrong and Buzz Aldrin are the first to step down from a landing craft.

Campaign aide Mary Jo Kopechne, 28, dies when a car driven by Sen. Ted Kennedy plunges into Poucha Pond on Chappaquiddick Island off Martha's Vineyard.

The Concorde supersonic jet makes its first flight.

YELLOW
FREIGHT SYSTEM
GMC
3512

Inflation's Impact

There were many influences shaping the trucking industry at the close of the 1960s. The National Master Freight Agreement, industry mergers, interstate highway construction and regulation all were significant. But the general health of the economy was emerging as perhaps the single most important factor.

Inflation was corroding the nation's well being as the 70s began. It appeared to be uncontrollable. Within the transportation industry, the primary inflationary catalyst was the price of petroleum. Yellow felt it first hand. Diesel fuel costs rose 350 percent during the decade.

The trucking company that carried the Yellow banner was now quite different. In 1960, Yellow Transit Freight Lines served eight states. Net income was less than half a million.

In 1969, Yellow Freight System served 30 states with nearly 7,300 employees and produced $162 million in revenue. Net income was more than $7 million. Furthermore, Yellow invested more in capital improvements in 1969 than it billed in revenue in 1961, $27.4 million.

Global View

Global tensions contributed to inflation and general strife. The United States had spent enormous sums – tax dollars – trying to end the conflict in Vietnam. Peace talks in Paris began in the late 1960s and were dragging on incessantly. Meantime, President Richard Nixon ordered U.S. military troops into Cambodia where the Vietnamese military was suspected of strengthening and training forces.

Domestic unrest over Vietnam that began in the 1960s spilled over into 1970. Campus disturbances pitted students against national guardsmen. Four students died at Kent State University in Ohio, two of them young women. Students at the University of Wisconsin bombed a research laboratory, killing a fellow student researcher.

Conflicts between laborer and management also rose in intensity during the year. United Auto Workers struck General Motors for 67 days. Military forces not involved in Southeast Asia were needed to move U.S. mail when 152,000 postal workers struck at more than 600 locations.

Not surprisingly, the most popular song of 1970 was Simon and Garfunkel's *Bridge over Troubled Water*.

Page 116 — *Confidence grew at Yellow Freight System during the inflation-driven 1970s. Yellow's trucks were moving shipments across 30 states at the beginning of the decade. Further expansion was on the horizon.*

1970

Public pressure forces the U.S. to reduce troop strength in Vietnam to below 400,000.

Four Kent State students are shot dead by National Guardsmen during demonstrations.

Burlington Northern is formed when several lines merge forming the longest railway system in the free world.

The Kansas City Chiefs win Super Bowl IV 23 to 7 over the Minnesota Vikings.

1971

The voting age is lowered from 21 to 18 with the passage of the 26th Amendment.

Page 119 — *Teamsters from Local 600 in St. Louis set up pickets during a work stoppage in 1970 that originally began in Chicago. (AP/Wide World Photos)*

Industry Pains and Gains

The trucking industry did not escape labor tension that year. Teamster locals in Chicago, bargaining independently from the National Master Freight Agreement, refused to accept terms negotiated between the rest of the union and carrier members of Trucking Employers, Inc. Their disagreements led to job actions.

The Chicago labor squabble in combination with the autoworker strike and a generally depressed national economy put a dent in Yellow's 1970 financial performance. Still, revenue went up more than five percent and net income rose slightly due to a tighter rein on variable costs and improved productivity.

Inflation is a double-edged sword for a company in a tightly regulated industry. As costs such as labor, fuel and revenue producing equipment go up, relief is granted by the regulating agency. Throughout the 1970s, Yellow would increase its rates more than once each year, sometimes by as much as seven percent. Annual contractual pay increases rose by double-digit rates. A 10.5 percent increase in April 1970 was augmented by a cost-of-living increase in July.

President Richard Nixon attempted to stop spiraling costs by freezing wages and prices. The slowdown was a temporary and, according to most economists, an ineffective stopgap. It certainly did not slow the pace at Yellow.

Yellow's revenue grew by 507 percent between 1970 and 1979, from $170 million to $863 million. Net income fell sharply in 1979 compared to 1978 because of severe economic pressures and another devastating labor disruption, but otherwise it had risen cumulatively by five times as well. Broken down, here is how each year's net income rose during the decade: *(see chart in left column)*

Net Income Growth During the 70s

Year	%
1970	+ 2
1971	+ 81
1972	+ 20
1973	+ 14
1974	+ 36
1975	+ 1
1976	+ 40
1977	+ 11
1978	+ 4

From 1971-1977, Yellow's operating ratio (O.R.), the percentage derived by dividing the company's operating expenses by its revenue, was below 89.0. That compares very favorably to the high 90s range of the current decade and would put the company among the best performers in both decades.

Yellow's stock split twice during the decade, both times 2-for-1, and the amount of money re-invested in trucks and terminals grew from $17 million in 1970 to $91 million in 1979, another five-fold increase.

Yellow ended the decade with 20,773 pieces of equipment – single and double axle tractors, 27-, 40- and 45-foot trailers, and straight trucks for city deliveries – after starting in 1970 with 8,255 pieces.

1972

President Nixon announces a "new economic policy" that imposes a wage and price freeze for 90 days.

The AFL-CIO refuses to cooperate with the wage freeze, claiming no faith in President Nixon's plan.

Amtrak takes over all U.S. passenger rail service in a federal effort to halt the decline in service.

Democratic party offices at the Watergate complex in Washington, D.C. are broken into; motive remains a mystery.

President Nixon is re-elected after defeating Sen. George McGovern, 49, of South Dakota.

NO CONTRACT
NO WORK
LOCAL 600

General offices crossed the state line from Kansas City, Mo., to Overland Park, Kan., in 1973. The 10-story structure filled quickly as Yellow continued to grow in the 1970s.

Wage scale During the 70s

Year	Teamster wages/hour	Weekly Health, welfare & pension contributions
1970	$ 4.43	$21.50
1971	$ 5.16	$23.50
1972	$ 5.74	$25.50
1973	$ 6.29	$33.50
1974	$ 6.70	$38.80
1975	$ 7.11	$43.50
1976	$ 7.76	$49.50
1977	$ 8.50	$55.50
1978	$ 9.38	$60.50
1979	$10.67	$74.50

The number of employees in the general freight division increased from 6,750 to 16,450, and the number of terminals grew from 101 in 1970 to 238 in 1979.

Growth was so fast, the company had to begin searching for new headquarters a year after completing an addition to its 10-year-old facility at 92nd and State Line. In 1973, the general offices, including CDO and an expanding computer information system, moved to its present-day 10-story site at 10990 Roe Ave. in Overland Park, Kan.

Similar growing pains were experienced in the field as the company continued to find more customers interested in shipping with an aggressive coast-to-coast carrier. New breakbulk facilities were built in Effingham, Ill., Charlotte, N.C. and Barstow, Calif. Additions were built at Yellow's other key locations.

The general freight division (including freight forwarding) continued to produce most of the revenue throughout the 1970s – from 90 percent at the start of the decade to 96 percent by 1979. The special hauling division shrunk because less steel was manufactured in the United States and because the company chose to focus on its core business.

Within the general hauling division, the balance between less-than-truckload and truckload freight remained strikingly constant throughout the 10-year period. LTL shipments – those weighing less than 10,000 pounds – accounted for two-thirds of the revenue and 97 percent of the total shipments. Yet, LTL accounted for only half the annual tonnage. The other half rode as truckload shipments, generating a little more than 30 percent of the revenue but a lot less handling cost.

This was typical of industry fundamentals at the time. Backhaul freight, those shipments generally moving from the west to the east or the south to the north and generally made up of raw goods or unassembled parts, moved in large lots – truckloads – for a significantly reduced rate. As debate about deregulating the industry intensified during the 1976 presidential election season, the logic behind selling the company's backhaul capacity as truckload rather than LTL came into question.

Interestingly, employee recollection about the company's preference for LTL vs. truckload freight is inconsistent. Some said Yellow was primarily a truckload carrier. Others said Yellow carried a lot of truckload freight, but regularly sought ways to abandon truckload in favor of LTL, a claim refuted by the fact that truckload freight accounted for more

1973

New Jersey voters reject a $650 million transportation bond issue because critics said too much was earmarked for highways vs. mass transit.

Tropical storm Agnes hits the Eastern U.S. causing the "worst natural disaster in U.S. history."

Popular movies include: Deliverance with Jon Voight, and Play It Again, Sam with Woody Allen.

A ceasefire in Vietnam ends U.S. direct involvement; U.S. bombing of Cambodia continues.

than 53 percent of the tonnage carried in 1979. Not only that, throughout the decade the company had increased the percentage of truckload freight hauled. Yellow would not make a strategic decision to alter this freight mix until after 1980.

Behind the Numbers

Yellow's versatile management team, a team that solidified in the 1960s, remained at the helm during the 1970s with these exceptions: Burl Cotton died in 1972 at the age of 64 after a year-long illness. The sometimes-surly character was kindly eulogized by his co-workers in the company's *Yellow in Motion* magazine as having had a keen nose for good food, a keen memory for old friends and a keen sense of how to run a truck line.

In 1976, Harold Edwards left the company. Hired during the Porter-Hardy era as a young accountant, Edwards was asked to stay when the Powell team bought Yellow out of bankruptcy, eventually becoming a vice president.

Mark Robeson, Yellow's premier industry diplomat and political insider, stepped down in 1976 as executive vice president, ending his day-to-day camaraderie with George Powell, Jr. and Don McMorris. It was Robeson, McMorris and Powell whom board member Dr. L.L. Waters called "the triumvirate," acting always in complete harmony. It was a team that had been together since the Riss & Company days during the late 1940s. Robeson remained on Yellow's board through 1982.

Following Robeson's departure from daily chores, Lloyd Brandt became executive vice president, triggering several additional promotions and the introduction of George Powell III to the officer ranks. Powell, a 1970 graduate of Indiana University, where Waters taught, joined the company soon after graduation. After experience in Yellow's terminals, Powell began his ascension.

In 1977, Ken Midgley retired. He was the neighbor to George Powell, Sr. who came at Powell's request for a 15-minute Sunday morning conversion in 1952 and gave Powell and the company legal counsel for 25 years thereafter. For most of that time he was secretary of the board.

Mark Robeson retired in 1976 but served on the board for six more years.

Operating Choices

Most strategic business decisions made during the 1970s were driven by the need to cope with inflation. The company was caught in a cost-price squeeze and was constantly searching for ways to manage

Achibald Cox, a Harvard law professor named special prosecutor to investigate the Watergate break-in, is fired.

Vice President Spiro T. Agnew resigns after charges of tax evasion; Gerald Ford replaces Agnew.

An energy crisis emerges when Arab nations impose an oil embargo.

Popular movies include: American Graffiti with Richard Dreyfuss, Bang the Drum Slowly with Michael Moriarity, The Exorcist with Ellen Burstyn, Last Tango in Paris with Marlon Brando, The Paper Chase with Timothy Bottoms, and The Sting with Paul Newman.

Marlboro

the effects. It meant the company had to become more productive.

One of those steps was freight-handling automation. A prototype was set up in Baxter Springs, Kan.

Double-bottom trailers, 27-feet long, had proven beneficial in linehaul operations, but some states in which Yellow had authority also had length-of-vehicle limits or restrictions on the number of trailers a tractor could pull. Eventually, in 1974, federal laws liberalized the vehicle length limitations on interstate highways, but the industry still needed further help from state legislatures. The geographic proximity of those more restrictive states forced Yellow to reduce the use of the "pup" trailers. Yellow de-emphasized doubles and moved to 45-foot trailers attached to double axle tractors for its best efficiency.

Another area of opportunity to conserve costs was in cargo claims. Better handling of customers' freight reduced the number of claims, but the growing concern in the 1970s was cargo theft. The issue became so daunting that Yellow developed its own internal security department that has evolved today into a small force of professionally trained detectives with law enforcement credentials. It is a force that many cities would love to have.

Safety continued to loom as a high-cost issue, especially when neglected. Ken Thompson, a former law enforcer himself, became the first vice president of safety in 1976 and was given credit for establishing a highway program that strengthened Yellow's position. His efforts placed Yellow among the safest trucking companies on the road, a position it still occupies today.

Yellow's drivers were recognized and honored for their safety achievements. In 1971, for instance, 422 drivers had driven 10 years without an accident, the equivalent of one million road miles. They were called Yellow's million milers. As a company, the drivers strung together 3,700,000 accident-free miles during the year, the best performance since 1961. By 1975, the company had 607 million milers and 25 drivers with 2-million miles of accident-free driving.

Drivers were better equipped to drive safely in the 1970s because tractors were becoming more reliable. Prompted by the need for better fuel efficiency and an opportunity to expand the size of its vehicles due to improved government regulations, Yellow replaced thousands of pieces of older equipment during this period. Most notably, in 1974, when size regulations changed and air quality standards stiffened, Yellow bought new and more expensive cab-over tractors.

This page — *Sets of double-bottom trailers provided efficiencies for the company, but many states had restrictions against them. Yellow de-emphasized the use of the doubles until federal laws provided new incentives in 1974.*

Page 122 — *Yellow Freight System employees identified as Gamberg and Silva, handled the critical chores of locating over, short and damaged freight (OS&D) and working claims issues with customers.*

1974

President Nixon resigns following embarrassment and futility due to revelations from the Watergate break-in.

Gerald Ford becomes president and pardons Nixon for his illegal activities.

Argentina dictator Juan Peron dies; he's replaced by his wife, Isabel, 43, who becomes the hemisphere's first woman head of state.

World oil prices rise dramatically as a result of OPEC's tough stance.

New Mercedes diesel city trucks helped the gradual conversion of city equipment to diesel power. Although linehaul tractors had been all diesel since 1955, many gasoline-powered city tractors were part of the fleet.

The power units could pull 45-foot trailers comfortably at 55 miles per hour, the nation's mandated speed limit for all vehicles because of the fuel crisis. A new 6-gear transmission and much lighter weight also helped the truck achieve four-percent better fuel economy while pulling heavier payloads.

At this point, Yellow also experimented with radial tires, eventually putting them on all tractors, which experts claimed improved driving safety and saved fuel, though the savings were mostly offset by the tires' higher costs.

When buying new 45-foot trailers, Yellow also opted for the smooth exterior wall on the box in order to cut down on wind resistance. It was another move to save on fuel costs.

Inflation, emissions control gadgetry, smooth-sided trailers and radial tires boosted the cost of a new 18-wheeler by $2,400. But the 45-foot trailer increased hauling capacity by 13 percent over the 40-foot trailer, another factor that helped to improve productivity.

Although government interests made the trucking industry a priority for receiving diesel fuel when shortages were occurring nationwide, there was still no guarantee that fuel was going to be available. Yellow took steps to improve its odds. Larger storage tanks were installed. When regular suppliers were unable to renew contracts for fuel because of uncertainties, Yellow bought directly from import vendors. The company expected to burn 72 million gallons in 1974, the pinnacle of the fuel crisis, so drastic steps were warranted.

In this same period, a new policy of converting gasoline-guzzling city units to diesel power also was imposed. New diesel tractors were purchased for city operations, but mostly they were converted from older linehaul tractors.

The Mergers Continue

Despite economic difficulties, growth did not stop. Yellow made three large-scale acquisitions during the 1970s and several smaller ones. The first purchase – Adley Express – was the most important.

Adley Corporation was a publicly traded company in 1972 when Yellow offered $6.25 per share and quickly escrowed 693,255 of 979,500 outstanding shares. Yellow's executives announced their intention to merge Adley Express into Yellow Freight System as soon as ICC permission was granted.

The acquisition extended Yellow's authority from the province of Quebec through New England to Georgia. It provided contiguous coverage to five

1975

A nationwide 55-miles-per-hour highway speed limit is imposed; federal aid is withheld from states that do not enforce.

Popular movies include: Chinatown with Jack Nicholson, and The Godfather II with Al Pacino.

Hank Aaron breaks Babe Ruth's career home run record of 714 lifetime round-trippers.

Saigon surrenders to North Vietnam; U.S. helicopters evacuate 7,000 Americans and Vietnamese.

Nixon advisors Mitchell, Haldeman and Erlichman receive prison sentences for their Watergate involvement.

states not served by Yellow and better coverage to those important states already part of the system, such as Massachusetts, New York, New Jersey and Maryland. There are several employees in Baltimore who remember the pain caused by the merger of Adley and Yellow.

"They hated us," said Ralph "Buzz" Amoss.

Amoss worked for Adley starting in 1963. He said many of the employees who were transferred from the old Adley terminal to the new facility built by Yellow in 1970, had seniority over Yellow's employees. Many employees were laid off temporarily during the transition.

To make matters worse, some wounds had barely healed from the merger of former Norwalk operations into the Baltimore terminal a little more than two years prior to the Adley purchase.

"After a time, everybody got along," said Amoss, one of many industry "legacies" working for Yellow. His father drove a truck for 50 years, he said, though Buzz Amoss chooses not to. He has worked on a freight dock 36 years because that is where he feels most comfortable.

"The big difference today is we don't handle the freight," Amoss said. "It's a lot less physical. Young guys don't realize how easy they got it."

He said he has moved lots of freight with a hand jack, a steel bar that was used to scoot and roll freight along the dock floor.

"You can come here and work out of shape nowadays," Amoss said, "you couldn't do that 30 years ago."

Frank DiPaula had been with Yellow for three years when Adley people were about to be merged in. DiPaula started as a clerk, became office manager and eventually switched to outbound supervisor.

DiPaula said Yellow families picketed the terminal. It caused a lot of problems initially. He said the Adley people who transferred to the terminal did not want to be there and the Yellow people did not want them there, because there were not enough jobs for both. However, layoffs for the most part were short-lived, although DiPaula said it took a year to mend the "rough edges."

The Young Breed

Expansion placed many demands on Yellow, especially for well-educated young people who were willing to learn the business from the ground up and supervise a unionized work force. By the time of the Adley merger, the Baltimore terminal had become one of the important training grounds and showcase facilities in the Mid Atlantic area.

This page, top — *Frank DiPaula, Baltimore outbound supervisor and 30-year veteran.*

This page, bottom — *Yellow acquired Adley Express in 1972, extending service into New England and the province of Quebec.*

The Chicago Rock Island & Pacific railroad files for bankruptcy: competition from trucks and barges is blamed.

Former Teamster boss Jimmy Hoffa disappears and is believed to have been murdered.

Popular movies include: Jaws with Roy Scheider, One Flew Over the Cuckoo's Nest with Jack Nicholson, Dog Day Afternoon with Al Pacino, The Man Who Would Be King with Sean Connery, and The Prisoner of Second Avenue with Jack Lemmons.

Popular songs include: Feelings, The Hustle, Love Will Keep Us Together, At Seventeen, Lyin' Eyes, and Jive Talkin'.

Proud of his GMC

Once Yellow began operating diesel tractors in the city, the company soon adopted a policy of retiring linehaul equipment to pickup and delivery operations in order to prolong the usefullness of its assets. However, Frank Averella currently drives a tractor that was purchased specifically for Baltimore's P&D operations in 1987.

Baltimore city driver Frank Averella loves his work and loves his truck. It makes no difference that he has driven a truck for 48 years and the one he drives now is 12 years old and has no power steering.

Averella, 66, is very proud of "his" 1987 GMC tractor. "It's so used to me, I hate for somebody to use it. That's my sweetheart," he said. Averella started his career with Shirks, the company bought out by Norwalk, which was then acquired by United-Buckingham and disassembled by Yellow and Ringsby all within a matter of a few years.

Claiming no desire to retire even though he has worked on a dock or driven a truck since he was 18 (he wore blue suede shoes then, he said), he hopes at age 70 to still be driving the tractor he pointed to proudly. One reason he is so proud of his GMC, he said, is that he can count on his hands the number of times that tractor "has been on a hook (needing repair)" in 12 years.

Among the men who remember their stops in Baltimore or who spent time supervising at the facility were Dave Letke, Dick Clepper and Jim Bair. All three became part of Yellow's training program in the early 1970s after graduating from college and all three made career stops at the Baltimore facility.

Letke later became president of Preston Trucking, an independent carrier owned by Yellow from 1993 to 1998, when it was sold to Letke and two other senior officers. He recalled the stiff qualifications for entering Yellow's training program. First, a college degree was mandatory and so was a haircut, he said. His hair was cut above the ears, as required, an hour before his interview. The haircut was a tough choice for a young man in 1973.

Part of the drill was to spend up to six months in a terminal observing several different functions, then to spend a week in Kansas City at a training center. Before the training week ended, Letke was offered a supervisor's position in Baltimore. He was on a plane that day and working that night.

Letke spent 10 years in the Mid Atlantic terminals, eventually becoming branch manager first in Washington D.C., then in Baltimore. Those advancements led him to management assignments in Lancaster, Indianapolis and Charlotte before receiving the promotion to head Preston Trucking.

Clepper and Bair attended classes together at the University of Maryland, 30 miles from the Baltimore terminal. Clepper is currently area general manager in Lancaster and now supervises the terminal where he, too, received his first impressions of the company. Standing at the terminal gate in Baltimore in early 1999, Clepper reminisced about being there 26 years earlier almost to the day. He remembered staying a few months and then taking an assignment in Boston.

Baltimore terminal manager Harvey Bruner was more like a banker than a trucker, said Jim Bair. Other trucking companies where Bair interviewed were not as genteel, he said. Baltimore's made a lasting impression.

Bair chose Yellow's training program over other carriers and worked in Richmond, Va., Wilmington, Del., and Lancaster as well as Baltimore before transferring to Maybrook, N.Y., where he is currently distribution center manager.

Out West, the same program masterminded by Jack Holder, had enticed Steve Defenbaugh. The current vice president of Yellow Freight's Southeast Group was hired at Barstow in 1969 when the terminal was a product of the Watson-Wilson merger. Defenbaugh

1970s Baltimore branch manager Dave Letke presents a box of cigars to city driver Frank Averella.

1976

Jimmy Carter defeats Gerald Ford to become President of the United States.

China releases 100,000 political prisoners following the deaths of Zhou Enlai and Mao Zedong.

Chicago's Mayor Richard Daley, 84, dies.

Conrail begins operations with 88,000 freight workers as the government attempts to keep rail freight service active in the Northeast.

A "swine flu" epidemic leads to widespread inoculations, which cause Guillain-Barre Syndrome; hundreds sue the government.

This page — *Braswell Motor Freight Lines was the last Yellow purchase before industry deregulation in 1980.*

Page 129 — *Steve Defenbaugh (far left) was a product of Yellow's management recruitment and training initiative in the early 1970s. He is shown with employees at Colorado Springs where he was terminal manager in the mid 70s. Defenbaugh is now vice president of the Southeast Group.*

went to Albuquerque for his training and eventually landed operations supervisor positions in Fresno and Los Angeles before getting his first terminal as manager in Colorado Springs.

"Growth was a lot of fun," said Defenbaugh. He said it is hard to imagine now how much excitement there was working for a $150 million company, then seeing it grow so quickly.

The South and Northwest

Two other major purchases were made during the decade. They helped Yellow fill in its coverage of the South and opened up new territory in the Pacific Northwest. In 1975, Yellow acquired Republic Freight System, a large forwarding operation. It was an important addition because it allowed Yellow to create a pathway to Florida's growing markets. The company opened terminals in Miami, Jacksonville, West Palm Beach, Orlando and Tampa, plus added New Orleans and New York City facilities. The drawback was that Yellow did not have authority to operate a linehaul system to the Florida communities, so it had to put trailers on the rail or hire contract carriers to take shipments in or pull trailers out of the state.

George Powell III said Yellow was attempting to set up intermodal capabilities for Republic's operation, but insisted that the railroad line become more reliable and offer timely service. The response from the railroad, said Powell, was, "Give us more business and we'll improve the service." He said it was indicative of railroad attitudes in the 1970s and a reason why shipping customers kept looking to the truck lines to expand their capabilities.

Owning Republic Freight System also allowed the company to establish terminals in the Pacific Northwest. The company could route freight in the same way it had used Yellow Forwarding in the 1960s to link its Midwestern and Southwestern markets to the East Coast. Trailers moved on rail or via authorized truckload haulers. Although the once prominent freight forwarder had fallen on bad times, its authority was worth the $100,000 investment. It permitted Yellow to establish customer relationships prior to acquiring full-service authority.

Buying Braswell Motor Freight Lines out of bankruptcy was the final major purchase of the 1970s. The transaction was subject to some question because Braswell was bought when it was starting to look more and more likely that an industry deregulation

1977

Congress creates a Department of Energy to broaden control over all energy forms.

President Carter calls for major energy conservation, saying the situation is "the moral equivalent of war."

West Virginia's New River Gorge Bridge is opened; it's the longest steel arch bridge in the world.

YELLOW
FREIGHT SYSTEM

Republic Freight System was a freight forwarding company that enabled Yellow to expand its service area without linehaul authority. Yellow transferred freight by purchasing piggyback rail service or linehaul service from an authorized trucker.

bill would pass Congress. If the industry was going to be deregulated, why invest in a carrier's authority that would soon be worthless?

Braswell's route authority stretched from Georgia to California and Illinois to Texas, covering 11 states. It was a gap that opened up another east-west pathway. It portended to be an important link between the textile states of North and South Carolina and the Gulf Coast states. It potentially could link Florida and Georgia to Texas and farther west. For many, the Braswell purchase made sense.

Yellow was busy all decade filling in other service gaps with the purchase of several companies. Among the 1970s purchases were all or a portion of these carriers:

Mid-South Transports, Inc. (Tennessee)
Central Motor Express (Tennessee and Alabama)
Eazor Express (Ohio & West Virginia)
Elgin-Chicago Express (northern Illinois)
Bay Cities Express (northern California)
Shane Truck Lines (northern California)
Carey Truck Lines (California)
LaSalle Trucking Company (California)
J.E. Miller Transfer & Storage Co (West Virginia and eastern Ohio)
Bartlett's Express (New Hampshire and Massachusetts)
Reich Bros. Long Island Motor Freight (New York)
Peoples Cartage (Ohio)
Schaller Trucking Corp. (Indiana)
Riteway Transport (Colorado and Utah)
City Drayage (California)

Working the Plan

The first decade under the Powell team was one of straightening up a tilting ship and then experimenting with ways to make it sail smoother. It was part of the philosophy to try different solutions. There were no recriminations if the solution produced inadequate results. According to George Jr., doing nothing got you nothing. Risks were allowed and indeed encouraged.

By the end of the 1970s, Yellow had become confident. Management had a good sense of company direction. In this period, a new planning group emerged headed by Ray Alderson.

Alderson's group mapped out alternatives for reaching national network coverage, clearly the ultimate goal to advance the company for the long term. Planning disciplines and technology tools that were not familiar to most in the trucking industry became vitally important. Computers and market research were relied on to identify and interpret facts that formed the basis of strategic decisions.

Where are businesses emerging? Are they likely to need inbound and outbound freight transportation? What cities appear to be growing faster than others are? Where are interstate highways projected to

1978

A New York power failure leaves the city in the dark for 25 hours; Con Edison is found guilty of negligence.

Congress enacts a ban on almost all aerosol products containing fluorocarbons.

President Carter creates "a framework for peace" in the Middle East with Israel's Prime Minister Begin and Egypt's President Sadat.

The president signs legislation making 70 the mandatory retirement age.

The Airline Deregulation Act phases out federal regulation, including control of routes and pricing power.

be built? These were questions the planning group asked as they looked for the right carriers to buy, the right spot to build and the right freight to solicit.

Still to come was the inevitable — deregulation. It would dramatically affect truck transportation and test Yellow's ability to adapt its business philosophies accordingly.

Jimmy Carter, a Democrat and fiscal conservative, and Congress were convinced that one way to curb runaway inflation was to get the government out of regulating transportation and allow free enterprise to rule instead.

The passenger airline industry was their first test, having deregulated in 1978. The action caused industry changes to happen quickly. In 1980, the president and Congress would decide to take similar steps in the trucking industry in an attempt to ease the economic pain felt by all consumers.

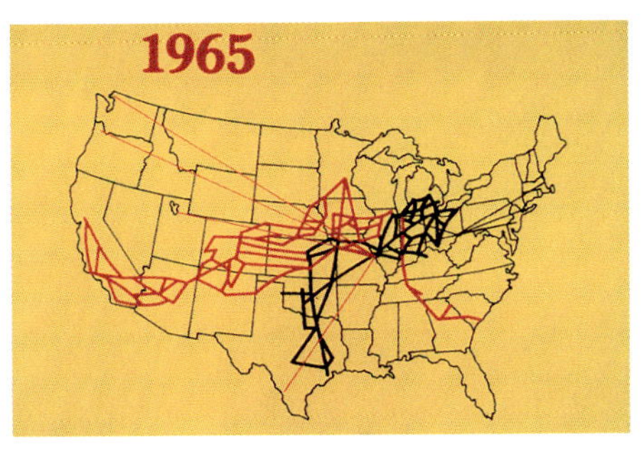

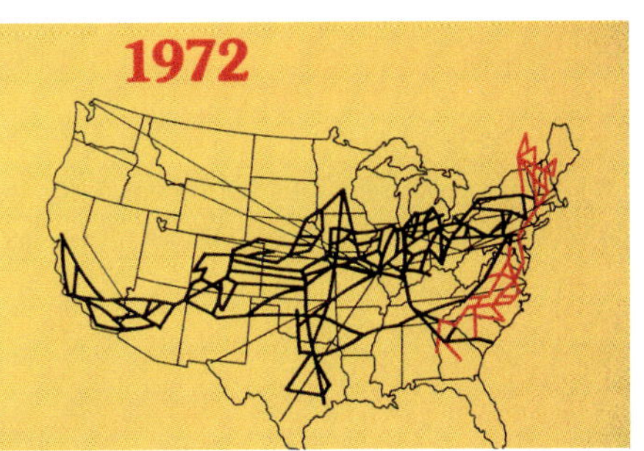

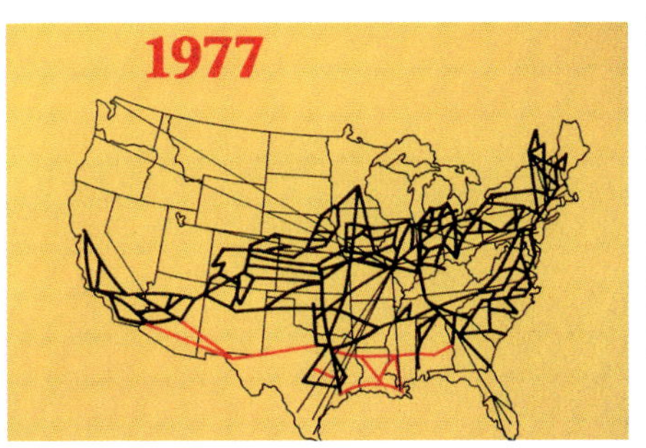

Yellow Freight System's coverage area grew rapidly in the 12-year period illustrated by these service authority maps. Revenue grew from $53 million to $648 million between 1965-1977.

1979

A melt-down scare at Three Mile Island nuclear generating plant near Harrisburg, Pa., causes the evacuation of area residents.

U.S. motorists form long lines at gasoline stations as shortages and exploding prices create panic.

The government guarantees $1.2 billion in loans to Chrysler Corporation to rescue the automaker from bankruptcy.

John Wayne, 72, dies of lung and stomach cancer.

Sony introduces the Walkman cassette player.

YELLOW

The "Go-Go" Years

The company's goal continues to be revenue growth through entry into new markets and expansion in existing ones. Yellow has the financial strength, the equipment, the personnel, and the terminal facilities to expand operations with minimal additional capital outlays. These ingredients, plus management's objective of achieving performance levels that are among the most favorable in the industry, make our outlook for the long term optimistic.

1980 Annual Report

George E. Powell, Jr.
Chairman of the Board

Donald L. McMorris
President

Double-digit inflation continued to hamper the American economy in 1980 with consumer prices rising more than 12 percent. The situation was made worse as the Federal Reserve attempted to get inflation under control by imposing extremely high interest rates. Business borrowers paid as much as 20 percent interest for bank loans.

The "stagflation" economy took its toll in other ways. Specifically, high unemployment. Millions of people were out of work at a time when costs were rising dramatically.

Before former actor and California Governor Ronald Reagan defeated Jimmy Carter in November, Carter administered part of his prescription for the chaos within the nation's economy. He imposed deregulation.

The Motor Carrier Act of 1980 went into effect July 1.

Since the early 1970s deregulation was talked about as a way to create more competition. The theory was that competition would lower the overall cost of transporting goods by letting market forces control prices. Furthermore, the theory went, competition would force carriers to broaden and improve services, all without the hammer of government intervention.

In 1935, when regulation went into effect, the situation was much different. The industry was in a slugfest and threatened to run amok. Policy makers were convinced that some kind of police effort was necessary to make sure that all shippers had equal access to service at an equitable price. Because of its newness and rapid growth, the government also saw trucking as a potential "profit center." It wanted a way to monitor the business in order to understand how to tax motor freight transportation without undermining its potential.

Once the Interstate Commerce Commission was established, the industry settled into a routine. Regulation meant that the carriers' capital investments were protected. In return for exclusive authority to

This page — *Freight movement has never been limited to daytime conveniences. It requires around-the-clock activities, especially in fast-paced urban centers such as this one in Chicago.*

Page 132 — *New terminals like this one in Lakewood, N.J., were part of the "Go-Go" growth of the 1980s. There were 235 terminals in the Yellow Freight network when the decade began and 640 when it ended. A new terminal opened every nine days during the 80s.*

1980

Iran holds 53 U.S. hostages for more than a year; eight soldiers die in an aborted rescue attempt.

The Motor Carrier Act curbs federal controls over interstate trucking.

Gasoline prices at the pump ($1.20 per gallon) have nearly doubled in two years.

Page 135 — *The Kansas City, Mo., terminal near the intersection of Interstate Highways 70 and 435 became a hub or "breakbulk" facility in the 1980s, serving several satellite terminals including Des Moines, Omaha and Topeka. (photo by Don Yaworski)*

provide service in a given geographic area, the truck line was obligated to provide service to all who asked. The ICC sanctioned a complicated system of rate tariffs and would approve rate increases as long as the carriers could demonstrate that costs for labor, equipment, supplies or other expenses had gone up.

Requiring relatively expensive government authority for a carrier to operate was a powerful barrier to competition.

But there was a victim of regulation – the consumer. The advocates of deregulation had long argued that highly regulated industries actually contributed to the spiral of inflation because protected industries had no incentive to keep their costs under control. The regulatory compact held that businesses that operated in the public interest, like truck lines, were entitled to recover all reasonable costs plus a reasonable margin of return on capital employed. The objective of those regulated companies was to convince government regulators that their costs were prudently incurred and thus should be eligible for recovery from customers.

Statistical evidence confirms that trucking regulation had contributed to inflation. In 1965, 15 years before deregulation, transportation accounted for 20 percent of the gross national product (GNP). In other words, 20 cents of every dollar earned in America was paid to transportation providers, their suppliers and employees. By 1995, 15 years after deregulation, the transportation portion of the nation's GNP had fallen to 16 percent. The nation was spending four percent less for transportation in relation to all other costs.[1]

There were certainly losers in the move to deregulate. Hundreds of mid-sized and larger transportation companies went out of business or were merged out of existence and thousands of jobs disappeared.

The Winners and Losers

Undeniably, deregulation was the biggest event to occur in the industry's first 60 years. Even as it unfolded in 1980 and for the next 10 years and longer, industry leaders, investors, employees and shippers puzzled over how to adapt. Regulation had been such an important part of the way business was conducted, that its behaviors stuck. They were hard to shed because systems were designed just to accommodate regulatory requirements. In 1980, however, those requirements were evaporating.

In the period of debate during the late 1970s, the industry unified in voicing its concern to President

1981

The Philadelphia Phillies win their first World Series defeating the Kansas City Royals in 6 games.

Former Beatle John Lennon is fatally wounded outside his New York apartment.

Mt. St. Helens erupts spewing volcanic ash and causing deaths and widespread havoc.

Iran releases 53 U.S. hostages after holding them for 444 days.

President Reagan, his press secretary James Brady and two others are wounded in an assassination attempt in Washington, D.C.

Cab-over-engine tractors enabled Yellow to pull double trailers and stay within most state length limits.

Carter and Congress, said former American Trucking Associations executive Bob Halladay. Yellow and the other big truck lines opposed deregulation with the rest of the industry, yet the big carriers suspected early on that they had an opportunity to become stronger if deregulation passed.

Was it a win-win situation for Yellow?

"Yes, probably; never thought of it that way before," said Halladay. The company was big enough to survive the cost of transitioning to a deregulated environment, he said, and its leadership team was among the smartest in the industry. Yellow also was in a good position after acquiring additional authority to grow stronger if Congress turned back the deregulation effort.

Yellow's leaders sided with the industry to fight deregulation mostly because it had invested nearly $35 million to gain authority to operate in the top 300 industrial and consumer markets.

It was a fight waged primarily by the trucking companies alone.

"What amazed us was how placid the Teamsters were," said George Powell, Jr. "It was amazing how they sat on the sidelines for as long as they did."

Powell said it looked like the Teamsters "put a bunch of money against the effort (to stop Congress from deregulating the industry)." However, he said, it was so late in the game that it had no impact.

The Gravity of the Matter

Deregulation nearly eliminated barriers to entry in trucking. New truck lines could operate with much cheaper labor and therefore offer customers lower rates. In 1980, with unemployment high, it was easy to find drivers who were willing to get behind the wheel of a truck for half of what a Teamster made.

For 45 years, carriers had patiently applied for expensive route authority. Now, with a swish of Jimmy Carter's pen, all those investments were meaningless.

Once deregulation was implemented, said Bob Halladay, the American Trucking Associations' efforts focused on making sure its members received tax credits. After all, these companies had paid millions to the government for route authority that was virtually worthless after July 1. According to Halladay, tax relief kept the carriers viable during the transition period.

A new wave of competitors did indeed materialize. They were small at first, nonunion, and very discriminating in their freight selection. They would only

The prime interest rate reaches 21.5 percent, the highest since the Civil War.

Popular movies include: Raiders of the Lost Ark with Harrison Ford, Arthur with Dudley Moore, Chariots of Fire with Ben Cross, The Chosen with Maximilian Schell, Reds with Warren Beatty, and The French Lieutenant's Woman with Meryl Streep.

want what was profitable and easy to handle. And, according to Don McMorris, company president at the time, the most vulnerable freight in Yellow's trailers was that shipped by truckload, not LTL.

It was the easiest freight for the startup trucker to cherry pick. With no investment in terminals, dock personnel, office staff or forklifts, a single trucker, or small trucking firm, could begin an operation with a used tractor-trailer rig or leased equipment for under $50,000. They could take freight to any destination and undercut major carriers who were competing with huge capital investments.

Long before the Motor Carrier bill was printed, McMorris had convinced his Yellow team to find LTL alternatives. Truckload freight that had filled the company's backhaul lanes was becoming less profitable. Truckload tonnage fell from 53 percent of the total tonnage in 1979 to 46 percent in 1980. Truckload revenue in 1980 was only 27 percent of total revenue, down from 32 percent the previous year. This same pattern continued throughout the decade. By the late 1980s, truckload shipments represented less than 20 percent of the total tonnage and less than 12 percent of the total annual revenue.

With the increased focus on LTL shipping, forklifts became critical in improving the efficiency of cross-dock operations. During the 1950s, Yellow had dabbled with forklifts as a way to master dock freight-handling processes. But the forklifts of that day were big, noisy, smelly and expensive. So the company mostly moved freight on the docks by handjacks and rolling bars, simple pieces of steel that allowed dockworkers to maneuver freight across a dock and into trailers.

In larger centers like St. Louis and Dallas, where freight was transferred often, Yellow installed draglines. These were carts on wheels that were pulled along an inlaid track. When freight was taken off a trailer, it was placed on one of the slow-moving carts. The cart rolled along the interior perimeter of the dock until it approached the outbound trailer. A dockworker would then pull the freight off the cart and load it.

Draglines were also expensive capital investments that George Powell, Jr. said never lived up to expectations. The dragline created a dependency that was often abused. Rather than improvise when the mechanism failed, employees often waited for repairs to get the line moving again, a huge waste of productive time. They also created a safety hazard since there was constant motion along an inlaid tracking system

Dragline carts were pulled along an inlaid track in the terminal floor. The encircling carts gave the dock an assembly line appearance.

1982

IBM introduces the first personal computer.

AIDS begins taking lives worldwide based on immune system abnormalities.

Argentine forces invade British controlled Falkland Islands.

The Vietnam Memorial is dedicated in Washington, D.C.; it shows the names of 57,692 men and women killed in the war.

Union Pacific merges with Missouri Pacific and Western Pacific.

This page, top — *Yellow's central dispatch operations (CDO) guided and monitored freight movement with the aid of computer technology.*

This page, bottom — *When linehaul units are loaded, they are parked on the "ready line," awaiting a driver at each distribution center or relay station.*

that was also part of the walking path and storage area on the dock. The draglines were abandoned after a relatively short life span.

Freight-handling efficiencies improved in the 1980s when forklifts became much more reliable. Many in the company felt forklifts were the single most important vehicles next to the truck itself.

The Hub and Spoke Solution

Deregulation handed George Jr. and Don McMorris a vexing business problem. How should Yellow Freight System operate in a new business climate that was still undefined? Furthermore, how would Yellow differentiate itself from all the other carriers that were now heaped together in the free-for-all? Two major decisions were made. The first dealt with the company's linehaul network.

Prior to 1980, linehaul drivers were stationed at several terminals throughout the authorized system. Their domiciles were arranged for the convenience of the linehaul operation based on customer volume and general freight-flow patterns. It was determined that the best way to win in a deregulated environment was to expand rapidly. The objective was to achieve full transcontinental coverage moving primarily LTL freight. But what was the best operating model for a transcontinental network?

Yellow chose a "hub and spoke" design, similar to those used by commercial passenger airlines following that industry's deregulation. It began by identifying 17 strategically located terminals. The terminals already were key centers in the old ICC authorized system. Among them was a new 132-door facility in Maybrook, N.Y., 80 miles northwest of New York City. It also called for converting similar consolidation hubs in these cities: Lancaster, Charlotte, Atlanta, Cleveland, Indianapolis, Nashville, Jackson, (Miss.), Chicago, St. Louis, St. Paul, Kansas City, Baxter Springs, Dallas, Denver, Phoenix and Barstow. In connection with the hub and spoke network, Yellow created new field executives called regional managers assigned to each hub.

Similar to its controversial 1950s operation in Marshall, Mich., each of Yellow's hubs, also known as breakbulks, had satellite terminals. The satellites routed their daily freight to their assigned hub. Even when a shipment's final destination was in the opposite direction, it went to the breakbulk to be consolidated with other shipments routed to the closest breakbulk near the destination city. It was a relay network designed for both over-the-road

Tylenol capsules laced with cyanide kill seven people; a man is arrested and the product returns with triple-sealed safety packaging.

Popular movies include: E.T., The Extra-Terrestrial with Dee Wallace, Tootsie with Dustin Hoffman, The World According to Garp with Robin Williams, Gandhi with Ben Kingsley, and The Verdict with Paul Newman.

efficiencies and dependable service. But there was an important catch. The network needed lots of freight flowing in all directions to keep the system well oiled and operating effectively.

That fact created added impetus for the company's second major post-deregulation decision – offering customers discounts off published tariff rates.

Give Me Five

The first year of deregulation was less than stellar. Revenue fell 10 percent, tonnage dropped 30 percent and the number of shipments handled was off 21 percent. Costs in the first quarter of 1980 were 53 percent higher than in 1979's first quarter. Seven tractors and trailers out of 100 were in mothballs because there was not enough business.

Company leaders gambled courageously by spending $39 million on capital improvements to get ready for the necessary change. Yellow opened 13 new terminals in addition to Maybrook and moved the Phoenix breakbulk to a new 81-door facility. The company and union agreed to the procedures for moving linehaul drivers to the 17 breakbulk hubs as well as a few relay stations, making them their new domiciles.

To complicate linehaul matters, there were still six states that prohibited heavier weights and 16 states forbidding 65-foot tandem trailer units, although Congress approved both. Many of the restricting states were in the heartland where truck traffic converged in high volumes. It was an important issue for lobbyists and lawyers. However, Yellow's more urgent need was to find freight.

Shippers were uncertain about what deregulation would mean for them, although some certainly expected relief from rates that had escalated by 14 percent in each of the previous two years alone.

Yellow's management was racing to find a solution. Ray Stewart, who at the time was senior vice president of finance, began a search for outside help. Stewart and others recognized they were treading in new territory when in came to open market pricing and needed an additional perspective on the team. Stewart had in mind Bob Burdick.

Burdick had worked for the Eastern Central Motor Rate Bureau since 1967. It was one of several price-setting agencies that collaborated with carriers during the regulated era. Stewart invited Burdick to meet with Don McMorris, Lloyd Brandt and Ray Alderson. They wanted to see if Burdick would bring needed insights to Yellow's traffic department. The department

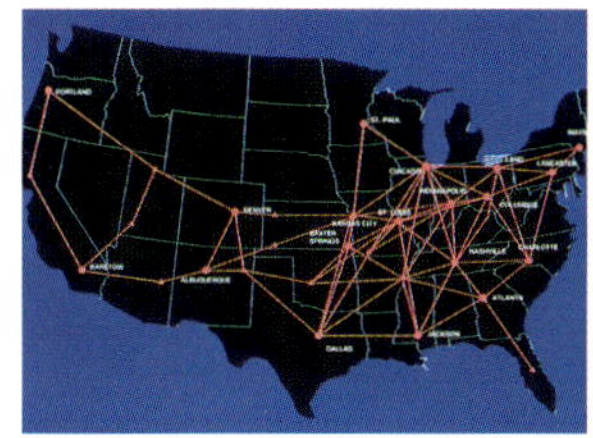

Moving trucks between major metropolitan areas during an era of rapid terminal expansion took precise planning and constant changes. This system map of the linehaul network revealed the main arteries of the freight-flow operation.

1983

President Reagan proposes a Strategic Defense Initiative (SDI) with laser-armed satellites to shoot down incoming missiles.

A Korean 747 jet is shot down by Russian missiles for allegedly entering Soviet air space; 269 passengers and crewmembers are killed.

The merger of two railroad lines creates Santa Fe Southern Pacific.

Black markets emerge as parents try to buy scarce Cabbage Patch dolls for Christmas.

First Lady Nancy Reagan coins the slogan "Just Say No" when promoting anti-drug sentiments.

This page, top — *Raymond A. Stewart, Jr.*

This page, bottom — *Robert W. Burdick*

divided later when half became known as "pricing." Yellow offered Burdick a loosely defined position that eventually became part of a new marketing department.

One of the obstacles Yellow had to overcome, said Burdick, was the truckload traffic. Roadway and Consolidated Freightways (CF), two larger rival carriers were already carrying more LTL and were a step ahead in preparing similar hub and spoke networks. The perception was that Yellow lacked the breadth of capabilities demonstrated by the other two carriers. They appeared to be better positioned to prosper during the transition, Burdick said.

In mid February 1981, Burdick met with George Brooks and Roamey Lathan, two middle level managers who reported to Glenn Brown in the traffic department. Brooks and Lathan were later assigned to pricing.

Brooks presented an idea to offer customers a discount off of Yellow's tariff prices with the condition that the customer must tender five shipments. The concept had a few more details than that, said Brooks, but that was basically it. He said there was nothing new in the idea, he just packaged it a little differently in response to discounts that were already available from other carriers.

According to Brooks, Roadway was one of the first to aggressively pursue larger shipment volume by offering discounts. As a result, Roadway took an early competitive lead, although most of the discounting was occurring east of the Mississippi River.

Roadway's historians saw it otherwise. In their book, *The Roadway Story*, they pointed the discounting finger at Mason-Dixon Lines and Overnite. Regardless, it started in the East and Yellow initially chose not to participate.[4]

By 1980, discounting began to creep westward and began affecting Yellow's heavier traffic markets. The loss of business carried over into the first quarter of 1981 when Brooks, Lathan and Burdick met. Burdick liked Brooks's plan and the three scheduled a meeting with Ray Alderson, senior vice president of operations. Alderson thought there was merit as well and asked the group to make a presentation Saturday morning to McMorris, Brandt and other officers.

McMorris saw the first glaring flaw. If Yellow offered a variable tariff discount based on a modest five shipments, Yellow could lose margin rather than gain volume. There were probably several customers that already tendered five shipments with each order. Burdick had come prepared. He told the Saturday

1984

The Reagan-Bush Republican team defeats former vice president Walter Mondale and running mate Geraldine Ferraro of New York.

CIA speedboats mine Nicaraguan waters to prevent Russian and Cuban arms from reaching El Salvador rebels.

U.S. economic growth is the highest since 1951, up 6.8 percent, but the U.S. budget and trade deficits rise to record levels.

Popular movies include: Amadeus with Tom Hulce, Beverly Hills Cop with Eddie Murphy, The Killing Fields with Sam Waterston, Moscow on the Hudson with Robin Williams, The Terminator with Arnold Schwartzenegger, and Under the Volcano with Albert Finney.

morning attendees that based on preliminary figures, the risk was a margin deterioration of about two to three percent if there was no increase in volume. He thought that scenario was unlikely. The consensus was to proceed with implementation and to keep the effort under wraps.

By the last weekend in March 1981, six weeks after Brooks had presented his idea to Burdick and Alderson, the company had prepared sufficient sales and marketing materials to share with the entire work force and its customers. Brooks said Glenn Brown gave his concept the name Yellow Effects Savings (YES). The marketing slogans became, "Give Me Five (shipments)," and "Just Say YES."

Burdick and Brooks credit John Dehan, currently an account manager in Kansas City, with putting together presentation materials and an effective marketing campaign for the roll out. Staff and officers traveled to numerous meeting sites where the campaign was shared with terminal management and sales representatives. Everything was cued up for a Monday morning surprise blitz.

Dehan said he had all of the materials sent by airfreight to the hotels where the weekend meetings were held, including Burdick's product knowledge document and Brooks's pricing explanation. The "big bang," said Dehan, was asking for more business to get the discount. It inspired a sales force that felt like it was getting beaten badly without a strong sales incentive. This was the potent incentive that they had been waiting for, Dehan said.

Roger Payne was an account manager in Rochester, N.Y., when YES was rolled out. He remembered a sales call on Monday after the weekend meetings. He stopped at Pfaudler, a customer he knew vaguely and waited while a P.I.E. representative concluded a presentation ahead of him. When the two men came out of the meeting, Payne was greeted with surprising glee. The customer said, "I know what you got in there," pointing to Payne's briefcase. Payne said the excitement surrounding YES was so pervasive on the street, it had preceded him on his sales calls.

The YES program hit with shocking success. Paul I. Greene, vice president of sales at Roadway in 1981, said, "(Yellow) just blew our socks off." He called the YES program effect "one of the most painful experiences that (Roadway) has ever had." By February 1982, Roadway had a similar pricing package it called All-Savers.[5]

Business volume at Yellow picked up immediately,

This page, top — *Virgil R. (Ray) Alderson*

This page, bottom — *John B. Dehan*

1985

An unemployed security guard kills 20 and wounds 16 in a San Ysidro, Calif., McDonalds.

Mikhail Gobachev, 54, is named general secretary of the Soviet Communist Party when Konstantin Chernenko, 73, dies.

An Ohio Savings & Loan fails, setting off a run on uninsured S&L savings nationwide.

Movie actor Rock Hudson dies of AIDS, heightening American awareness of the deadly disease.

Oil prices collapse, putting pressure on Texas and Oklahoma financial institutions, which backed local exploration.

Burdick said. Customers seemed sincerely thrilled by the offer. But YES alone was not the reason Yellow's position in the industry rose sharply during the 1980s.

The steps Yellow took to prepare for the effects of deregulation were similar to those taken by competitors Roadway and CF. The difference appeared to be in the desire to succeed and an enormously successful roll out of the hub and spoke system.

Yellow had risen from nowhere in 1960 to be among the largest companies at the time of deregulation. Although George Powell, Jr. said it was never a goal to be the largest carrier in the nation, his employees seemed to pursue the number-one ranking with gusto. Within 18 months after the introduction of YES, Yellow was closing in on its once stronger rivals. It was especially gratifying, said Burdick, because it was commonly known that CF's sales force boasted at the time YES was introduced that it was the beginning of Yellow's end.

Despite its poor first quarter, by the end of 1981, Yellow's revenue had jumped 21 percent. The number of shipments rose by the same amount. Progress on the hub and spoke system continued at full throttle, including the addition of 88 terminals, pushing the total terminal count to 347. The company bought 1,809 new linehaul trailers with the first roll-up doors used by Yellow. All additional trailers after that also were to be roll-ups.

The momentum was stoked again. Growth started in the 1970s was just the forerunner. The 1980s kept an intense fire burning. Rumors that Yellow was incapable of shedding its truckload albatross were misguided. Yellow's forces were re-energized. Employees were inspired to excel. The success of the YES effort and the new hub and spoke network was a blast that rocked the industry and shattered the uncertainty caused by deregulation.

Rochester sales rep Payne said there was a special moment in about 1983. He was attending a meeting at which the normally quiet and somewhat shy leadership laid out further plans. Bob Burdick arose and said he knew it was not a goal to be the largest LTL carrier, but it was time to move past the long-standing leader, Roadway, and stake a well-deserved claim on industry leadership. Payne said the declaration was inspiringly explosive. Management employees let out a cheer that seemed to accelerate enthusiasm even more.

"We blew by Roadway at 100 miles per hour," said Payne. "It was amazing."

By 1983, Yellow surpassed $1 billion of revenue.

This page — *Roll-up trailer doors were first used in 1981. They saved time when trailers were docked for loading and unloading. (photo by Dave Bahm)*

Page 142 — *This terminal in Melrose Park, Ill., was opened in 1979, setting the stage for a new generation of similar suburban facilities that fed a growing hub and spoke network.*

Popular movies include: Agnes of God with Jane Fonda, Cocoon with Don Ameche, The Color Purple with Whoopi Goldberg, Out of Africa with Meryl Streep, Prizzi's Honor with Jack Nicholson, and Purple Rose of Cairo with Woody Allen.

The Royals beat the Cardinals in 7 games to win the World Series.

Compact discs and CD players become the new music source.

British scientists say there is a large hole in the Earth's ozone layer over Antarctica caused by air pollutants.

City scences used in service flyers helped Yellow promote its coverage area.

By 1988, Yellow surpassed $2 billion of revenue. Burdick described the era as the "go-go" years at Yellow. Careers advanced quickly. Customer entertainment was lavish and regarded as first class. The carrier that Roadway and CF saw as the also-ran, ran by them on its way to becoming the largest LTL carrier in North America. These statistics illustrate the growth: *(see chart below).*

During the six-year "go-go" period, 1983-1989, bottom line earnings dipped twice in 1984 and 1987 as a result of special charges related to rapid expansion, and in 1989, Yellow increased its workers' compensation reserves by $27.7 million. By all other measures of growth, Yellow was the star of the industry.

Sadly for thousands of industry employees, part of Yellow's good fortune during the 1980s came at their expense. As predicted by opponents of deregulation, many companies were poorly prepared for competition, either unwilling or incapable of expanding and attracting new business. Overwhelmed by lost revenue and unyielding debt, labor, maintenance and service expenses, they were driven out of business in droves.

The situation was actually made worse for many of the carriers following settlement of the 1985 NMFA union contract. Recognizing that nonunion carriers were starting to capture more of the LTL market with lower prices, the Teamsters agreed to company proposals to establish new-hire wages that would allow them to hire first-time employees for under scale. For those new hires, wages would go up each year until reaching contract scale after the second full year of employment. The catch was that companies could not hire new entry-level employees at a terminal with laid-off workers.

Yellow was one of only a handful of benefactors. For others, it was another competitive disadvantage because they were unable to grow and had several employees on layoff. They had to put those employees back to work at full scale when Yellow, expanding

	1983	1984	1985	1986	1987	1988	1989
Revenue*	$1,089,105	$1,380,042	$1,550,313	$1,713,731	$1,759,992	$2,016,466	$2,219,755
Net income	$49,185	$44,103	$55,536	$69,719	$41,284	$68,962	$47,785
Assets*	$564,531	$666,380	$747,904	$862,359	$923,867	$1,020,724	$1,081,665
Shipments*	7,894	10,430	10,846	12,909	14,229	15,145	16,037
Tonnage*	3,692	4,977	5,086	5,966	6,863	7,770	8,413
Employees	15,550	19,550	20,750	23,400	25,500	27,200	29,200
Terminals	437	508	533	599	610	618	640

(000)*

1986

U.S. warplanes bomb Libya's Muammar Qadaffi's headquarters in Tripoli in retaliation for terrorist bombings in West Germany.

Seven astronauts die when space shuttle Challenger explodes 73 seconds after liftoff.

The Senate overrides President Reagan's veto of economic sanctions against South Africa; GM and IBM divest South African subsidiaries.

Two days after being drafted by the Boston Celtics, University of Maryland basketball star Len Bias, 22, dies of cocaine overdose.

Inside trading rocks Wall Street; guilty participants are sentenced to prison terms.

Mobile Safety Classroom

Safety issues had been top of mind since A.J. Harrell began painting Yellow's trucks orange. This Mobile Safety Classroom was more than a training facility on wheels, it became an important community relations vehicle as well. School-aged children were fascinated by its novelty.

In 1984, Yellow increased its safety presence with the introduction of a mobile display vehicle that traveled from terminal to terminal, allowing employees to watch videotapes of important safety messages. It became a very popular community relations tool, especially with police departments and state highway patrols. Yellow called the converted rig its "safety training trailer." At the same time, quality control teams were established to help terminal management train employees in safer, more efficient handling of freight.

Yellow Freight System, Inc. of Delaware became the new parent company in 1983 when it was apparent that the marketplace was changing again due to deregulation. The new structure gave the company greater corporate flexibility.

rapidly in 1985, could hire new employees with a cost advantage of up to 25 percent.

Well-known unionized carriers were among those to go out of business. Some were more fortunate due to mergers with healthier firms. Companies affected included: East Texas, Lee Way, McLean, Navajo, P.I.E., T.I.M.E.-D.C., Transcon, Specter and Western Gillette. In the 1990s, the list grew with the demise of St. Johnsbury, Churchill, Carolina, ANR-Advance and Preston Trucking.

Yellow Strengthened

For the first time, Yellow offered services to all 48 contiguous states and parts of eastern Canada. Hawaii had been part of the service for several years because of Yellow's freight forwarding business. Intermodal rail and ocean carriers took freight to the islands. Alaska was added in 1987 by using the same methods. Meantime, the company re-instituted daily linehaul schedules to improve service throughout the system.

During the 1980s, the company revised its equipment purchasing policies and created a premier maintenance network. Shops were expanded in Cleveland, Denver, Atlanta and Barstow. A disciplined, preventive maintenance program was implemented that stressed pride in equipment appearance as well as safety. Employees did extensive repair work that had previously been vendor tasks. Yellow also bought Northcutt, Inc., a Wichita firm that specialized in repairing trailers and trucks. Yellow Freight System had become its primary customer.

Uncertainty about the future prompted many carriers to set up holding companies. It was a way to create more corporate flexibility in order to respond to growth opportunities. Yellow followed the trend on June 1, 1983, when it established Yellow Freight System, Inc. of Delaware, which became the organization's parent company.

Also during 1983, the Surface Transportation Assistance Act went into effect, allowing Yellow and other carriers to use twin trailers or 48-foot vans on all federally funded highways. The change added more efficiency to Yellow's expanding LTL operation and motivated the company to convert linehaul trailers to more 28-foot pups. Seventy-two percent of the trailers were pups by 1984 and 81 percent in 1986.

The weight capacity became a uniform 80,000 pounds. Fuel taxes increased by five cents a gallon and other fees and taxes went up as well.

Oil and gas exploration, in which the company

1987

Nintendo video games debut to receptive U.S. buyers and players.

Soviet leader Gorbachev seeks economic reforms, claiming the current system is stopping economic growth rather than stimulating it.

U.S. naval ships are deployed to the Persian Gulf to protect oil tankers from fighting between Iran and Iraq.

The Reagan Administration is accused of selling arms to Iran and using funds to support Nicaragua's contra forces.

President Reagan and Soviet leader Gorbachev sign a medium-range nuclear weapons disarmament pact.

invested immediately after the fuel shortages of the 1970s, officially ended in 1984 with the shut down of Overland Energy, Inc.

In other steps, the company renamed its special hauling division, calling it Freightcor Services, Inc., a holding company for the various functions – steel and thermo-protection primarily. Freightcor and Delaware Trucking, the company's truckload operations that had been operating unprofitably, were sold in 1986.

Also in 1986, Yellow combined the freight forwarding operation with Yellow Freight System and bought Custom Courier Services Ltd. in British Columbia. The Canadian carrier was renamed Yellow Freight System of British Columbia. Its acquisition permitted expansion of direct service to the province.

The company had previously bought rights to operate GMW, Inc. in Winnipeg, Manitoba, in 1982. It also purchased RBS Enterprises, which permitted expansion of services between the United States and the province of Ontario. Its subsidiaries International Carriers Limited (ICL) and International Carriers, Inc., had offices in both countries. The carrier was later renamed Yellow Freight System of Ontario, Inc.

Era Ends

By the time deregulation became reality, the same management team had been running the company for nearly 30 years. They had guided the company through many challenges. This one, however, may have been the toughest. And the difficulty was only magnified when the old gang began to break up.

The first blow was the death of George Powell, Sr. in December 1981. More than any one person, the elder Powell had put his personal stamp on Yellow Freight System when he boldly rescued the carrier from bankruptcy in 1952. He had broken with management tradition in the industry by surrounding himself with smart, young people who were good businessmen first and foremost. He relied on them to make solid business judgments, even if they were not truckers by experience. He drew ridicule from others in the industry for his tactics, but in the end, he proved it was a wise choice.

George Sr. had done more than make his mark on the industry. The Kansas City community lost a longtime civic leader who had been instrumental in galvanizing efforts ranging from construction of Kansas City International Airport and Harry S. Truman Sports Complex to bond issues and fundraisers

Freightcor Services, Inc. became a subsidiary company that specialized in steel and thermo-protection hauling. Freightcor was sold in 1986.

The Dow Jones Industrial Average plunges 22.6 percent in one day, worse than the crash of 1929.

Congress overrides President Reagan's veto of a highway appropriations bill.

Chrysler acquires American Motors.

The Twins win the World Series in 7 games against the Cardinals.

PTL minister Jim Bakker resigns after an affair with church secretary Jessica Hahn; he used church money to pay for her silence.

George Powell, Sr. rebuilt Yellow when it appeared to be crumbling. He also helped the company's headquarter city – Kansas City – grow and develop into a more livable city, too.

for arts and education. His greatest contributions to Yellow, though, were the people he attracted and the people he kept.

One person with Yellow when the company was rescued was Lloyd Brandt. He rose in the organization beside Powell's best and brightest recruits, eventually reaching executive vice president and board member. Brandt retired from his job in 1981 and from the board in 1984 along with Dr. L.L. Waters. Ray Alderson rose to take Brandt's place as executive vice president-operations, and Ray Stewart was named executive vice president-finance and administration.

After 16 years at the helm and more than 30 years with the Powells, Don McMorris retired in 1984. Ray Stewart replaced him as president of the company. McMorris remained a member of the board of directors and was joined by George Powell III in that capacity.

After joining Yellow in 1966, Ray Stewart had been on a fast track to the top mainly due to his contributions on financial matters. His versatile background aided his ability to lead the company. A clash between Stewart and others in the executive ranks led to his resignation three years later in 1987.

George Powell III followed in the footsteps of his father and grandfather to become president of Yellow Freight System mid way through 1987. George III was another of the 100 former students of Dr. Waters to work at Yellow, taking various assignments beginning in the early 1970s. He inherited the Powell work ethic and soft-spoken diplomacy. He chose as his closest advisors highly motivated operators focused on performance excellence. He considered M. Reid Armstrong his closest ally. Armstrong had been a division vice president in the Southeast and soon rose to senior vice president – terminal operations at the general office.

Although George III took over management of an organization that was growing in strength and growing in size, he faced critical decisions. Principally, he had to declare whether Yellow would stay the course as a bona fide LTL carrier committed to unionized labor or diversify as Roadway and CF had begun to do with their nonunion subsidiaries. Pressure mounted as the company continued expanding.

Growing with a ZIP

The company opened additional hub and spoke breakbulks in the mid-to-late 1980s. Added were Portland, Ore., and Columbus, Ohio, in 1984; Detroit

1988

Vice President George Bush defeats Democratic challenger Massachusetts Governor Michael Dukakis to become president.

The U.S. warship Vincennes mistakenly shoots down an Iranian passenger plane, killing 290 citizens.

Moscow agrees to withdraw military forces from Afghanistan after 10 years of intervention.

The first transatlantic fiber optical cable links the U.S. with England and France.

Popular movies include: Big with Tom Hanks, Dangerous Liaisons with Glenn Close, Midnight Run with Robert De Niro.

and Memphis in 1985; Salt Lake City in 1986; Northern California (eventually, Tracy) and Elizabeth, N.J., in 1987; and Nashville and Buffalo in 1988. By 1989, the total network consisted of 640 terminals surrounding 25 hubs.

Safety was an important issue during the rapid growth, but it was an area that could also be neglected easily in lieu of other priorities. It was easy to focus on solving productivity issues because success often led to quick career advancements. There was nothing sexy about getting employees to drive safely or pick up freight by bending knees rather than the back. Still, men like Ken Thompson and Bill Brooks, a long-time operations man and former division vice president, made safety their passion for parts of their careers at Yellow.

In concert with the physical growth, Yellow applied new operating and marketing strategies.

A new computerized dispatch system was a significant step that allowed linehaul managers to optimize delivery schedules by assigning dispatch priorities to all trailers.

Reducing freight claims was another priority. The company introduced a system of assigning "pro stickers" as a way to more efficiently assign a freight bill number to each shipment at time of pickup. It helped terminals know that there were multiple shipment pieces, alerting freight handlers not to split the shipment when trying to maximize the use of the trailer cube. Although cube utilization also was an operating priority, it was more costly overall to make two city runs delivering the split shipment than to keep all pieces together. The pro stickers were instrumental in reducing claims from lost and split shipments and damage from excessive handling.

Quality control experts had been trained to monitor freight claims by creating an exception report. Detection of repeated errors allowed quality control personnel to concentrate their efforts on terminals with problems.

Yellow also introduced a marketing innovation called Zone Index Pricing, or "ZIP." With the introduction of U.S. postal Zip codes, the trucking industry was able to implement more precise pricing schedules because of the greater precision in calculating lengths of haul. "ZIP" Disks were computer memory storage disks distributed to customers. They carried programmed pricing information, based on postal Zip codes, that customers could use when preparing their shipping orders.

The "ZIP" Disk became an important tool.

This page, top — *George Powell III became president of Yellow Freight System in 1987.*

This page, bottom — *The "ZIP" disk became an important tool for customers in the 1980s, helping them plan and budget their shipping costs. ZIP stood for Zone Index Pricing. Computer disks were prepared with pricing based on length of haul between U.S. Postal Zip codes.*

Popular songs include: Don't Worry, Be Happy, So Emotional, Sweet Child O' Mine, and Faith.

The Dodgers beat the Oakland A's to win the World Series in 5 games.

The Redskins whip the Broncos 42 to 10 in Super Bowl XXII.

The U.S. first-class post rate is increased to 25 cents per ounce.

Others On the Move

Don McMorris and George Powell, Jr. had worked side-by-side for more than 30 years when McMorris retired as president of Yellow Freight System in 1984.

Yellow Freight System executives advancing during the 1980s: Forrest Burm, senior vice president – maintenance; Paul Eaton, senior vice president – linehaul; Phil Spangler, vice president & treasurer; David Loeffler, vice president – controller; Larry Berkowitz, assistant treasurer and Bill Martin assistant secretary. Dale Merriman, who headed the special hauling division, retired after 21 years with Yellow. James Murphy replaced him. By 1983, George Powell, III had become senior vice president – operations and sales, Loeffler was senior vice president – finance and administration and Bill Martin was named vice president – legal. Ray Alderson retired after 29 years in 1983 and Ray Stewart assumed responsibility for the general freight division. Bob Burdick, with his rate bureau experience, was named senior vice president – marketing in 1984.

Following deregulation, most carriers created proprietary pricing programs that were kept top secret from the rest of the industry. Yellow took the opposite tactic. It put its Tariff 500 prices on the ZIP Disk and allowed any customer or carrier to use its pricing design. Yellow's T-500 pricing schedule is still preferred by many shippers because of its easy use.

Contract Time

Eighty percent of Yellow's work force was represented by the International Brotherhood of Teamsters, which meant pay, benefits and work rules for 20,000 employees were to be negotiated in the 1988 National Master Freight Agreement. Labor costs were one of the hot embers fueling inflation. At Yellow, and elsewhere in the industry, union labor consumed 55-60 percent of the revenue, and the total work force expense pushed the figures to 65-70 percent.

As long as shipping rates continued to rise, the cost of employment could be absorbed without affecting profits. However, with nonunion competitors improving their services and expanding their coverage area primarily in regional markets, they were able to undercut LTL rates alarmingly. Their work-force cost was their greatest edge.

Most nonunion truck lines began after 1980. They assembled work teams during high unemployment, so many companies paid 50 percent less than Yellow. Consider again that Yellow spent up to 60 percent of its revenue on labor. Comparatively then, nonunion carriers had up to 30 percent of its revenue to use as leverage against union competitors. They could discount rates in an attempt to acquire larger market share or bank much larger profits with which to grow their organizations. In fact, they did both.

It took most of the decade, but deregulation was beginning to take a toll on the surviving union carriers. The carriers had three options: one, start their own nonunion regional carriers to compete with the upstarts, an action referred to as doublebreasting. Two, they could negotiate costs out of labor contracts by seeking wage cuts, benefit reductions or work rule changes. Or three, they could attempt significant productivity gains and service enhancements to justify higher wages and higher shipping rates.

Yellow initially rejected the doublebreasting option that Roadway and CF chose soon after deregulation. From the time the Powells entered the trucking industry, they had maintained a better-than-average relationship with their employees and the union, often winning the Teamsters' support on matters

Communicating with more than 25,000 employees spread across North America became an important challenge. Several tools were created, including magazines, fact sheets, videotapes and audiotapes that were designed especially for linehaul drivers.

1989

Canada's Supreme Court rules that a law restricting abortion is unconstitutional.

Ethnic divisions threaten stability and Communist control in the Soviet Union.

Chinese students demonstrate in Tiananmen Square for more democracy; hundreds are killed in a military attack.

The Berlin Wall built in 1961 comes down as political policies liberalize.

Iran's Ayatollah Khomeini, 86, dies; Japan's Emperor Hirohito, 87, dies.

such as the purchase and merger of other carriers. For this reason, Yellow chose instead to seek compromises with the Teamsters and to improve operating efficiencies.

The tiered wage structure that was established in 1985 proved to be a critical advantage for Yellow and other union carriers positioned to grow. When contract negotiations began in late 1987, the union was in a less cooperative mood. Roadway and CF had made significant progress in building their own nonunion carriers and the Teamsters were upset by the threat to their work.

Art Bunte was an officer and lead negotiator for Trucking Management, Inc. (TMI) during the 1988 contract negotiations. TMI was the organization that evolved from the original employer group that Ray Beagle helped organize in 1964, known then as Trucking Employers, Inc. (TEI). Bunte said he worked harder on the 1988 contract than any prior to it. Teamsters General President Jackie Presser had overseen the 1985 contract that established the tiered wage structure, but was now extremely ill. Though the negotiations were difficult, partly because of Presser's ill health, the new NMFA eventually settled with a seven percent wage increase the first year and three percent increases the second and third years.

Following settlement, Yellow resigned from TMI and declared it would negotiate the next contract on its own. It was an important and very risky decision. Yellow was counting on the strength of its relationship with the Teamsters in order to implement the company's next strategic plan.

Popular movies include: The Accidental Tourist with William Hurt, Born on the Fourth of July with Tom Cruise, Crimes and Misdemeanors with Woody Allen, Do the Right Thing with Spike Lee, Driving Miss Daisy with Jessica Tandy, My Left Foot with Daniel Day Lewis, and Sea of Love with Al Pacino.

The A's blank the San Francisco Giants in a World Series that is delayed 11 days because of an earthquake.

Michael Milken, 42, is indicted on 98 counts of stock manipulation and securities fraud when dealing with "junk" bonds.

Safety Success

Safety Vice President Ken Thompson presents the ATA Sontheimer Award to Bob Blassingame of Tyler, Texas, in 1983. The award is given to the ATA's National Truck Roadeo contestant whose driving record, skills, attitude and personality best exemplify all professional truck drivers.

Yellow encouraged employees to participate in driving-skill contests sponsored by ATA. Yellow produced several finalists and grand champions over the years. The company also placed skillful employees on ATA's America's Road Team, a group of drivers who became industry spokesmen and women and whose driving records demonstrated their commitment to highway safety.

Larry Lemke from Peoria, Ill., was one of the first Yellow representatives chosen in 1986 followed by John Brubaker from Lancaster, Pa.

Driving a truck 100,000 miles a year without causing an accident is an importantant accomplishment. Ten of those years back to back earned Yellow employees million-miler recognition. To pool a group of drivers together in one domicile and all of them drive 100,000 miles accident free is a remarkable feat, but in 1985, drivers in Albuquerque, N.M., did it. They set a new company record by driving more than 6-million miles without an accident, which was the equivalent of 60 drivers hauling freight for a year accident free.

Building Relationships with Communications

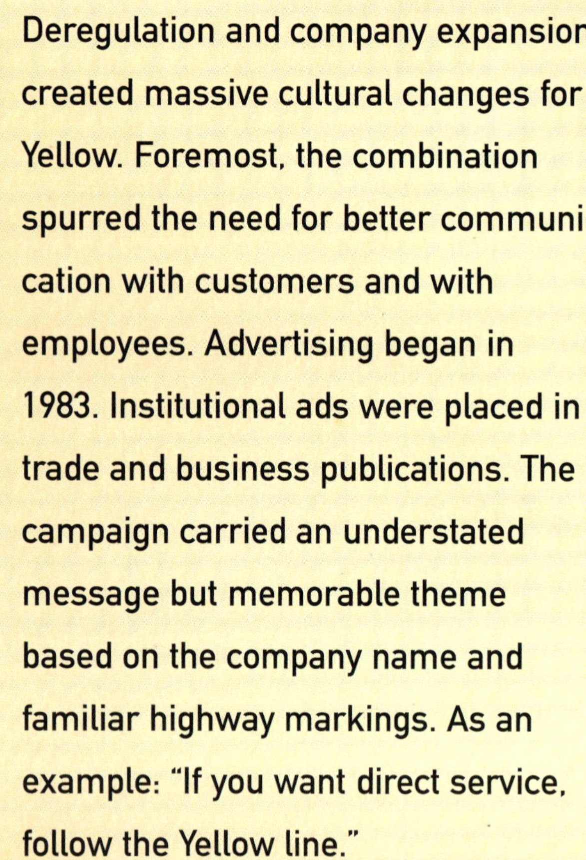

These communications tools helped the company advertise its services to customers and keep employees informed. With employment expanding and the business changing rapidly, communicating company priorities relied on swift distribution of facts and instructions.

Deregulation and company expansion created massive cultural changes for Yellow. Foremost, the combination spurred the need for better communication with customers and with employees. Advertising began in 1983. Institutional ads were placed in trade and business publications. The campaign carried an understated message but memorable theme based on the company name and familiar highway markings. As an example: "If you want direct service, follow the Yellow line."

The fact that it took three years from the time of deregulation until Yellow invested in advertising was an indication of how accustomed shippers and the industry were to regulation and its influence. It was not until low-cost start-up carriers had grown big enough to offer better service and unfettered prices that pressure began to mount on Yellow. Customers began to rejoice at the change because new carriers brought a different attitude, a friendlier, agreeable we-can-do-that approach rather than "this is where we go and how much it costs."

Recognizing the influence upstart companies were having on shippers, Yellow looked for ways to rally its work force to counter the efforts of the new competition. A campaign was created to make everyone aware that "Every One Counts." The message's double meaning was that each customer counts and therefore service cannot be neglected to any one customer.

Yellow's marketing department became the intelligence unit assigned verify customer desires through search and then to devise ways operations to accommodate those nts with services that could be omoted through advertising. Bluntly, vas foreign to a company and lustry that had operated so long der government regulation.

mployee communications experi-ced a few of the same obstacles e also to cultural issues. The principal drance was size. The company had wn from fewer than 7,000 employees erating 100 terminals in 1970 to 200 employees and 618 terminals 988. The culture was different. e pace was faster and managing business was more complex. To company messages distributed an entire work force called for new ernal communications methods.

Yellow in Motion magazine was a quarterly icon that was first published in the early 1970s. Although it was well known, it could not carry the entire weight of timely, persuasive messages that were necessary to influence cultural behaviors.

Electronic tools such as audio and videotapes were deemed better instruments for persuasive communications. Yellow invested several thousand dollars in television sets with VCR players and installed them at each terminal. The company hired professional television news producers to assist corporate communications coordinators with the first YFS Network. The format was a news magazine program, but the stories were exclusively about Yellow, its employees and customers. Produced quarterly, the program was distributed via internal truck mail.

Linehaul drivers, who made up a quarter of the field work force, worked irregular schedules, which made meetings difficult to attend. Communicators accepted the limitation and instead devised a different tool based on the fact that drivers spend a lot of time in one place – the cab of their tractors. Audio tapes were produced with popular music and specific stories about maintenance and driving safety interspersed with the same kind of business messages assembled in YFS Network. The audio programs were named Yellow Line Radio.

23985

Building Relationships with Communications

These communications tools helped the company advertise its services to customers and keep employees informed. With employment expanding and the business changing rapidly, communicating company priorities relied on swift distribution of facts and instructions.

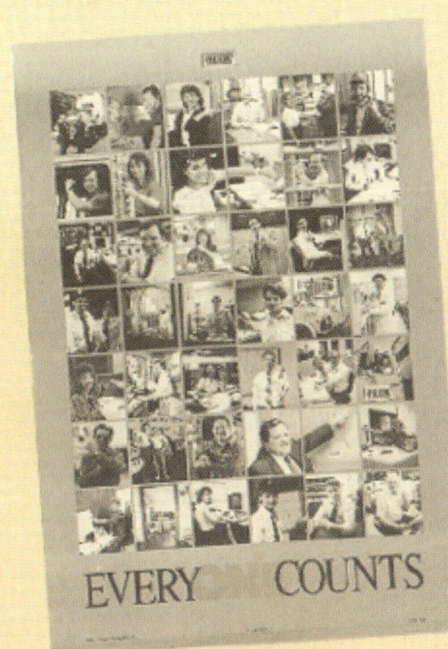

Deregulation and company expansion created massive cultural changes for Yellow. Foremost, the combination spurred the need for better communication with customers and with employees. Advertising began in 1983. Institutional ads were placed in trade and business publications. The campaign carried an understated message but memorable theme based on the company name and familiar highway markings. As an example: "If you want direct service, follow the Yellow line."

The fact that it took three years from the time of deregulation until Yellow invested in advertising was an indication of how accustomed shippers and the industry were to regulation and its influence. It was not until low-cost start-up carriers had grown big enough to offer better service and unfettered prices that pressure began to mount on Yellow. Customers began to rejoice at the change because new carriers brought a different attitude, a friendlier, agreeable we-can-do-that approach rather than "this is where we go and how much it costs."

Recognizing the influence upstart companies were having on shippers, Yellow looked for ways to rally its work force to counter the efforts of the new competition. A campaign was created to make everyone aware that "Every One Counts." The message's double meaning was that each customer counts and therefore service cannot be neglected to any one customer.

Yellow's marketing department became the intelligence unit assigned

Safety Success

Safety Vice President Ken Thompson presents the ATA Sontheimer Award to Bob Blassingame of Tyler, Texas, in 1983. The award is given to the ATA's National Truck Roadeo contestant whose driving record, skills, attitude and personality best exemplify all professional truck drivers.

Yellow encouraged employees to participate in driving-skill contests sponsored by ATA. Yellow produced several finalists and grand champions over the years. The company also placed skillful employees on ATA's America's Road Team, a group of drivers who became industry spokesmen and women and whose driving records demonstrated their commitment to highway safety.

Larry Lemke from Peoria, Ill., was one of the first Yellow representatives chosen in 1986 followed by John Brubaker from Lancaster, Pa.

Driving a truck 100,000 miles a year without causing an accident is an importantant accomplishment. Ten of those years back to back earned Yellow employees million-miler recognition. To pool a group of drivers together in one domicile and all of them drive 100,000 miles accident free is a remarkable feat, but in 1985, drivers in Albuquerque, N.M., did it. They set a new company record by driving more than 6-million miles without an accident, which was the equivalent of 60 drivers hauling freight for a year accident free.

Being Different Didn't Pay

Corporate Direction: Priorities for Tomorrow
(1990 Annual Report)

Many of the preparations for the next decade are under way. We are successfully "re-engineering" systems and processes to reduce overall transit time, further improve on-time deliveries and intact shipments, and handle the quick-response needs of the just-in-time and flex manufacturing markets.

These improvements will permit an expansion of our business base into markets requiring shorter lengths of haul. They will make it easier for customers of all sizes to do business with us. They will enable us to offer a broader package of services to our customers than ever before, including logistics and more customer-specific agreements. They will ensure our being the best at what we do by utilizing the talents of our employees to the fullest and by bringing us closer to our customers.

A recession in 1990 ended eight years of record-breaking economic growth in America. Iraq's invasion of Kuwait drew world ire. Oil prices spiked. On Wall Street, the Dow Jones Industrial Average fell 20 percent between July and October then recovered half its losses by year's end, closing at 2633.66. The economy was troublesome for Yellow at the start of the decade. But those difficulties paled in comparison with decisions the company needed to make about its future.

Sights Set On Compromise

When the starting gun for deregulation sounded in 1980, Yellow Freight System was out of the blocks quickly. By de-emphasizing its truckload business in backhaul lanes, Yellow had reduced its vulnerability to "cherry picking" by low cost, startup carriers. A highly efficient hub and spoke network was built in an amazingly short time. Many customers testified that it was the industry's premier network system. And while controversial to some in the industry, Yellow's volume discount pricing program, dubbed YES for Yellow Effects Savings, had been a resounding success.

But there was a drawback. The investment was enormous. While still financially healthy, Yellow lacked the cash held by its two traditional rivals, Roadway and CF.

Consolidated Freightways had just sold a valuable possession, Freightliner, the truck manufacturer. The transaction left the company sitting on hundreds of millions of dollars in cash. Roadway had built its hub and spoke network earlier and also held about $300 million in cash.[1]

Page 156 — *Pre-shift meetings have been an important communication process for several years. In addition to making specific daily assignments, supervisors are able to share relevant company news and changes in policy or procedures.*

1990

Iraqi forces invade Kuwait; the U.N. imposes economic sanctions and a military conflict ensues.

The Soviet empire crumbles as the Communist Party relinquishes its hold as the political power base.

East Germans vote in the first free elections since 1932; reunification follows.

Nelson Mandela, South African resistance leader, is freed from prison after 27 years; South Africa's Separate Amenities Act is repealed.

Oil prices soar in response to the conflict between Iraq and Kuwait.

George Powell III cuts the ribbon with Jacksonville Mayor Tommy Hazouri to open the new Florida hub.

By the late 1980s, market trends had become clearly defined. Nonunion LTL carriers were filling a niche by moving freight in shorthaul, mostly overnight and second-day lanes. They could not afford national networks to compete against the "big three," Yellow, Roadway and CF, but most proclaimed that they did not need them.

Regional shipping patterns were growing in strength as the retailing and manufacturing sectors increasingly adopted just-in-time distribution and lean inventory replenishment strategies. The new carriers met a demand while investing less capital in equipment, systems and facilities and paying lower overall wages and benefits.

Recognizing this trend, George Powell III and his advisory team examined alternatives. Should they create nonunion subsidiaries as an insurance policy for the future? Or, should they choose another way that was more in keeping with the Yellow tradition?

The easiest strategy was to embrace the industry movement toward low-cost, nonunion labor. With their hub and spoke networks further advanced than Yellow's, Roadway and CF did just that. Using their cash reserves, they began to create new nonunion companies. Teamster protests notwithstanding, they were successful.

Looking at strengths rather than vulnerabilities, Yellow opted for another strategy. It was unique. It rested on a strong faith in the abilities and skills of its management and workforce.

People at Yellow knew they worked for a compassionate organization. While good performance was expected, they could also expect fair treatment. It was an environment that did not exist at most companies in the industry.

Management decided to pour its energy, planning and finances into building the best operating network in the industry. The strategy was risky. It meant Yellow would remain extremely vulnerable to competition from low-cost nonunion carriers who, if their service was at par with Yellow, held huge pricing advantages.

Can We Talk?

Yellow's objective was to capitalize on its massive hub and spoke network. In fact, it opened a new hub, its 26th, in Jacksonville, Fla., during 1990 hoping to take advantage of the growing Florida population and port capacity to the Caribbean.

The management team believed that a huge terminal network would deliver competitive advantages. Enormous sums had been invested in constructing

Smoking is banned on virtually all U.S. domestic flights.

Popular movies include: Dances with Wolves with Kevin Costner, Ghost with Patrick Swayze, Goodfellas with Robert De Niro, Hamlet with Mel Gibson, and Mr. and Mrs. Bridge with Paul Newman.

The 49ers whip the Broncos 55 to 10 in Super Bowl XXIV.

The Supreme Court rules that a pregnant teen must inform her parents before having an abortion.

or leasing a Yellow terminal in nearly every significant metropolitan area throughout the U.S. and Canada.

The terminal count in 1990 was 631. More terminals meant more capacity to handle freight. The philosophy of the day was, "If there's a Kmart in the community, Yellow ought to be there, too."

Yellow wanted to use this capacity to run two operations side by side – the traditional longhaul LTL business and a new, lower cost regional LTL business.

"The main strategy was to move into the regional markets," said Reid Armstrong, who was senior vice president – operations in 1990 and the man George III trusted most. "We needed a regional contract more like the cost of the regional competitors; not the exact cost, but enough to give ourselves some relief from the NMFA in order to grow the company and compete."

Armstrong said the goal was to work with the Teamsters to grow as a unionized company in exchange for wage and work-rule concessions. The end result would be more Teamster jobs. To sweeten the offer, Yellow proposed a plan that would allow new regional freight handlers to move to higher paying jobs with the longhaul operation within a certain period of time.

The plan was very different from the strategy followed by Roadway and CF. That is one reason why Yellow withdrew from TMI after the settlement of the 1988 NMFA. Yellow anticipated negotiating the 1991 contract on its own. Furthermore, Yellow wanted to establish its own grievance mechanism, which would further distance the company from the most volatile issue in TMI grievance hearings – doublebreasting.

Once again Yellow was playing odd man out. It had become part of the company's image.

"We plan to develop profitable growth opportunities that leverage our existing pickup and delivery network, as opposed to launching separate subsidiaries. We think our approach will avoid the confusion of having separate operations within the company competing with one another, provide more flexibility to enter markets of varied lengths of haul, and allow us to concentrate our expertise and technology on markets of most productive volume.

"Industry trends and issues support our logic in taking this course of action. Driven by customer preference, the nature of the LTL business is changing. Customers are reducing the number of carriers they use and want to minimize transactions and simplify the process as they attempt to manage their inventories better and decrease costs. Businesses are becoming more time-sensitive to stay competitive.

"The freight transportation universe also has become global, so that competition will be even keener in the years ahead. That dictates both challenges and growth opportunities in the world marketplace, which we feel we are prepared to manage prudently. All of these factors point to a redefinition of Yellow's role in the industry based on our intention to stay focused on our single network core business."

1990 Annual Report

Heavy winter snowfall in the Northeast and Mid Atlantic slowed movement in the yard and even on the docks, especially effecting the hubs in Maybrook, Buffalo and Lancaster.

General Motors introduces the Saturn car to challenge Japanese automakers that have seized one-third of the U.S. auto market.

America's economy goes into recession after eight years of boom.

A jury acquits the Cincinnati Arts Center and its director of obscenity charges stemming from an exhibit of Robert Mapplethorpe's photographs.

Rescuing the U.S. savings and loan industry costs taxpayers $500 billion.

Page 161 — *City P&D units have the flexibility to pick up and deliver regional freight with longhaul freight, said Yellow's management. Yellow proposed creating parallel operations to handle both regional and longhaul services in 1989, but the proposal was turned down by the Teamsters because it sought lower wages for the regional startup.*

Other Views

TMI saw Yellow's move in a different light. TMI Executive Director Art Bunte said he and others in the industry anticipated that union negotiators would use the split in ranks to their advantage.

The split also put the Teamsters in an untenable situation. As much as union leadership might have sympathized with Yellow and understood company plans to protect union jobs, Bunte said they could not show favoritism that would risk alienating dues-paying members who worked for other carriers.

Bunte said that Yellow might have miscalculated these political realities. No matter how much faith their own Teamster employees put in Yellow, the company still had only a minority of the vote compared to the rest of the industry and a still smaller vote in proportion to the entire Teamster union membership. Union leaders were elected officials who faced many of the same political realities as members of Congress – they were prone to listen to their loudest and most powerful constituencies. It was naïve, Bunte said, to expect the Teamsters to take such risks on behalf of one carrier, no matter how good management's intentions.

Nevertheless, Yellow proceeded to make contact with the Teamsters. The carrier wanted to open discussions about the plan.

Billy McCarthy had become general president following the death of Jackie Presser in July 1988. McCarthy took over at a time when the federal government was mustering another action against the union for allegedly conspiring with organized crime figures. The government claimed that the union, the Mob and some carriers had arranged financial kickbacks in exchange for more favorable Teamster contracts. It was not the best time to be presenting creative proposals.

By March 1989, the government had solicited from the union's board a consent decree following accusations that the Mob had influenced union policy. It put the government in the middle of union affairs. Federal officials declared that the union would mount democratic elections for Teamster office holders slated for late 1991. McCarthy first appeared to be a candidate, then surprised everyone by withdrawing.[2]

Yellow looked at the field of three candidates and chose to present its case to R.V. Durham, a likeable union leader from North Carolina. Yellow wanted to be in position to establish its regional operation as soon as elections were completed.

1991

Soviet President Gorbachev suspends the Communist Party ending 74 years of rule.

Croatia and Slovenia declare independence from Yugoslavia; fighting erupts.

U.S. bombs fall on Iraq in an attempt to get Iraqi troops to withdraw from Kuwait.

Eastern Airlines and Pan Am quit flying.

U.S. first-class postal rates jump to 29 cents per ounce.

YELLOW

George Powell III used videotape recorded messages distributed quarterly on YFS Network to share his business strategies with employees. Producer-host Pauly Hart interviews the company president.

Durham faced Walter Shea, a long-time IBT insider who had served five general presidents before McCarthy fired him. The other opponent in the race was Ron Carey, who was considered a long shot even though he had entered the race early and was campaigning aggressively.[3]

Carey was relatively unknown among the truck lines. He had led a New York local that was dominated mostly by UPS workers. Carey himself had been a UPS driver.

Yellow was confident that the Teamsters under Durham would give the plan fair consideration. But Ron Carey dashed those hopes. He beat Durham and Shea in the election and was officially sworn in as general president in 1992 with the government watching happily from the sidelines. Yellow was placed back on square one but kept the plan in motion.

"The democratic election totally politicized the internal process of the Teamsters," said George Powell III. "We were caught in the middle of that."

Contact was made with Carey soon after he was installed in office. A meeting was set up to talk about Yellow's plans. There was some satisfaction knowing that Carey promoted himself as the bearer of union democracy. He criticized former Teamster leaders for ruling the union as dictators and vilified their corrupt relationship with the Mob.

Though Carey was an unknown, management was hopeful that he truly believed in democratic solutions and would allow Yellow employees to decide the fate of their company by voting on the regional and truckload tiered-wage proposal. Powell and Armstrong were willing to find out. They were especially confident of Yellow employee attitudes. They had surveyed employees and found that 80 percent were in favor of company plans. Moreover, Carey's biggest concern expressed during his campaign was doublebreasting.

"We were unique," said Powell, "the only pure play. We felt the union had a basis to give us something different."

Carey left no doubt where he stood during the meeting. He rejected the idea.

Armstrong said the abrupt failure was extremely disheartening and quickly closed the books on years of planning. It left the company with a bleak outlook. Customers and employees were upset as well. They saw merit and a number of advantages in working under a flexible union contract.

Armstrong said Carey did not have the perspective

Popular movies include: Bugsy with Warren Beatty, The Silence of the Lambs with Anthony Hopkins, Thelma and Louise with Geena Davis, and Truly, Madly, Deeply with Juliet Stevenson.

Earvin "Magic" Johnson, 32, shocks the world by announcing he has AIDS.

The Supreme Court rules nude dancing can be banned without violating first amendment rights.

A bystander videotapes Los Angeles police brutalizing Rodney G. King, 25, leading to the dismissal of Police Chief Daryl F. Gates.

to make a fair decision. Carey's UPS background was different from that of others in key union positions. Most of them had come from the trucking sector. Men like Durham and Shea had dominated the union, although truckers made up less than 10 percent of Teamster membership. According to Armstrong, Carey did not understand the unionized trucking sector or the competitive pressures it faced.

This issue was dead. Roadway and CF expanded at the expense of union jobs, but the union denied Yellow an opportunity to add them. The frustration ran deep. A compromise with the Teamsters, which meant membership growth, seemed like a win-win proposition. Instead, it was discarded unceremoniously.

The Preston Acquisition

Despite the setback, the company wasted little time implementing an alternative growth strategy. Before 1992 ended, Yellow had reorganized its corporate structure using its Delaware company that in 1993 was renamed Yellow Corporation.

The reorganization was a precursor to a tender offer to buy Preston Corporation. In November 1992, the company offered to buy the 5.8 million outstanding shares of Preston for $4.13 per share. The transaction closed in February 1993 with Yellow acquiring the stock of Preston Corporation for $25.3 million, including transaction fees and assuming $135 million in Preston Corporation debt.

Preston, a holding company with a long history similar to Yellow, owned four trucking companies. The namesake carrier, Preston Trucking, was a unionized regional carrier operating in the Northeast and Upper Midwest, producing $400 million in revenue. However, it was operating with small losses in very competitive business corridors at the time of the acquisition.

Saia Motor Freight Line, the next largest Preston subsidiary, was a profitable nonunion regional carrier headquartered in Houma, La. At the time, it was generating revenue of about $120 million.

The other Preston subsidiaries were Smalley Transportation, a nonunion regional carrier in Tampa, Fla., operating in the red with less than $40 million in revenue, and CSI/Reeves, a relatively small specialty carpet hauler with headquarters in Calhoun, Ga.

"We felt that we paid a price that would justify the ultimate (ownership)," said George Powell III. "We felt with our management experience, we could greatly improve Preston's operations."

Preston Trucking had critical structural problems,

Having exhausted other attempts to establish regional service, Yellow entered the market by purchasing Preston Corporation. Its two largest operating subsidiaries were Preston Trucking and Saia Motor Freight Line.

1992

Anita Hill, 35, charges that Supreme Court nominee Clarence Thomas, 45, sexually harassed her.

Oil prices drop as the U.S. and its U.N. allies get the upper hand on Iraq following its military aggression in Kuwait.

The U.S. population reaches 250 million; the world population hits 5.5 billion.

Jeffrey Dahmer confesses to killing at least 11 people after body parts are found in his Milwaukee apartment.

Arkansas Governor Bill Clinton, 46, defeats George Bush to become President of the United States.

CALIFORNIA REPUBLIC

according to Powell. The problems were well known because of the publicity they generated in trade publications.

"Wage rates were competitive, but we couldn't predict the price wars that broke out in the Northeast," Powell said. "It substantially deteriorated the pricing environment up there. It became an issue all over the country."

Powell appointed Leo Suggs to be president of Preston Trucking, with a priority charge to restore profitability. Powell picked Jimmy Crisp to take over Smalley. Crisp had been Yellow Freight System's regional manager in Charlotte. Smalley and Saia were merged shortly after the acquisition and Crisp was named president of the enlarged nonunion regional operation.

Yellow was now playing on the "doublebreasted" ball field. The company had tried to avoid this by establishing unionized regional and truckload operations, but Ron Carey was not interested. Yellow was then several years behind Roadway and CF in developing regional operations. But that was no longer an issue for Yellow Freight System. Yellow Corporation now had sole responsibility for expansion into regional markets where operating costs were much lower.

New Order at Yellow Freight System

Not surprisingly, Reid Armstrong became president of Yellow Freight. George III wanted his closest advisor near at hand. As top executive for the flagship operation, representing more than 80 percent of corporate revenue, Armstrong now had the most critical job in the company. He also was appointed to Yellow's corporate board.

Revenue continued to rise in 1991, but profits fell sharply. Net income in 1991 was $26.6 million, compared with $65.3 million in 1990. The decline was mainly due to severe industry-wide price discounting and increases in Teamster wages and benefits.

Revenue slipped in 1992 but net income inched up slightly to $29.5 million as the company jettisoned high-cost freight in favor of loads with better yields. Capital expenditures dropped, too, as Yellow wrapped up construction of the hub and spoke network. The final stages included opening the Jacksonville hub and a new hub facility in Tracy, Calif. The terminal count at year-end 1992 was 608, down slightly from the year before as a result of some system pruning.

In 1993, corporate revenue jumped to $2.8 billion from $2.3 billion the year before. Revenue benefited from the first full year of contributions from Preston

This page — *M. Reid Armstrong became president of Yellow Freight System when the corporation expanded to include four additional subsidiaries in 1993. George Powell III remained president of Yellow Corporation.*

Page 164 — *Although more competition and an economic slowdown affected Yellow's business, the company continued to expand its coverage with the opening of the Tracy, Calif., breakbulk in 1992.*

President Bush pardons Reagan Administration's Defense Secretary Caspar Weinberger, 75, for his role in the Iran-Contra affair.

Three admirals are forced to resign as the Navy is criticized for allowing sexual harassment of female officers during the Tailhook convention.

Mall of America opens in Bloomington, Minn.; the world's largest mall with 400 stores, it took seven years to build.

Popular movies include: Malcolm X with Denzel Washington, Unforgiven with Clint Eastwood, and Scent of a Woman with Al Pacino.

Trucking, Saia, Smalley and CSI/Reeves. Profitability suffered though as net income dropped to $18.8 million.

Financial pressures were increasing. Low-cost competitors were chipping away at market share with their pricing strategy. Yellow worked harder at taking out cost. The effort led the company to Total Quality Management (TQM).

TQM had captivated America's business culture by 1990. At Yellow, the goal was to use TQM tools, such as statistical process control, to create a common language among users for isolating and solving problems. Roger Payne, the former Rochester sales rep during the 1981 YES campaign, led the new quality department. His department taught operations and sales leaders new procedures that improved the monitoring of work effectiveness. It empowered people while assessing new accountability for work performed. These efforts were built on the teachings of W. Edwards Deming, father of the quality movement.

Applied to central rating, as an example, where freight tariffs were scrutinized, TQM's processes boosted the department's accuracy ratio and saved $1 million in reprocessing costs. At the Nashville hub, process improvements on the dock cut 1.5 hours of handling time per shipment. Improvement ideas came from an employee task force.

TQM helped employees from Detroit and Jackson, Miss., to open dialogue between the two groups. It sparked inventive solutions to quality issues at both locations. Despite being very different business locales and geographic cultures, both hubs were able to learn and apply the same process and management skills.[4]

Yellow's work to invigorate its service quality received wide recognition. Yellow received the Ford Excellence Award and recognition from customers like Motorola, Kendall Company, Westinghouse Electric Corporation, Huffy Bikes, Target Stores, Stanley Works, Siemans Energy and Automation, Corning, Inc., Merck and Co., Inc., Federated Department Stores, Cadbury Schweppes and the Tennant Company. *Distribution* magazine honored Yellow with the 1990 *Quest for Quality* highest rating among all longhaul carriers.

The Capital Advantage

For a number of reasons, the 1990s evolved as the "Technology Decade." Technology became one of Yellow's most powerful competitive trump cards.

In the early 90s, Yellow developed a sophisticated

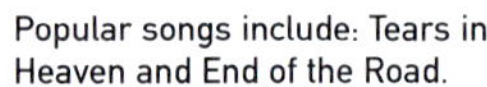

Popular songs include: Tears in Heaven and End of the Road.

The Chicago River floods the city's downtown structures through its freight tunnels, causing power blackouts and mass transit closures.

Hurricane Andrew strikes Florida, killing 15 and destroying the homes of 250,000 people.

U.S. unemployment has jumped to 7.8 percent, the highest since 1983.

Four L.A. police officers accused in the brutal beating of Rodney King are acquitted causing widespread riots and looting; 52 die.

Technology Assisting Customers and TQM

After TQM training, Revenue Accounting employees found ways to improve their services by learning and applying new computer skills. Their success earned (seated) Debra Johnson, Dana Hiatt, Lyla Bremer, (standing) Jana Lathrop, Terry Benjamin and Jan Baird recognition in Yellow in Motion, Yellow's company magazine.

EDIPartners™ evolved in the 1990s. Using mainframe-to-mainframe or PC-based computer technology, EDIPartners allowed customers to trace, rate and create freight bills. The program would even help customers with cash management and planning functions. It was designed to completely integrate the shipper's information resources with Yellow's for quicker analysis and better freight transportation decisions. Another kind of technology introduced during this period, which tied closely to Yellow's Total Quality Management (TQM) practices, was Yellow's package design and testing lab. If shippers wanted to know that their boxes and crates were protecting their products adequately, Yellow could tell them. Lab technicians used sophisticated instruments to test the overall quality of packaging and also to identify where boxes or crates might be vulnerable. One piece of equipment would simulate a truck ride to see how the product in its container withstood the bumps and sways inside a trailer.

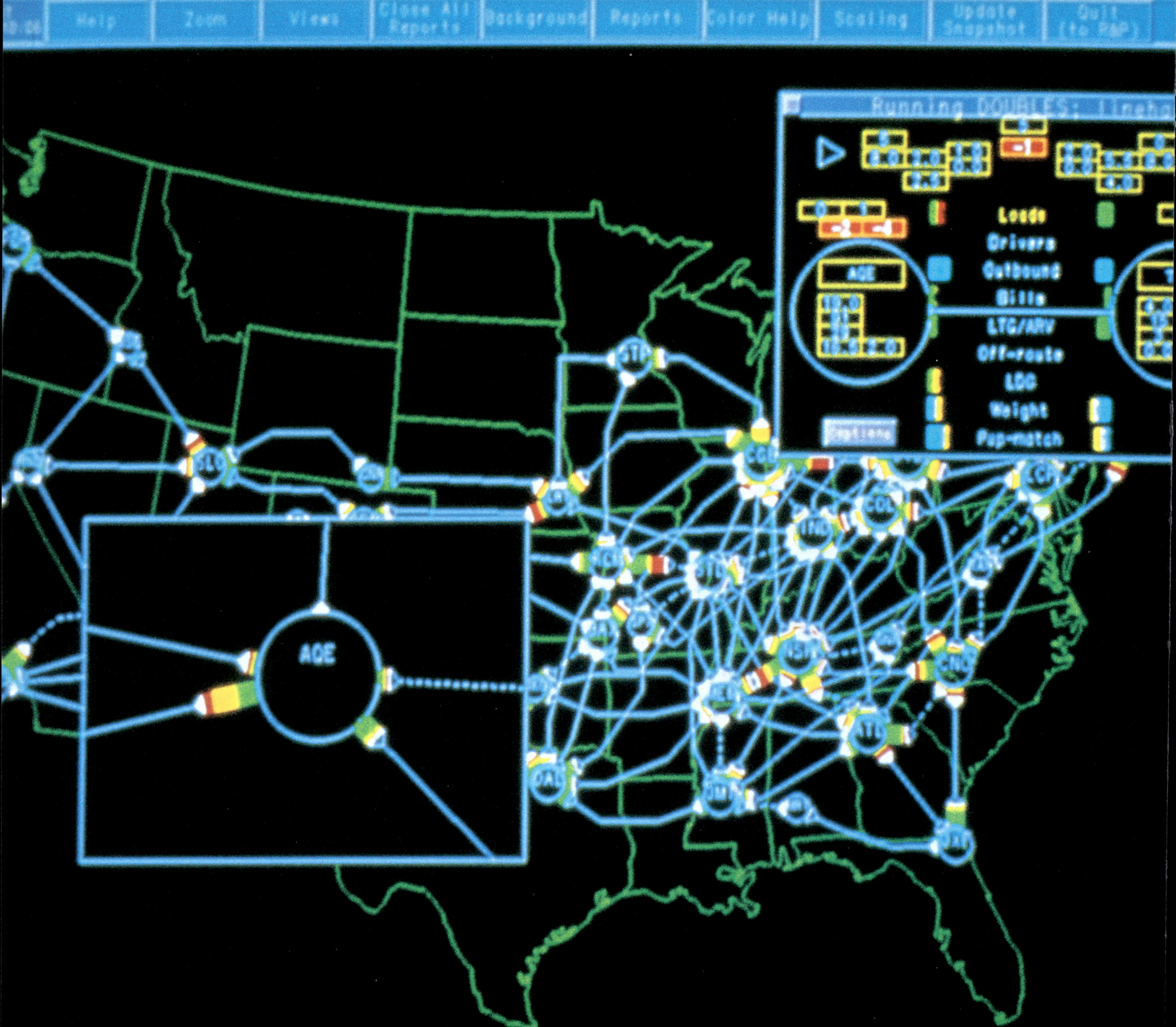

Help
Zoom
Views
Close All Reports
Background
Reports
Color Help
Scaling
Update Snapshot
Quit (to R&P)
Leads
Drivers
Outbound
Bills
LTC/ARV
Off-route
LDC
Weight
Pup-match
AOE

computer program named SYSNET®. Designed by Warren B. Powell (no relation to Yellow's leadership family), a graduate student at Massachusetts Institute of Technology, SYSNET was created to both monitor and plan freight movement throughout the continental network. Powell, who eventually became a professor at Princeton University, still monitors SYSNET progress and practical success.

The computer program protracted a long tradition of linehaul innovations. Practices established by Ray Alderson, Paul Eaton and Grady Haley, among others, were passed down to a new generation. Robert L. (Bob) Bostick, a no-nonsense trucker who began his career as a teenager in the 1950s, inherited the linehaul team. Knowing the exact results he expected, he turned authority over to an inquisitive group in linehaul planning to master the technology.

John Braklow, director – network planning, learned and implemented the program. He made several trips to Princeton to confer with Powell and colleague, Hugo Simão, while the team continued to improve the program.

One critical advancement came in 1994 when the team created a graphical-based tool for linehaul operations. It enabled central dispatch operations to visualize the network and predict among other things where logjams might occur, allowing preventive action to be taken. The program did more than examine load capabilities. It also helped central dispatch operations manage drivers and equipment.

SYSNET did exactly what the company desired. It added efficiency and improved management of a complex part of the company's business. It allowed its users to obtain information about the best load patterns and linehaul routes. It kept thousands of tons of customer products moving between cities in a timely, error-free manner.

Customer Relationships

Over the years, Yellow's sales representatives have also served as frontline customer service agents. Last minute shipping changes, billing errors and cargo claims often get reported to sales reps before customer service experts are called. Sales reps have to have a thorough understanding of company policies and procedures to perform their duties effectively.

The industry may be unique in that many account managers earn their promotions to sales responsibilities through experience in operations or administrative positions. As selling skills improve, some earn further

This page — *Atlanta dock supervisor Jim Wilson enters data in the DOCS communication system that gives city yard hostlers information about the status of a trailer.*

Page 168 — *The SYSNET screen reveals many details about Yellow's linehaul schedules, giving CDO information about freight movement throughout the network.*

1993

- Vietnam agrees to turn over war records of American's still unaccounted for during the 10-year conflict.
- England's Prince Charles and Princess Diana separate after 11 years of marriage.
- NBC Tonight Show host Johnny Carson retires after 30 years.
- A bomb explodes in New York's World Trade Center killing six and filling the 110-story structure with black smoke; 100,000 people evacuate.
- A plot to assassinate former President George Bush during a visit to Kuwait is thwarted.

This page — *Account Manager Randy Cox goes over Yellow's routing schedule with Mike Frey of Koch Labels in Evansville, Ind.*

Page 171— *Yellow employees have assisted others in their communities, often volunteering their time. Here, Charleston, S.C., driver Mike Flynn loads drinking water bound for Sullivan's Island where Hurricane Hugo struck violently in September 1989.*

promotion to corporate and national accounts.

Companies like General Motors, Ford, Chrysler, General Electric, DuPont, Goodyear, IBM, Sears, Kmart and Wal-Mart require enormous time commitments and a variety of solutions to multiple transportation and logistics challenges. They move massive amounts of products in and out of major distribution centers throughout North America.

The skills of corporate account managers have grown to match customer needs. They offer experienced advice and counsel to senior managers who make strategic transportation decisions for their companies.

Prior to deregulation, selling was based almost solely on a different kind of relationship. Knowledge was important, but maybe not as important as a big expense account. Rates were similar at all carriers. Service was about the same, albeit on regulated routes. And customers took what was available, not necessarily what was best for their businesses. Transportation was not something used strategically.

Newton Graves and Don Roberson were among those to rise to leadership positions in the new corporate sales hierarchy. By the early 1990s, approximately 45 national and corporate account managers were responsible for half of Yellow Freight's $2.3 billion revenue.

Most had some experience in operations. They knew the business and knew Yellow's capabilities. A surprising number had even worked on the docks and driven trucks during summer employment when attending college. The business was in their blood, and as one employee described it, it flowed Yellow.

With An Eye on Costs

When Reid Armstrong took command of Yellow Freight System, he promoted Bob Bostick to senior vice president – operations; J. Kevin Grimsley, a former division vice president and product of the management training program of the early 1970s became senior vice president – marketing and sales; and Gail Parris was elevated to senior vice president – administration. Kermit Scarborough was a senior vice president responsible for leading the labor department. The field operation was condensed from five to four divisions and headed by Fred Major, Ralph Nowell, Dick Wright and Steve Defenbaugh.

The Yellow Freight management group faced daunting challenges. Profits were eroding as regional, mostly nonunion competitors, grabbed more market share. Unable to compete on price, Yellow had to lower costs and improve its value.

One million gays and lesbians march on Washington to protest delays in enforcing a court ruling to permit homosexuals in the military.

Government lawmen storm an armed Branch Davidian facility near Waco, Texas; the structure is set on fire, killing 80 cult members.

The worst winter storm in 17 years deposits up to 50 inches of snow in the East and plunges temperatures to 2 degrees in Birmingham, Ala.

Popular movies include: Schindler's List with Liam Neeson, The Fugitive with Harrison Ford, In the Line of Fire with Clint Eastwood, Jurassic Park with fake dinosaurs, and The Piano with Holly Hunter.

27431
27431
YELLOW
84974
P106938
2D 86

New International Services

Yellow Freight System established a unique alliance with Royal Frans Maas in order to offer customers international trade capabilities between North America and Europe.

Consistent with its objective to expand its core business to areas with more growth opportunity, Yellow announced in 1992 an alliance with Royal Frans Maas, a Dutch transportation provider with operations in Western Europe. The two companies introduced an international service called YFM Direct. The service was built on a marketing plan to offer door-to-door convenience between the continents using one bill of lading.

Rather than a separate forwarding operation with its own sales force, which Yellow operated in the 1970s and 1980s, YFM Direct was offered as part of Yellow Freight's shipping arsenal. Research had shown that many of Yellow's domestic shippers also sent products overseas and bought supplies from overseas vendors.

Earlier, services between Canada and the United States were extended, especially to the Maritime Provinces.

ı Mexico, a carrier partnership abled the formation of a subsidiary, low Freight Mexicana, which ened service to the Mexican interior.

ıternational shipping was just other arrow in the account manag-s quiver. Today, Yellow's internation-offering has a new identity, new nagement and new operating ilosophies.

Peter Brown heads YCS International. own has more than 30 years of international transportation leadership and expertise. As a global freight forwarder and NVOCC company, YCS International, a Yellow Corporation subsidiary, works closely with Yellow Freight System in transporting import and export shipments throughout the system and with the respective gateways.

This dynamic combination in conjunction with overseas alliance partners in Europe, Latin and South America, the Caribbean and Asia/Pacific Rim countries enables the Yellow family of companies to provide a unique international connection. The companies provide instantaneous rate quotes, Internet-based track and tracing capabilities, and a consistent level of reliable services that meet the demands and expectations of today's international marketplace.

Yellow in Motion magazine told employees in 1993 about a new threat from non-traditional competitor UPS.

Once again, attention turned to the labor contract. With the contract due to expire at the end of March 1994, the company mounted an all-out effort to assess where costs could be removed from a new NMFA with the least impact on employees.

Yellow rejoined TMI in 1993 and worked closely with the organization to create a communication plan that would help employees and the union leadership understand the magnitude of issues facing the industry. The member carriers agreed on common bargaining goals that included putting more trailers on railroad flatcars for longhaul transport, changes to restrictive work rules such as mandatory overtime for dockworkers, and more flexibility in the use of part-timers. All the changes, if implemented, would save TMI carriers millions of dollars annually.

UPS, by then a serious competitor, already operated with half its Teamster employees working part time at reduced wages. In an annual report, UPS had said $6 billion of the LTL freight market moved in small enough sizes to fit within its self-imposed limits. The carrier said it was coming after a portion of that LTL market because it was a good fit with its primary parcel package business.

Eight times bigger than Yellow in 1993, UPS had the wherewithal to take freight from the truckers, especially if it was allowed to compete as a union competitor with less cost. From Yellow's perspective the Teamsters had granted UPS an unfair competitive advantage that was going to cost trucking industry Teamsters their jobs. Yellow, Roadway, CF, ABF, Carolina, Preston and others wanted part-timers for the same reason UPS had them – to lower costs at peak periods on the dock.

Employee surveys showed that Yellow had a difficult task ahead. Teamsters did not understand nor believe that changes were necessary. Communications intensified. The strategy was to build a case with employees explaining that the situation was dire. It was mandatory that the company lower its cost structure to a more competitive level in order to survive. The communication program made it clear that costs could be saved with minimal impact on employees' wages and benefits.

Regrettably for Yellow and the other carriers, Ron Carey resisted. Negotiations failed and in late April, Carey took 70,000 Teamsters out on strike for 24 days before the two sides got back together and compromised.

Both sides learned a sorrowful lesson – the customer had options. By this time, it was the customer, not

The Florida Marlins and Colorado Rockies become major league baseball franchises.

The "Brady Bill" requires a 5-day waiting period for handgun purchases.

Janet Reno becomes the first woman U.S. Attorney General.

The FDA reports that cigarettes cause 6,000 deaths annually from second-hand smoke.

Fifteen percent of Americans live below poverty level; the highest percentage in 30 years.

the government, nor union leadership, nor the carriers who had the upper hand. The outrage of shippers appeared to surprise union leaders. But once they foresaw lost jobs and dues shrinking, they included an article in the contract that promoted ongoing discussions about marketplace influences.

Two percent of Yellow Freight business did not return after settlement. For a company with razor thin operating margins, it was a devastating loss. Customers wanted no part of labor interruptions when there was a surplus of carriers that could get the job done.

Yellow finished 1994 with a net loss of $7.9 million, mostly due to the strike. It was the first time that Yellow had finished a year in the red since 1952, the year the Powell management group rescued the company from bankruptcy.

Moving Past the Strike

Yellow reacted quickly to appease shippers after the 24-day strike ended in May. But the damage was done.

Still, there were important gains from the 1994 contract led by the fact that the new agreement covered four years rather than three. It was the first four-year contract since the NMFA was created in 1964.

The new contract also gave Yellow many of the operational advantages it had sought. The company won the right to put more trailers on piggyback rail cars, cutting linehaul expenses by as much as $30 million annually.

Yellow also implemented a change of operations that converted more linehaul units to sleeper teams. Combined with the intermodal improvements, it enabled the company to reduce its relay movement along Interstate 80 and concentrate its east-west relay network along Interstate 70.

The external demand for service improvements and the internal push for cost savings gave new momentum to a system-wide network consolidation effort. Smaller terminals in major industrial centers like Boston, Philadelphia and Baltimore were closed and freight pickup and delivery operations moved to one larger terminal serving the entire city. The resulting freight density allowed the company to schedule more direct routes to destination cities, bypassing one or more breakbulk terminals. In addition to faster service, there was less cross-dock freight handling, fewer cargo claims for damaged or missing shipments and lower overall expense. The company ended the year with 509 terminals, down nearly 100 from two years earlier.

1994

Michael Jordan retires from basketball after the Bulls win their third straight title and in the wake of his father's murder.

Computer users start to link to the World Wide Web in droves as a new communications phenomenon catches on.

The "Great Flood of 1993" destroys $12 billion in Midwest property, kills 50 and leaves 70,000 homeless.

Former CIA agent Aldrich Ames is sentenced to life in prison for spying for the Soviet Union.

Teamsters strike against LTL truck lines lasts 24 days.

TIME
OR NO
TIME
TEAMSTERS LOCAL 710
LOCAL 710
ON STRIKE
YELLOW FREIGHT
NO RAIL
NO PART TIME
DRIVE

The network development enabled the company to introduce new services. Metroliner became a special 2-day service between major metropolitan markets. Express Lane gave shippers an alternative to airfreight.

New Blueprint

While the company scrambled to lower operating costs and improve service, it also was looking beyond the immediate need. Survival in the new competitive environment required a long-term view. The Yellow Freight system had to be re-engineered. Again.

By 1994, intense planning sessions and internal debate had produced a concept that management was ready to commit to. Known by the acronym BASICS (Building A Solution for Integrated Customer Service), the program incorporated both a massive technology investment and organizational redesign. Though it would take years of effort and $100 million to execute, Yellow Corporation's board of directors courageously approved management's plan. Work started immediately.

Tracy Regional Manager James Welch and Doug Waggoner, who also had extensive field and sales experience, were the point men in the BASICS project, reporting daily to senior management. Months of prior analysis by employees, aided by a consulting group, concluded that several steps in Yellow's service process could be eliminated if a number of tasks were centralized and supported by state-of-the-art information technology systems. They also concluded that customer service overall could be improved by creating two large inbound call centers where customer service representatives would be available to deal with specific customer requests and problems.

Centralization also would enable Yellow to capture customer information more quickly and more accurately. Processes could be streamlined and administrative costs reduced while productivity improved through smarter freight flow planning.

Management had learned from the strike that most employees had little grasp of Yellow's seriously weakened competitive condition. Communication was essential. Everyone needed to know that they had a role to play and a stake in the outcome. A program dubbed *Blueprint for Change* served as the framework for communicating the company's plan of attack through technology development, centralized customer service operations and accelerated network development.

Two customer service centers were opened in 1995. In January, about 100 employees began eight weeks of training in Des Moines and then were taking live

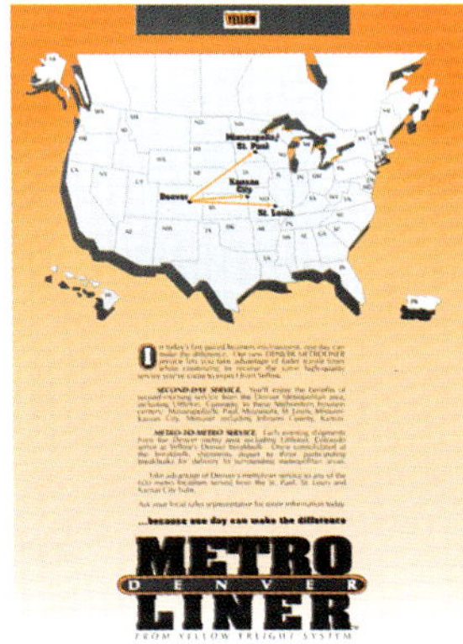

This page — *Regional service created new demands for faster transit times, especially between major metropolitan areas. Yellow's first regular expedited city-to-city service was branded Metroliner.*

Page 176 — *Teamster pickets were set up April 6, 1994, shutting down Yellow Freight's Chicago terminal and all others as well. The Chicago distribution center is the company's largest and busiest facility employing more than a thousand people. The strike lasted 24 days and caused permanent customer flight resulting in revenue losses for the year. (AP/Wide World Photos)*

Former football star and actor O.J. Simpson pleads not guilty to murdering his former wife and her male friend.

Republicans win a majority of the seats in the U.S. House of Representatives for the first time in four decades.

The Supreme Court rules that pro-life protestors can be sued for blocking access to abortion clinics.

Former President Richard Nixon dies; his funeral is attended by 5 living U.S. presidents: Clinton, Bush, Reagan, Carter and Ford.

Popular movies include: Forrest Gump with Tom Hanks and Disney's animated film the Lion King.

Tracy, Calif., Regional Manager James Welch and Regional Sales Manager Bill Schwar, Jr. were both promoted to positions at the general office. Today, Welch is vice president of Yellow's Central Group and Schwar is director of exhibit services.

calls by April. A few months later a second facility opened in Sioux Falls, S.D.

Some shippers and employees resisted the change. They were more comfortable handling customer service matters at the local terminal. Prior to 1995, customers who needed anything at all simply called their closest terminal, where they often spoke with the person nearest the phone when it rang.

Frustrations ran high, according to Reid Armstrong, because employees felt handcuffed by lack of information. There were a few locations where calls were not handled courteously.

"In general, our people were doing a good job," said Armstrong. "They were the best in the industry at customer service."

Centralizing the function improved it though, and saved costs. The centers achieved success well beyond expectations. They became so efficient that new responsibilities were added and further productivity gained. The company learned that the real-time information captured through a centralized information clearinghouse would allow the company to achieve a number of efficiencies related to managing and planning the movement of hundreds of thousands of shipments per day. Most impressive was the addition of the call-for-pickup function. With customer pickup calls going to the centers, city dispatchers were freed to manage their work more effectively.

The customer service centers became showcase operations within short order. Their techniques and constant process improvements earned the centers recognition not just within the transportation industry, but among all customer service operations. They became an ongoing source of pride and continued to create additional cost savings and customer convenience.

Another part of the BASICS concept was to put technology into the hands of pickup and delivery drivers. Yellow had already begun to use bar coding to help it manage freight at its breakbulk hubs, which had been renamed distribution centers. Dockworkers and dock supervisors used infrared scanners to log receipt of freight bills as they pulled shipments from trailers and transferred them to city operations or consolidated them for relay purposes. Putting similar capabilities into the hands of city drivers could expedite processes.

Transit Time Improvement

Despite the achievements of programs like

1995

The World Series is cancelled because of a players' strike in mid season.

The Cowboys beat the Bills for the second Super Bowl in a row, this time 30 to 13.

It is revealed that former President Ronald Reagan has Alzheimer's disease.

Jacqueline Kennedy Onassis, widow of President John F. Kennedy, dies in New York City.

A federal office building is bombed in Oklahoma City; 168 people die and hundreds more are injured.

BASICS, customers continued to migrate toward carriers that were providing faster service. Shippers were under pressure to reduce inventory costs and one way was faster movement to market. Yellow Freight answered in July 1995 with a comprehensive transit time improvement dubbed *Further, Faster*™, and a specific segment called *2-Day USA*™.

Consolidation of terminals made it possible to reach the 2-day goal where it was established. On longer routes the objective was to shave at least one day from standard times involving the largest 100 markets. The program was introduced with promotional fanfare. However, it failed to generate enough additional revenue to cover increased operating costs.

The service depended on tightly controlled departure schedules that often resulted in trailers leaving only partially full. More trucks were put into service to meet commitments, which meant more jobs were created at additional cost. Had the revenue increased, costs would have been covered. But the company had moved too aggressively. Customers failed to respond to the improved transit times with the acceptance hoped for.

Other efforts running concurrent with transit time improvement were freight movement management (FMM) and a process improvement program called Best Practices. FMM was designed to tackle a costly concern about service failures, a major source of customer dissatisfaction.

Nearly 11 percent of Yellow's shipments were moving with some level of freight handling or paperwork error that created cargo claims or rework. As an example, Yellow was docking about one million shipments per year requiring appointment calls. They did not include trapped freight for large corporate accounts. The additional handling was calculated to cost $12 million in labor expenses alone and still did not take into consideration extra damages due to repositioning the stored freight on overcrowded docks. Full Circle Training involved employees in designing solutions once FMM identified the problem. The corrective actions began to strengthen Yellow's operations and helped trim more waste-related costs.

Layoffs Necessary

All of the efforts in 1995 to remove costs and increase revenue failed to reach necessary levels. In the third quarter, the focus shifted almost entirely to the cost side. A dramatic cost-reduction effort was implemented that included elimination of jobs and

Yellow Freight System was the first LTL carrier to centralize customer service. Here, Doug Toth, customer service representative in Des Moines, demonstrates the company's new computer-generated process techology to visiting company executives.

O.J. Simpson is acquitted of slaying his former wife and her male friend.

The Intergovernmental Panel on Climate Change, sponsored by the U.N., confirms that the Earth is warming.

Popular movies include: Apollo 13 with Tom Hanks, Braveheart with Mel Gibson, Leaving Las Vegas with Nicholas Cage, Dead Man Walking with Susan Sarandon, and Sense and Sensibility with Emma Thompson.

Popular songs include: Kiss From a Rose, No More "I Love You's," Let Her Cry, and Have I Told You Lately That I Love You.

George Powell III spent 25 years with the company his grandfather and father also headed. In 44 years, the Powells and their protégés transformed Yellow from a Midwest regional carrier, producing $7.5 million in revenue in 1952, to the largest North American LTL truck line with revenue of $2.3 billion.

a cost-saving target of $75 million. For the second year in a row Yellow Corporation lost money. The net loss at year-end 1995 was $30.1 million.

With Yellow Freight's regional management teams gathered at the general office in January 1996, George Powell III made an unexpected and dramatically emotional announcement. He was resigning as president and chief executive officer of the corporation after 25 years with the company. The board immediately began a search for a new corporate leader.

CD-ROM discs carry full-length feature films.

Rose Kennedy, 104, matriarch of the famous political family, dies of pneumonia.

"Superman" actor Christopher Reeve is paralyzed when thrown from his horse in Virginia, injuring his neck.

Microsoft launches Windows 95 program software amid a worldwide and highly publicized midnight blitz.

Conservative company dress codes in America are relaxed; employees begin wearing casual attire, especially on Fridays.

New Customer Parntership

Bottom Left — *Goodyear's Peter Webb, senior transportation systems analyst, goes over presentation materials with Dirk Abernathy, corporate account manager for Yellow on the Goodyear account.*

Bottom Right — *Yellow Freight President Reid Armstrong (left) and Goodyear Vice President Rick Adante examine reports during an employee presentation. Data confirmed cost savings for both companies due to a partnership campaign to tighten transportation processes.*

Another route to cost savings went through one of Yellow's longest standing corporate relationships. Goodyear Tire and Rubber and Yellow were natural customers of one another. Both wanted the same thing – to preserve their relationship and to reduce their costs. Management teams from both companies were assembled to find new ways to accomplish their shared mission. Their plans were presented to senior officers and endorsed. Innovative partnering created savings, better service and thus, profits for both. It became a model for carrier and customer cooperation.

YELLOW
YELLOW
LOCAL GVW
71213
341-855

Re-Inventing the Company

The Board's Decision

Yellow Corporation's board of directors faced a critical decision in 1995. The board had suspended the per-share cash dividend at mid-year, contributing directly to a 50 percent decline in share prices. Still, the action was far from enough. Operating losses continued to mount.

The board directed each subsidiary to cut costs. Progress was monitored carefully. When it appeared that cost cutting would fall short of goals, more drastic action was planned.

"It was not a pleasant situation, especially for those of us on the board that had known the Powell family for a long time and had been close to them," said John C. McKelvey, president and chief executive officer of Midwest Research Institute. McKelvey was elected to Yellow's board in 1977 and prior to that had worked with Yellow on several research projects.

McKelvey said the cultural tone and high moral values that the Powells brought to Yellow made the board's dilemma especially difficult. The character of the company was a direct reflection of the Powell character, which was a source of pride for all employees, and rightfully so.

"But we had to sit down and face the facts," he said. "We needed fresh views and fresh approaches."

"We had a responsibility to shareholders and employees," said Howard Dean, chairman and chief executive officer of Dean Foods Company and a board member since 1987. "We were concerned about the long-term viability in an industry that was way over capacity. Everybody was hurting. It wasn't our top management's fault."

Dean said the board's view was that shareholders and employees have other options. To compete for investment dollars and the best work force, the company had to be strong competitively. The task was made even more difficult, Dean said, because of the "very restrictive labor contract. We needed to go a new direction."

It caused the board to look for a new management group with perspectives and a base of experience not necessarily rooted in the trucking industry. The plan was reminiscent of the path taken by George Powell, Sr. in 1952 when he built his new management team

Page 182 — *Few consumer goods get to a store shelf without riding on a truck. The familiar orange and white vehicles with the Yellow name are among the most recognized trucks on North America's streets and highways. (photo by James Hoffman)*

1996

President Bill Clinton retains his office by defeating former Sen. Robert Dole of Kansas.

Popular movies include: The English Patient with Ralph Fiennes, Jerry McGuire with Tom Cruise, Shine with Geoffrey Rush, Fargo with Frances McDormand, The People Vs. Larry Flynt with Woody Harrelson.

Popular songs include: Blue, Change the World, Because You Loved Me, Exhale, Give Me One Reason.

The Yankees beat the Braves in 6 games to win the World Series.

George Powell, Jr. spent 44 years with Yellow. Following his father from Riss & Company to rescue Yellow Transit from bankruptcy in 1952, George Jr.'s first title was controller. He was 26.

with good business people who would learn the trucking business as they went.

A New Leader

By March 1996, the board had decided on a course of action. A. Maurice Myers, a 55-year-old airline executive, was tapped as the man to lead Yellow into its next era. Myers was formally named president and chief executive officer of Yellow Corporation on April 1, and in June was elected chairman of the board, replacing George Powell, Jr. Powell retired at the mandatory age of 70 after 44 years of service to Yellow.

Myers was familiar with the problems facing Yellow. He had witnessed them in the airline industry where he had spent most of his career. As president and chief operating officer of America West Airlines, he had overseen that carrier's emergence from bankruptcy.

Prior to 1994, when he joined America West, Myers had spent several years in Hawaii running Aloha Airlines. He was named president and chief executive officer of Aloha in 1985, having held other positions before his promotion. Prior to that, Myers had worked for Continental Airlines, Merrill Lynch & Company and Ford Motor Company.

Running Aloha Airlines seven years after the industry was deregulated probably gave Myers his closest look at what presiding over Yellow would be like. Aloha and Hawaiian Airlines had been challenged by an upstart carrier with low prices. According to Myers, the aggressive new carrier had caused Aloha's board to consider liquidating.

"When I arrived, we owned about 38 percent of the market on the islands," Myers said. "By the time the job was complete, we were the dominant carrier with close to 60 percent.

"That whole experience was learning how to deal with a competitive marketplace," he said. "The company needed to change from an internal to an external focus – a customer focus."

Yellow faced the same challenge. Although deregulation had occurred nearly 16 years earlier, it had taken until the mid 1990s and the final phase – intrastate deregulation – to apply its heaviest pressure. Yellow had thrived throughout the 1980s by capitalizing on the weaknesses of other unionized carriers who were unwilling or unable to compete. With most of those weaker carriers gone from the marketplace, it was now a toe-to-toe battle with emerging nonunion competitors, three established unionized longhaul LTL carriers, UPS and even FedEx.

The Cowboys defeat the Steelers 27 to 17 in Super Bowl XXX.

The "Blizzard of 96" covers the East Coast from Virginia to Massachusetts in 1-3 feet of snow; airports close and damage is estimated at $1 billion.

Eccentric millionaire John E. duPont is charged with murdering gold-medal wrestler Dave Schultz at DuPont's Newton Square estate.

A crude pipe bomb explodes on the busy grounds of the 1996 Olympic Games in Atlanta; two die and 111 are injured.

Call Me Maury

On April 26, dressed in an open-collar shirt and dark blazer on casual Friday, Myers drew a huge crowd of curious employees to his first town hall meeting. They wanted to see him, hear his first impressions and learn what he expected from them.

Myers began by telling everyone they could call him Maury. He then explained the steps the company needed to take.

First, he said, Yellow needed to operate more efficiently to compete with the lower cost, nonunion competition, where salaries and benefits were as much as 40 percent lower than Yellow Freight's union scales. This gap could be substantially closed by instituting a package of "best practices" that had been designed by an outside consulting company, hired by the board of directors. The goal was to reduce operating expenses by as much as $200 million per year. And to provide leadership by example, all management employees' salaries were frozen for the year.

The second step was to re-energize the revenue machine. "We've got to start making money. We have a plan to reduce costs," Myers said, "but, we can't save our way to prosperity."

And, a third immediate goal was to pay down debt. Within a short time, three buildings at headquarters were declared excess and sold, funds were repatriated from Canadian operations and the debt began to shrink. His goal was to pay down $100 million by the end of the 1996. That goal may have been too modest. The company actually paid down $158 million in debt by yearend 1996.

Myers gave credit to the Powells for building Yellow into one of the country's leading transportation companies. He said that Yellow had a rich history and that the company needed to change so that all employees could again be proud of their company and secure in their jobs and future.

Myers said that a "pay-for-performance plan" would be initiated so that all non-contract employees would share in the company's resurgence. And to be sure everyone knew that things were changing, Myers ordered "symbols of excess" eliminated. Expensive art was taken down in the headquarters building and sold. Garden fountains were turned off and the company executive car was raffled off with the proceeds going to charity.

Regarding the similarities between trucking and passenger airlines, Myers noted that both faced the

Dressed for "Casual Friday," April 26, 1996, the corporation's new president and CEO told a large audience of curious and anxious general office employees to, "Just call me Maury." (photo by James Hoffman)

TWA Flight 800 explodes off the coast of Long Island, N.Y., killing all 228 people aboard.

Liggett Group, Inc., the fifth largest tobacco manufacturer, admits cigarettes are harmful; settles the largest class action anti-smoking suit.

Eleven-to-one underdog Evander Holyfield defeats Mike Tyson in an 11th round technical knock out.

A 3,000-lb. truck bomb kills 19 U.S. airmen and injures 160 people in Saudi Arabia; Islamic militants are suspected.

30 African-American churches are destroyed in random arson-set fires across the South; racial bigotry motives suspected.

This page, top — *A. Maurice Myers joined Yellow Corporation in April 1996. The company's board of directors hired Myers to be president and chief executive officer. A short time later he was elected chairman of the board when George Powell, Jr. retired.*

This page, bottom — *William F. (Bill) Martin, senior vice president-legal, Yellow Corporation.*

same struggles in emerging from the grip of decades of government regulation. The challenge was to transition from an operation driven to a marketing oriented culture. Using American Airlines as an example, Myers said the company met the challenge with innovative marketing that leveraged its state-of-the-art SABRE reservations system.

"In trucking, we've seen price become the primary driver of buying decisions," Myers told employees. "The same thing happened with the airlines. People started putting up with less legroom and less food and were willing to line up in front of a gate and race for their seats," he added. "In trucking, there is probably more of a premium attached to reliable service but there are a lot of parallels."

Though it was too early to articulate a vision for the company, Myers warned everyone to expect change as a way of life.

Revitalizing a languishing stock was another challenge. With the dividend suspended, Myers had to find a way to attract new investors willing to take a chance on a quick turnaround. A strong economy, corporate debt reduction and productivity improvements at Yellow Freight were his allies.

Presiding Over Yellow Freight

After George Powell III resigned from corporate management, he later left the board. His departure stunned Reid Armstrong, Powell's "right hand man," who was then president of the corporation's largest carrier. Armstrong elected to retire, but said that he remained hopeful, even in departing, that strategies in place would help the company turn the corner.

Myers presided over Yellow Freight for the next six months as he searched for Armstrong's replacement. He also began forming his Yellow Corporation holding company team.

H.A. "Bert" Trucksess, an experienced finance executive who had moved to Yellow Corporation from Preston, continued as the corporation's senior vice president and chief financial officer. Myers described Trucksess as having the best executive name in the trucking business and said he was fortunate that Bert was willing to join the new team.

William F. "Bill" Martin, Jr. also agreed to continue as senior vice president of legal and secretary of the corporation. Myers said, "Bill has long provided wise counsel to this company on a wide range of issues and I'm pleased that he has agreed to be part of the new team."

Daimler-Benz introduces a prototype cell-powered minivan it calles NECAR II.

Former CIA director William Colby is missing; his capsized canoe is found near his vacation home at Rock Point, Md.

A Michigan grand jury acquits Dr. Jack Kevorkian of assisted suicide although he admits he helped two elderly patients inhale carbon monoxide.

Jessica Dubroff, 7, trying to become the youngest pilot to fly across the continent, dies with her father as her Cessna 177B crashes.

Sam Woodward, a former transportation consultant, truck line owner and associate of Myers, joined the team as senior vice president of operations and planning.

Search Ends

In early September 1996, William D. "Bill" Zollars accepted the challenge of steering Yellow Freight System back to profitability. A former University of Minnesota football player, Zollars still looked fit enough to put on pads and a helmet when Myers introduced him to employees.

Zollars officially started work on Sept. 16. He first had to close up his office at Ryder Integrated Logistics, Ryder's fastest growing business unit, where he had spent two years as senior vice president. Before joining Ryder, Zollars had worked 25 years for Eastman Kodak.

Zollars exuded quiet confidence about the future. "My management style is uncomplicated," he said at the time, "team oriented, visible and active."[1]

At Ryder, Zollars was part of the executive team that created the leading company in integrated logistics. While at Eastman Kodak, Zollars had gained a depth of experience that included five years as a manager in Europe.

Zollars spent the first few weeks at Yellow getting to know the employees and familiarizing himself with day-to-day operations. Those observations helped him quickly launch his first major initiative – a system-wide reorganization.

The upshot was a major downsizing of staff that included an early retirement offer for 153 long-tenure employees and a de-centralization of Yellow Freight's sales and operations management. The key elements were establishing five geographic business groups and eliminating two of the six layers of management. The goal was to put Yellow Freight closer to its customers.

Zollars named five field generals who were Yellow veterans: Ron Gilleran in the Northeast, Steve Defenbaugh in the Southeast, Dick Wright in the North-Central, Mike Smid in the Central and Kevin Grimsley in the West. Each group vice president picked their sales and operations leaders in the reorganized structure. At the general office, he added an outside perspective with the hiring of Greg Reid, senior vice president of marketing, Deborah Kass, senior vice president of human resources and Hiram Cox, senior vice president and chief financial officer. They joined senior officers Kermit Scarborough, labor, and Ralph Nowell, operations. Nowell, a 34-year

This page, top — *William D. "Bill" Zollars was named president of Yellow Freight System in September 1996. He became the 10th president of the company behind Harrell, Nash, Hardy, Powell Sr., Powell Jr., McMorris, Stewart, Powell III, and Armstrong.*

This page, bottom — *H.A. (Bert) Trucksess, senior vice president - chief financial officer, Yellow Corporation.*

1997

Scientist Dr. Ian Wilmut of Scotland successfully clones a lamb, Dolly, from cells extracted from the utter of a sheep.

Mars lander Pathfinder settles on the planet's surface and sends remarkable video pictures back to Earth.

A White House scandal surfaces when President Clinton,52, is accused of having an affair with a 24-year-old intern; the president denies the affair.

Teamsters strike UPS; sides differ on future use of part-time employment.

This page — *(seated left to right) Steven E. Defenbaugh, Southeast Group vice president; James L. Welch, Central Group vice president; Dan Goodwill, president – Yellow Freight Canada; (standing) Ronald E. Gilleran, Northeast Group vice president; and Richard J. (Dick) Wright, Jr., North Central Group vice president. (Dick Wright retired in September 1999 and Maynard F. Skarka, Jr. replaced him. A predecessor to Kevin Grimsley, Western Group vice president, who was promoted to president of WestEx, a Yellow Corporation subsidiary in 1999, had not been named.) (Photo by Ron Coppock-King)*

Page 189 — *(seated left to right) William D. (Bill) Zollars, president; Mike Smid, senior vice president – operations; (standing) Hiram Cox, senior vice president and chief financial officer; Deborah Kass, senior vice president – human resources; Gary Beggs, vice president – express services; C. Kermit Scarborough, senior vice president – labor relations; Greg Reid, senior vice president – marketing. (Photo by Ron Coppock-King)*

Yellow veteran, retired in 1998. Smid took his spot and James Welch replaced Smid as head of the Central Group.

One hundred thirty-one employees accepted the early retirement offer, including former officers and employees in key roles. Those eligible were non-union employees who were 55 and had at least 20 years of service with Yellow. Don Roberson, vice president of corporate sales, who had spent 37 years with Yellow, was one of the retirees. So was Fred Major, a former division vice president who had spent 27 years with the company, and George Brooks, the pricing director who was the mastermind of the YES concept. Brooks had spent 30 years with Yellow.

A New Yellow

The changes went deeper than a management shuffle. Freight handling, productivity and service improved. Operating expenses were reduced and revenue began to grow again. Third and fourth quarter results looked encouraging. It allowed the company to break even for the year, although Yellow Corporation took a one-time charge of $27 million after taxes to pay for the early retirements and operating changes.

As 1997 began, Yellow Freight was preparing to go to the Teamsters with the largest change of operations in company history. The change to be implemented in April would reduce linehaul costs by increasing the use of rail from 18 percent to 27 percent of total over-the-road miles. The change also doubled Yellow's contingent of driver sleeper teams and called for relocating as many as 1,000 employees.

The 1997 change of operations produced a first, as well. Linehaul movement that normally went from east to west changed along the Interstate 80 link between Cleveland and Chicago and between Elizabeth, N.J., and Cleveland. Those routes reversed. Several triple-trailer runs were scheduled each day along that route and those, too, reversed. Drivers from Chicago began pulling freight east to Cleveland and returned with the westbound freight. Cleveland's drivers did the same, driving east to Elizabeth.

The change went flawlessly. Customer shipments continued to move close to schedule, although 10 percent of Yellow Freight's linehaul drivers were themselves moving to new domiciles.

Popular movies include: As Good As It Gets with Jack Nicholas, Good Will Hunting with Robin Williams, L.A. Confidential with Kim Bassinger, The Apostle with Robert Duvall, Wag the Dog with Dustin Hoffman, and Titanic with Leonardo DiCaprio.

The Green Bay Packers beat the New England Patriots 35 to 21 in Super Bowl XXXI.

A civil jury finds O.J. Simpson liable in the deaths of his former wife and her friend, Ronald L. Goldman, murders for which Simpson was previously acquitted.

75
EST.1924

This page, top — *Thomas L. "Tom" Smith joined the corporation in February 1997 as president of Yellow Technology Services, which later was renamed Yellow Services, Inc. (photo by Ron Coppock King)*

This page, bottom — *Yellow Freight System's Internet site became a critical communication and marketing tool seemingly overnight. The Web address, www.yellowfreight.com, gives customers with computers a virtual and convenient source for conducting business with Yellow.*

New Leader for Technology

Shortly after he arrived, Maury Myers made it clear that technology would be used as a competitive weapon. It was another lesson learned from his airline days, where he had watched high-cost established airlines defend their turf against low-cost, start-up carriers by utilizing technology.

He hired Thomas L. Smith, a former colleague from the airline industry, to lead the effort, naming him as president of Yellow Technology Services, a company name which Smith later changed to Yellow Services to encompass the broader responsibilities his unit acquired.

Myers said Smith possessed a rare talent. He was good at leading technology groups and getting them to understand their importance to the core business. Myers said in most business cultures, individuals responsible for information technology face issues that are foreign to mainstream executives. They have difficulty communicating effectively to bridge the gap. Smith understood the business and technology sides and was able to improve the working relationship.[2]

The technology strategy was designed to capitalize on the advantages already created by the Yellow Freight inbound customer call centers in Des Moines and Sioux Falls. None of the company's traditional competitors had committed to that approach. The task for Smith and his technology team was to add service functionality to the call centers while also utilizing the Internet to create a "virtual customer service center" that freed the company's 500 call center employees to spend more time solving problems for customers.

"The real advantage we gain from the customer service centers is that we now have a massive pool of real-time information available to help us plan and manage shipments moving through our network," said Yellow Freight President Zollars. "It's a big advantage from a customer relationship and a customer experience standpoint."

Success in '97

Implementation of operating changes and Zollars' new group structure did not interfere with Yellow Freight's performance. Aided by a strong economy, the company had its most profitable year since 1990. Yellow Freight System finished 1997 with operating income of $82.7 million on revenue of $2.54 billion. As a subsidiary of Yellow Corporation, Yellow Freight no longer reported a net income figure.

A mass suicide in San Diego claims 39 cult followers of "Father John," who said they would be reunited aboard a UFO behind Hale-Bopp comet.

Congress reprimands and fines House Speaker Newt Gingrich $300,000 for improper use of charitable tax-exempt contributions.

Tiger Woods, 21, is the youngest winner of golf's prestigious U.S. Masters tournament.

Princess Diana of England is killed in a high speed automobile accident in Paris.

The bottom line results were helped substantially by $145 million in cost savings from the operations changes and overall productivity gains from ongoing Best Practices effort.

Other carriers in the Yellow Corporation family also had good years. The corporation as a whole reported 1997 net income of $52.4 million on revenue of $3.35 billion. The earnings improvement caught the attention of the investment community and Yellow's stock price rose steadily until it had tripled earlier levels. Investors were happy and so were supervisors, managers and nonunion staff. New Pay for Performance incentives were yielding excellent bonus checks. In 1997, Pay for Performance checks to employees totaled $26 million.

New Challenges That Look Like Old Ones

Some of the 1997 momentum began to fade in the fourth quarter when customers began diverting some shipments to nonunion carriers. It was a signal that unionized carriers and the Teamsters had better reach an early settlement to the 1998 National Master Freight Agreement or a lot of business would go elsewhere. The contract with the International Brotherhood of Teamsters did not expire until March 31, 1998, but shippers were already hedging their bets in October. A shift by Home Depot, one of Yellow Freight's largest customers, was especially agonizing.

A disruptive Teamsters strike at UPS in August 1997 had heightened shipper anxieties. Many shippers also had clear memories of the problems they faced during the 24-day strike in 1994. During normal times, shippers have many alternatives for moving their goods by truck. But many nonunion carriers began warning shippers that these were not normal times. They had better make an early commitment if they expected to receive service during a work stoppage by union carriers.

Fourth quarter revenue began to slip. To further complicate the situation, the Teamsters were in a political quandary. General President Ron Carey had been accused of illegally using Teamster money in a scheme to funnel it back to his re-election treasury. The contest was held in late 1996 at which time Carey narrowly defeated James P. Hoffa, son of the Teamster leader who created the first National Master Freight Agreement in 1964.

By late 1997, the government had accumulated enough evidence to disqualify Carey from running again after overturning his 1996 victory. Carey had

1998

Bobbi McCaughey gives birth to seven healthy babies, the first living septuplets; McCaughey was using a fertility drug to get pregnant.

Ennis Cosby is murdered in an apparent robbery attempt; Cosby is the son of TV superstar Bill Cosby.

Swiss banks, businesses and the government set up a fund to compensate victims of the Nazi Holocaust.

The House of Representatives impeaches President Clinton for immoral conduct stemming from an affair with a White House intern.

The Senate condemns the president's behavior but refuses to remove him from office.

YELLOW
YELLOW
WORLD HEADQUARTERS
ROE AVENUE

attended pre-negotiation discussions with Bill Zollars, Kermit Scarborough and their counterparts at Roadway, CF and ABF. Those sessions went well, but the industry was uncertain about who had authority to schedule and conduct formal talks for the union after Carey was disqualified.

During this period, Zollars and the presidents of other union carriers formed the Motor Freight Carriers Association (MFCA) to represent their interests in Washington and with the Teamsters. They hired Timothy P. Lynch as its president and chief executive officer. They folded TMI into the organization. Art Bunte, TMI's executive director and chief negotiator with the union, joined the MFCA staff.

Lynch, a former Roadway employee and long-time ATA executive, brought other former ATA staff members with him. The group was well positioned to manage lobbying and industry affairs.

Negotiations Settle Quickly

Formal negotiations started in December 1997. The Teamsters' general freight director led the talks on behalf of the union. The issues were very similar to those bargained in 1994 – intermodal use, part-timers, work-rule changes and a general need for economic relief in order to compete with lower-cost carriers. Negotiators settled nearly two months ahead of contract expiration, but shipper anxiety had already created problems for Yellow and its MFCA/TMI counterparts.

Freight diversion during negotiations erased millions from the bottom lines of unionized carriers. At Yellow Freight, tonnage declined 3.6 percent during the 1998 first quarter. The decline contributed to a small first quarter net loss for the corporation as a whole.

The recovery was slowed but not stalled. Business began to come back in the second quarter and by year-end 1998 Yellow Freight had more than made up for the earlier defections. The company also continued to make strong headway with productivity improvements, shaving millions of dollars in additional costs through technology-aided operational process improvements.

Meantime, Chairman Myers was maneuvering his growing regional carriers into a more competitive position.

At mid-year 1998, Yellow Corporation finally ended its relationship with Preston Trucking by divesting the Northeastern regional carrier to a group of its senior managers. The group included Preston President

Page 192 — *World headquarters in Overland Park, Kan., employs more than a thousand people working for Yellow Corporation, Yellow Freight System, Yellow Services, and YCS International. It has been home to the company's general offices since 1973. (photo by Ron Coppock-King)*

U.N. involvement in the Serbian aggression in Kosovo escalates; the U.N. warns that an air offensive will be used if Serbian forces are not withdrawn.

Popular movies include: Skakespeare in Love with Geoffrey Rush, Saving Private Ryan with Tom Hanks, Life is Beautiful with Roberto Benigni, Affliction with Nick Nolte, One True Thing with Meryl Streep, and Primary Colors with John Travolta.

Popular songs include: My Heart Will Go On, Uninvited, Fly Away, The Boy Is Mine, and Intergalactic.

A U.S. Marine jet flying at low altitude clips a ski-lift cable at an Italian resort sending 20 people to their deaths after a 300-foot fall in the gondola.

Dave Letke, a seasoned trucking executive who had earned his stripes in the Yellow Freight management organization.

Preston had turned a small operating profit only one time in the five full years that it was a part of the Yellow portfolio. It's operating woes continued after the sale. Citing a cash crunch and an inability to recover business lost during the 1998 Teamster contract negotiations, Preston shut its doors for good in July 1999, a little more than a year after Yellow had sold it.

The 1998 divestiture allowed Yellow's corporate management to re-tool its regional expansion strategy with a focus on acquiring profitable operators that specialized in various service niches.

Going for the Gold

Meantime, at Yellow Freight System, the facts spoke clearly. Where Best Practices were implemented effectively, Yellow Freight's terminals improved their efficiency. They lowered operating costs and did a better job of serving customers. However, Bill Zollars recognized that participation was sporadic and therefore undermined the broader success. He made implementation of improved processes and procedures mandatory.

"Shortly after I arrived, I could see that everybody was trying to do the right thing," Zollars said. "But we had as many processes as we had terminals around the country. There were some really good best-practice kinds of activities going on, but there was a lot of inconsistency around the network. There was a lot of variation; not much dependability; not much accountability.

"So we started from scratch and went back and re-engineered everything from the ground up. We took apart every process we had, decided the best way to do it and then institutionalized it across the company."

The program was called Gold Certification. The first step was to determine what was feasible. Testing began at Cleveland.

Rick Brenneman, area general manager in Cleveland, had been with Yellow since it acquired Adley Express in 1972. He was one of a few active Yellow managers who had worked for the old East Coast carrier.

Although Brenneman had all the outward characteristics of a trucker's trucker, his team-player attitude made him a good choice to test Zollars' concepts. If you could convince Brenneman the idea was workable, you would not have to work hard convincing anyone else. He would do it for you.

Two boys, 13 and 11, collaborate to kill schoolmates in Jonesboro, Ark.; five die in the shooting massacre allegedly triggered by scorned love.

Unabomber Theodore Kaczynski is sentenced to four life terms and 30 years for killing three people and injuring 29 others with his home-made bombs.

Record-setting mergers include Citicorp and Travelers; NationsBank and BankAmerica Corp.; Daimler-Benz and Chrysler Corp.

Three East Texas white men are charged with the brutal slaying of James Byrd, Jr., a black man who was maliciously dragged behind a truck.

The effort began with pickup and delivery processes. Cleveland's employees found all the reasons to resist the program. New disciplines threw a wrench in the way things had been done for years. New accountabilities seemed more like distrusting managers looking over drivers' shoulders at every step of the way.

Brenneman's blunt but fair determination drove the program to success. His review of the processes helped industrial engineers shape the program for broad distribution. The goal was to distribute the program to other large terminals where success could impact Yellow's overall operation quickest. The first phase was to get the largest 100 terminals in general compliance with pickup and delivery (P&D) Best Practices. Once achieved, the terminal earned Silver Certification that entitled it to begin the next step.

Five teams of three management employees, including an area general manager, a terminal manager or operations manager and an industrial engineer, were to focus on implementing new Gold Certification processes at designated terminals within the five business groups.

The teams had seven weeks to work with terminal management, P&D drivers and dispatchers to establish the new standard operating procedures. Once installed, the terminal had a specific time frame in which to improve results in order to be certified. With Gold Certification, the terminal and employees received special recognition and benefits.

Rick Brenneman was picked to be Gold Team manager for the North Central Group and his Cleveland distribution center became the first terminal in the system to earn P&D Gold Certification. Meantime, parallel efforts were started for dock processes and linehaul operations. As they progressed, efficiencies drove costs out of the system and improved service standards.

Reinventing the Company

As operating processes were re-tooled to improve overall performance, a new marketing strategy was emerging.

Senior Vice President of Marketing Greg Reid had directed researchers to peer into the minds of Yellow Freight customers. A veteran marketer with broad experience in industries ranging from consumer packaged goods to third-party logistics, Reid wanted to know who was making shipping transportation decisions and what motivated those decisions. With the information, Yellow could create new services

Terry Nichols is sentenced to life in prison for his role in the Oklahoma City bombing of a federal office building in 1995; 168 people died.

The Chicago Bulls win their sixth NBA title of the decade.

Cal Ripken Jr. ends his playing streak at 2,632 straight games, easily surpassing Lou Gehrig's long-standing mark.

A gunman kills two security guards at the Capitol; screaming tourists duck for cover.

This page, top — *NASCAR driver Tony Raines piloted Yellow Freight System sponsored racing machines in the company's inaugural entry into NASCAR events in 1998.*

This page, bottom — *NASCAR driver Mike Skinner*

Page 197 — *Greg Reid, senior vice president – marketing, puts his enthusiasm to work leading the company's annual meeting for sales and operations management.*

that satisfied customer demands and shape its advertising messages to sell them.

Once basic information was in hand, Reid's objective was to prepare a strategic marketing plan that could be shared with the entire organization. The results confirmed his belief that business-to-business transportation buyers make decisions like any other consumers. Selling messages had to appeal to basic human instincts by using humor, honesty and simplicity.

Not surprisingly, researchers also confirmed the strength of the Yellow name. After more than 70 years in business, shippers were very familiar with Yellow Freight, even if they were not currently using the carrier. It was a true asset.

Researchers also confirmed a fact that many sales executives had instinctively known for years – Yellow's customers tended to be sports fans. In fact, the research showed that they tended to be four times more likely on average to be active sports participants or observers. It was an insight that led Yellow Freight to NASCAR.

Yellow dipped its toe into the Winston Cup circuit in 1998 by sponsoring a Winston Cup car for five races and co-sponsoring a Ford F-150 pickup on the NASCAR Craftsman Truck Series.

The company changed teams and NASCAR racing circuits in 1999 when the company became primary sponsor of a car owned by Emerald Performance Group competing in the Busch Grand National series of races. The new driver was Mike Skinner with strategic racing support coming from Darrell Waltrip. Yellow also sponsored a Busch series race in Atlanta – the Yellow Freight 300 – that Skinner won in Team Yellow's orange and white No. 19 Chevrolet Monte Carlo. The race was broadcast live on ESPN.

Business Firsts

The marketplace was changing and research was proving it. Customers wanted a transportation service provider that would deliver a broad range of services. Deliveries, and pickups for that matter, had to be on time, with no excuses. Damaged or missing shipments had to be kept to a minimum. Operating flexibility was a must.

"Our customers keep asking us to do more and we have to meet that request," said Zollars. "Most of our customers are experiencing the phenomenon of shorter and shorter product life cycles. You had better get it on the shelf or get it on the World Wide Web while the window's open because the window is getting shorter all the time."

Celebrity deaths include Frank Sinatra, Lloyd Bridges, Sonny Bono, Tammy Wynette, Roy Rogers and Gene Autry.

A third of the world – 1.7 billion people – watch France defeat Brazil in soccer's World Cup finals; the TV audience is 12 times bigger than America's Super Bowl audience.

Senator John Glenn, 77, returned to orbit to conduct scientific studies on the effects of space travel and weightlessness on aging.

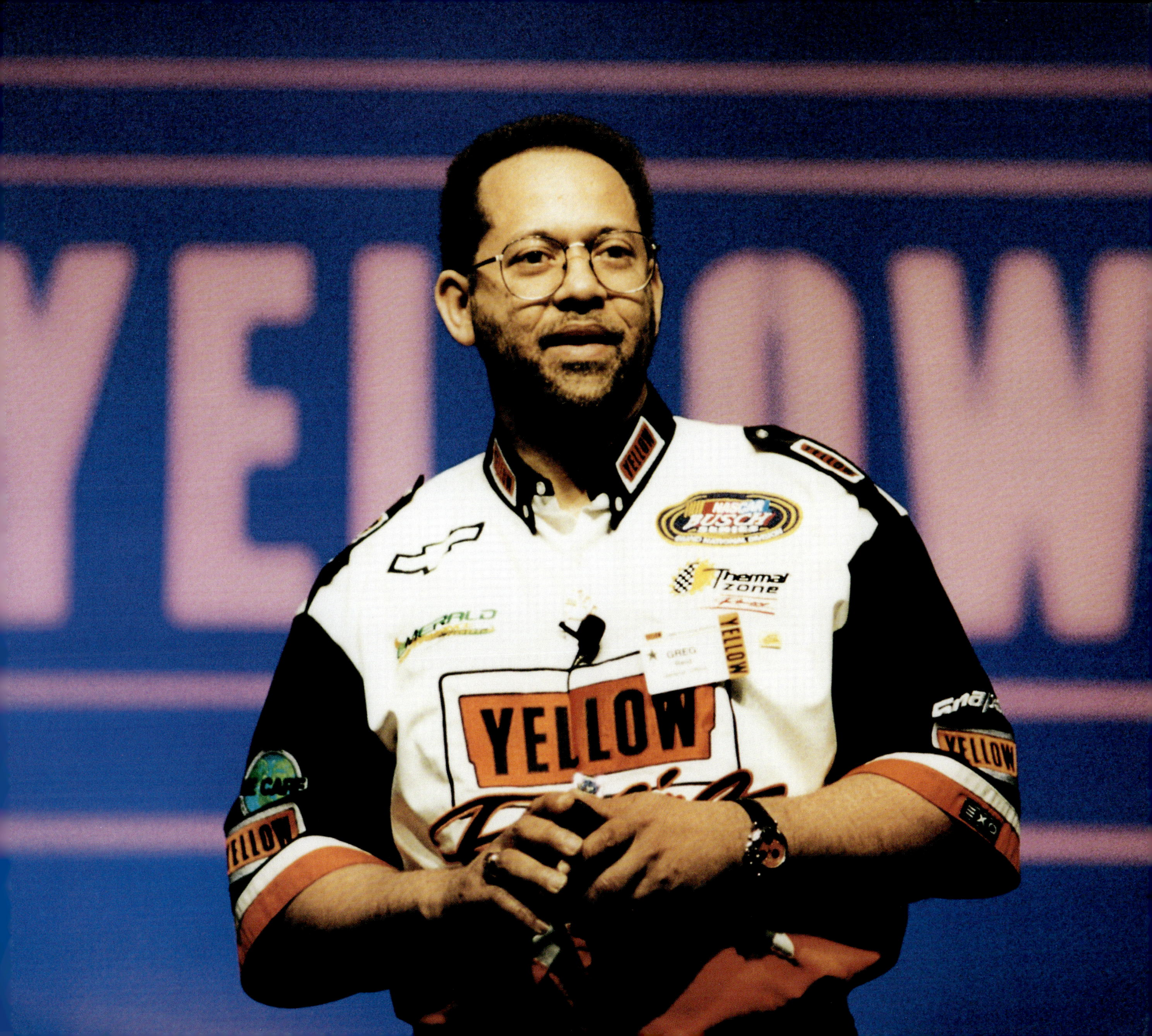
YELLOW

Among the firsts for Yellow Freight System in 1998 was sponsorship of a television commercial. The 60- and 30-second spots promoted the company's new Exact Express™ service.

Yellow Freight responded with new services that offered a range of options backed by aggressive satisfaction guarantees. Midway through 1998, Yellow launched a new time-definite, expedited service called *Exact Express*™.

Exact Express was significant because it was the first service in the company's post-deregulation history that had been designed and introduced after extensive input from customers. *Exact Express* worked because Yellow had succeeded in buttoning down its operating system, Best Practices, Gold Certification and other efficiency programs. According to Myers, a company can execute a service as demanding as *Exact Express* only when operating disciplines are standardized throughout the network.

It Takes Communication

In 1996, Maury Myers closed corporate offices located a short distance from Yellow Freight's headquarters and moved back to the Roe address. The move was financial as well as symbolic. He believed it was important that senior management remain closely connected to daily operations.

Myers' operating philosophy, influenced by quality management guru Deming, resolutely demanded timely and frank communications. He instructed corporate communicators to purge its programs of what he viewed as clutter.

Relationships with employees, especially in a union environment, require trust, said Myers. Employees cannot trust a company that is constantly feeding them propaganda. There is a way to persuade people and help them understand the company's mission with the truth, he said.

Opinions matter, according to Myers. They are part of two-way communications that teach a company about itself – where it is failing, where it is succeeding and whether its employees are satisfying customers and providing value for shareholders.

A courageous board of directors made very difficult decisions in 1995. The board deserves credit for excellent governance, Myers said. The Powell family had operated Yellow well for a long time. Loyalty notwithstanding, the board upheld its responsibility to represent shareholder interests first, realizing that operating profits were the only way to provide the service customers expected and the security employees wanted.

The board had been clear in its direction to Myers: get the company back on track. That first step was

1999

White House intern Monica Lewinsky, 25, is given immunity from prosecution for her "full and truthful testimony" regarding her affair with President Clinton.

A 54-day UAW strike against GM ends with GM losing $2.8 billion in sales and employees $1 billion in wages; nobody won, says the UAW president.

The National Basketball Association cancels the first 99 games of the season because of a labor dispute between players and owners.

Two Colorado high schoolers shoot and kill fellow suburban Denver students during a self-proclaimed anti-jock rampage.

ANR-Advance and Preston truck lines shut down; 8,000 trucking jobs eliminated.

accomplished largely through operating cost reductions totaling nearly $200 million within two years.

The second step, said Myers, was to build a strategy for long-term prosperity. The plan was two-pronged. The first prong was to develop a strong regional portfolio in order to compete against its growing rivals.

Shortly after the divestment of Preston Trucking, Yellow bought Action Express, a small nonunion regional carrier serving the Pacific Northwest. And in June 1999, it made a tender offer to acquire Jevic Transportation, a company headquartered in New Jersey with service concentrated in the Northeast.

The portfolio of regional nonunion companies now spanned the entire country with operations in each quadrant of the compass. It was envisioned that the regional companies could now compete in the fast growing overnight and second-day markets nationwide.

The other half of the two-pronged strategy was revitalization of Yellow Freight.

"The number one objective is to bring Yellow Freight's core service up to best-in-class levels," said Myers. "You have to be the best to remain competitive with the new carriers that have entered the market, the regionals that have been stealing market share for years. It just has to be excellent."

The future for Yellow Freight would be built on the operating excellence established in the 1990's. Bill Zollars and his team established a vision for the carrier to capitalize on its superior network infrastructure and process efficiencies. Three distinct tiers of service were developed.

The first is the core service, known today as *Standard Ground*™. Even at this basic level, said Zollars, Yellow Freight has created a competitive edge with improved transit times and service quality on nearly 60,000 city-to-city lanes. Improvements were possible due to Yellow Freight's re-engineered processes and redesigned freight movement network, free of the bottlenecks that normally plague transportation systems. The result is a superior service made easier to access through Internet and toll-free customer service centers.

The second tier, said Zollars, is *Definite Delivery*™, a guaranteed delivery of the core service for a 15 percent premium. Launched in July 1999, it is designed for those customers who need delivery assurances whether a shipment moves over a 2-day lane or 5-day lane. To add even more value, the service is backed by state-of-the-art computer technology that allows operations management to continuously monitor a

Marketing brochures distributed by the sales force and drivers help Yellow Freight System promote its new services as they are introduced in the marketplace.

John F. Kennedy, Jr., 38, his wife and her sister die in a single-engine plane flown by Kennedy when it plunges into the ocean near Martha's Vineyard.

Popular movies include: Star Wars Episode I: The Phantom Menace with Liam Neeson and Notting Hill with Julia Roberts.

The U.S. Women's Soccer Team wins the World Cup title in a dramatic shoot-out victory over China.

George W. Bush takes an early lead in the race to gain the GOP nomination for the 2000 presidential election.

shipment's progress. Customer service representatives will proactively notify customers in advance if there is a potential problem.

The third service level is *Exact Express*, said Zollars. The premium air and ground service achieves competitive advantage through its variable transit times, including same-day and next-day delivery, even down to the precise hour, along with the 100 percent satisfaction guarantee.

"Constant shipment monitoring, proactive notification and guaranteed delivery are more than just benefits," said Zollars. "They're tangible promises to our customers, and part of our ongoing effort to offer greater convenience, more services and greater reliability.

"We are committed to deliver the most outstanding services possible, not only to support our customers' supply chain management, but to provide them peace of mind."

Further Changes in 1999

New opportunities for Yellow Corporation Chairman Maury Myers created additional changes for the company in November 1999. Myers was named chairman, president and chief executive officer of Waste Management, Inc., a Houston-based firm with revenue in excess of $13 billion.

Yellow Corporation's board of directors immediately named Bill Zollars as Myers' replacement. Yellow Freight System's president, hired by Myers in 1996, became chairman, president and chief executive officer of the corporation on his 52nd birthday.

"I feel Yellow is now well positioned for a solid future and it is time for Bill Zollars to have his opportunity at the top spot," said Myers. "Zollars has been fully involved with the company's strategy development and will carry on with the established plans to unlock value from the company's portfolio."

Then and Now

In a span of a lifetime, the name Yellow has grown from a hand-painted Model-T taxicab in Oklahoma City to ride proudly on thousands of powerful trucks moving on highways throughout North America. The carrier started on a single, unpaved path along U.S. Route 66 to Tulsa, carrying oil rig parts and general commodities. It withstood the Great Depression thanks to smart, conservative men who figured out how to manage scarce resources and still make a profit by delivering the service customers wanted.

This page and page 200 — *Yellow's 75-year evolution has been dramatic. Technology has been the force behind many of Yellow's changes. It will remain an important force as a new century and new millennium usher in new demands and new opportunities.*

First Lady Hillary Rodham Clinton announces intentions to become a resident of New York in order to run for the U.S. Senate.

Kosovo residents return to their homeland after U.N. forces stop Serbian aggression; hundreds of massacred Kosovo Albanians are reburied.

Page 203 — *The Yellow Freight truck is an icon upon which a new company designed for a new century will carry the company's legends and legacy forward. (photo by James Hoffman)*

Surviving and prospering, the Yellow name continued to spread. Planned growth took it into new regions. World War II presented huge operating challenges. With much of its fleet dormant because tires and mechanical parts were unavailable, employees kept the company moving almost through sheer willpower alone. Then misguided plans to exploit the financial health of Yellow caused it to falter. But the name was not tarnished.

A rescuer quickly bandaged Yellow and moved the carrier to Kansas City, where it flourished.

Almost as if destined to become a leader through the will of its people, Yellow rose when others fell. Certainly, there were plenty of concerns along the way. George Powell, Sr. contemplated throwing in the towel in the 1960s because he saw maneuvers by a powerful union creating a long-term threat to the company's financial health. Yet, he put his trust in Yellow's employees and carried on.

Deregulation could not stop it, and indeed fueled determination. Still, Yellow today exists in a dynamic marketplace that cannot be taken for granted.

The name and company endure. The company continues to renew itself, as it has throughout the decades.

The company has been a stable pillar for generations of people whose paychecks enabled them to buy homes and educate children and then, in later years, to retire in comfort. New leaders and an entrusted board of directors intend for Yellow to remain a prominent fixture in the world of commerce.

On December 31, 1999, Yellow celebrates the completion of 75 years of service. Through its re-invention, Yellow expects to be a new company for a new century. The name has survived because the company has operated 75 years with a strong heart. And, yes, its people are truly proud that the blood it pumps is indeed Yellow.

A tornado, rarely seen in Utah, causes one death and heavy destruction as it skips across downtown Salt Lake City.

Joltin' Joe DiMaggio, the Yankee Clipper, voted "the greatest living (baseball) player," dies at age 84.

Thousands die and many more are seriously injured in an earthquake that struck Istanbul, Turkey.

Three U.S. soldiers are captured and held by Serbian forces; pictures are sent to U.S. media, but all three are eventually released.

Jordan's King Hussein dies; Crown Prince Abdullah, 37, declares he is "an extension of His Majesty's outlooks... and beliefs."

YELLOW
12654
12654
P175945

Chapter One

1 James F. Filgas, and L.L. Waters, Yellow in Motion: A history of Yellow Freight System, Incorporated, (Yellow Freight System, Inc., Overland Park, Kansas, 1987) p. 4-5.
2 Ibid., p. 5.
3 Ibid., p. 7.
4 Mildred Harrell, A Tribute to Cleve Harrell, (unpublished), p. 6.
5 Ibid., p. 12. Additional information supplied by Jan Cooke in an oral history interview conducted Feb. 17, 1999.
6 Filgas, p. 8-9.
7 Ibid., p. 9-21.
8 The Oklahoma Motor Carrier, 40th Anniversary Issue, June 24, 1973, p. 3-30.
9 Filgas, p. 18-20.
10 Ibid., p. 10-13.
11 James Trager, The People's Chronology: A Year-by-Year Record of Human Events from Prehistory to the Present, (Henry Holt and Company, New York, New York, 1994) p. 819-824.
12 Filgas, p. 14.
13 William Glenn, Notes on Interviews with Mr. A.J. Harrell and Mr. Evans Nash, (unpublished, 1958) p. 6.
14 Glenn, p. 15-16.
15 Ibid., p. 12.
16 Ibid., p. 16-17.
17 Ibid., p. 11-12.
18 Ibid., p. 31-32.
19 Ibid.
20 Georgia Pauline Harrell Severs, oral history interview conducted March 22, 1999.
21 Glenn, p. 17.

Chapter Two

1 Glenn, p. 27.
2 Filgas, p. 24-25.
3 Glenn, p. 28.
4 Ibid., p. 29.
5 Filgas, p. 27.
6 Ibid., p. 37.
7 Ibid., p. 38.
8 Ibid., p. 48-49.
9 Ibid., p. 49-51.
10 Ibid., p. 52-54.

Chapter Three

1 The Powell Family Foundation, The Sky is the Limit: A Biography of George E. Powell, (The Powell Family Foundation, Overland Park, Kan., 1988) p. 36.
2 Filgas, p. 50-52.
3 Ibid., p. 64-65.
4 Ibid., p. 77.
5 Ibid., p. 85-87.
6 U.S. Department of Transportation, Transportation in the United States: A Review, (Bureau of Transportation Statistics, Washington, D.C., 1997) p. 292-295.
7 Wendell Cox and Jean Love, The Best Investment A Nation Ever Made: A Tribute to the Dwight D. Eisenhower System of Interstate and Defense Highways, (American Highway Users Alliance, Washington, D.C. June 1996) p. 1-3.
8 Ibid., p. 4-5.

Chapter Four

1 Rosalyn A. Wilson, Transportation in America: Historical Compendium 1939-1995, (Eno Transportation Foundation, Inc., 1997) p. 10-19.
2 Filgas, p. 107.
3 Arthur A. Sloane, Hoffa, (The MIT Press, Cambridge, Mass., 1991) p. 316-318.
4 Filgas, p. 108-109.
5 Ibid., p. 118-119.
6 Ibid., p. 122-124.

Chapter Five

(Statistical information from company Annual Reports: 1970-1979)

Chapter Six

1 Wilson, p. 3.
2 Deleted through edits.
3 Deleted through edits.
4 Philip L. Cantelon and Kenneth D. Durr, The Roadway Story, (Montrose Press, Rockville, Md., 1996) p. 205-206.
5 Ibid., p. 220-221.

Chapter Seven

1 Cantelon and Durr, p. 213.
2 F.C. Duke Zeller, Devil's Pact: Inside the World of the Teamsters Union, (A Birch Lane Press Book; Carol Publishing Group, Secaucus, N.J., 1996), p. 312.
3 Ibid., p. 313
4 Yellow Freight System Annual Report, 1990, p. 5-6.

Chapter Eight

1 YFS Week, "New President: Yellow Freight System Hires Zollars," September 13, 1996, p. 1.
2 YFS Week, "New Leader for YTS: Thomas L. Smith Named President," February 14, 1997, p. 1.

Point in Time Bibliography

Bernard Grun, The Timetables of History: The New Third Revised Edition: A Horizontal Linkage of People and Events, (Simon & Schuster, New York, New York, 1991), p. 484-633.
Chronicle of America, (DK Publishing, Inc., New York, New York, 1997), p. 928-939.
James Trager, The People's Chronology: A Year-by-Year Record of Human Events from Prehistory to the Present, (Henry Holt and Company, New York, New York, 1994), p. 761-1136.
Laurence Urdang, Editor, The Timetables of American History: Updated Edition, (Simon & Schuster, New York, New York, 1996), p. 304-449.
Life: The Year In Pictures 1998, (Time, Inc., New York, New York, 1999), p. 6-155.
Our American Century: Events That Shaped the Century, (Time-Life Inc., Richmond, Virginia, 1998), p. 74-184.